African
American
Communication

LANGUAGE AND LANGUAGE BEHAVIORS SERIES

Howard Giles
SERIES EDITOR
Department of Communication
University of California, Santa Barbara

This series is unique in its sociopsychological orientation to "language and language behaviors" and their communicative and miscommunicative consequences. Books in the series not only examine how biological, cognitive, emotional, and societal forces shape the use of language, but the ways in which language behaviors can create and continually revise understandings of our bodily states, the situations in which we find ourselves, and our identities within the social groups and events around us. Methodologically and ideologically eclectic, the edited and authored volumes are written to be accessible for advanced students in the social, linguistic, and communication sciences as well as to serve as valuable resources for seasoned researchers in these fields.

Volumes in this series

1 THE POWER OF SILENCE: *Social and Pragmatic Perspectives*
   Adam Jaworski
2. AFRICAN AMERICAN COMMUNICATION: *Ethnic Identity and Cultural Interpretation*
   Michael L. Hecht, Mary Jane Collier, and Sidney A. Ribeau
3 POWER IN LANGUAGE: *Verbal Communication and Social Influence*
   Sik Hung Ng and James J. Bradac
4. DISCOURSE AND LIFESPAN IDENTITY
   Nikolas Coupland and Jon F. Nussbaum, Editors

Volumes previously published by Multilingual Matters in the series Monographs in the Social Psychology of Language and in the series Intercommunication may be obtained through Multilingual at 8A Hill Road, Clevedon, Avon BS21 7 HH, England.

African American Communication

Ethnic Identity and Cultural Interpretation

**MICHAEL L. HECHT
MARY JANE COLLIER
SIDNEY A. RIBEAU**

LANGUAGE
AND
LANGUAGE
BEHAVIORS
volume 2

SAGE Publications
International Educational and Professional Publisher
Newbury Park   London   New Delhi

Copyright © 1993 by Sage Publications, Inc.

For information address:

SAGE Publications, Inc.
2455 Teller Road
Newbury Park, California 91320

SAGE Publications Ltd.
6 Bonhill Street
London EC2A 4PU
United Kingdom

SAGE Publications India Pvt. Ltd.
M-32 Market
Greater Kailash I
New Delhi 110 048 India

Printed in the United States of America

Library of Congress Cataloging-in-Publication Data

Hecht, Michael L.
    African American communication : ethnic identity and cultural
    interpretation / Michael L. Hecht, Mary Jane Collier,
    Sidney A. Ribeau.
        p. cm.—(Language and language behaviors series ; 2)
    Includes bibliographical references and index.
    ISBN 0-8039-4515-9 (cl).—ISBN 0-8039-4516-7 (pb)
    1. Afro-Americans—Race identity. 2. Afro-Americans—
    Communication. I. Collier, Mary Jane. II. Ribeau, Sidney A.
    III. Title. IV. Series: Language and language behaviors : v.2.
    E185.625.H39   1993
    305.896′073—dc20   92-35510

93 94 95 96   10 9 8 7 6 5 4 3 2

Sage Production Editor: Astrid Virding

Contents

Acknowledgments

This work was supported by a wide variety of colleagues. Research projects with Judith Martin, Linda Larkey, and Ruth Butler have furthered this project immensely, and their comments along with those of Christina Gonzalez and Howard Giles have contributed greatly. Jill Johnson's work as a research assistant has been invaluable. Among all these people we would like to single out Linda Larkey whose assistance throughout the preparation of this book cannot be underestimated.

We thank also the participants in our studies who have informed us about African American communication and corrected us when we misinterpreted their social world.

We thank Fran Mularski and Janet Soper of the Auxiliary Resource Center in the College of Public Programs at Arizona State University for preparing this manuscript. Their work has been invaluable.

Michael L. Hecht

I would like to thank Albie, Susan, and Bella Hecht, Donnie and Lenore Perlmutter, and Diane Schneider for their support throughout my life and for the diversity they have provided. Thanks to Stan Jones for introducing me to the study of intercultural communication and to Joe DeVito, friend and mentor, for the intellectual and personal values he has modeled. Thanks also to Sidney and Mary Jane, co-authors and friends.

Mary Jane Collier

I wish first to acknowledge my two co-authors. The three of us have been collaborating on various projects since 1982 when we coded our first qualitative data about communication competence across ethnic and interethnic conversations. Our dialogue about African American communication and identity continues to be engaging, collegial, and stimulating. I also wish to thank the many, many students, colleagues, and friends who participated in our research studies, read drafts of the manuscript, supported our efforts, and were so willing to engage in dialogue about their identity and communication processes.

Sidney A. Ribeau

Thanks to those who made my contribution to this project possible—my family, who support me unconditionally; Michael L. Hecht, my patient colleague and friend; Pat, my partner; Janis Woolpert, my transcriber; and God, my constant guide.

Preface

Many academic research projects begin as creative enterprises that culminate in a finished product, in this case a book. Informal conversations among the authors regarding the lack of information that explains African American communication led to our first empirical study of this group. These conversations, which included discussions of African American popular culture, sports figures, and rhetoricians all seemed to conclude with an awareness that something unique characterizes the African American experience in the United States and that this should be exhibited in communication and other expressive forms. Conversations such as these were reinforced by classroom teaching experiences and examples in the media of communication breakdowns/problems that suggested differing communication systems that lead to alternative interpretive frameworks.

There seemed to be a great deal of attention given to interethnic communication problems, but little data to help us better understand this phenomenon. We initially conceptualized a number of studies to help better understand the complexity of African American/European American communication, a practical task that was ambitious and premature. What was needed, we decided, was a data-based explanation of African American communication that could be used first to explicate the communicative behavior of this important American co-population. A series of studies has evolved into this text, an attempt to describe and interpret African American communication.

The work is important for a number of reasons, a few of which will be mentioned here. The book is a serious attempt to provide a cultural analysis of African American communication from the perspective of the group. Emphasis is given to the identity, rules, and strategies that characterize communication for group members. It is a look from within. Group-specific cultural data are used along with culturally sensitive social psychological theory to provide an analytical framework for group behaviors. Analytical constructs were selected because of their congruence with African American life and culture. Finally, we provide an extensive review of the literature and recommendations designed to assist one in understanding African American communication in a context that extends beyond the Eurocentric paradigm.

The text presented here is a beginning. It suggests an approach and provides information necessary to begin an important dialogue in the communication discipline, ethnic studies, and other fields concerned with the centrality of culture and communication as it relates to human behavior.

The three authors came to this book from diverse yet intersecting paths. Below we attempt to situate the book in the experiences of the authors.

Michael L. Hecht

I was born and raised in New York City. My family home was in a section of the borough of Queens where diversity was represented more by religious and nation-of-origin differences than by racial distinctions. During these early years my exposure to ethnic diversity was mainly through my interest in basketball. But my cultural background as an Eastern European Jew raised in the post-World War II era taught me about prejudice and stereotyping. As a child I met holocaust victims and was warned about the dangers of discrimination and racism. Through these experiences I gained an awareness of membership in an oppressed culture. Although Judaism may be an "invisible" culture, one easily hidden, it nevertheless comes with a history that rivals any group for its tragic treatment at the hands of the dominant class.

My focus on intercultural communication, and particularly interethnic communication, was shaped through undergraduate and master's classes at Queens College under Stan Jones. Jones, one of the early communication ethnographers, observed the proxemic and touch behaviors of African American and European American children and examined cultural walking styles. While at odds with my early positivist bent, these cultural experiences sparked an interest that survived the intellectual training of my doctoral program.

It was during these doctoral years that I met Sidney A. Ribeau and we became friends. Later, while working at separate universities in Los Angeles, we decided to combine my work in communication competence with his work on African American culture, and thus began our line of interethnic research. This line and my understanding of ethnicity were enriched through a second friendship with Michael Sedano, with whom we co-authored a paper. And into this world came a doctoral student, Mary Jane Collier, eager to develop new understandings of ethnicity and culture through a unique combination of rules and systems theories. The three co-authors first worked together on studies related to Collier's dissertation work. My work on interethnic communication was encouraged by my move to Arizona State University's Department of Communication, which was building a doctoral program around intercultural communication as one of its prime foci.

The specific idea for this book developed at a conference at Bristol, England, when a colleague, Bill Gudykunst, introduced Ribeau and Hecht to Howard Giles, who was editing this series on language and social behavior. Contact with Giles, Bourhis, and Sachdev stimulated our thinking and encouraged us to continue establishing linkages between our work and ethnolinguistic identity theory. With the encouragement of Giles, this book project was begun.

Mary Jane Collier

I am a White woman who grew up in a White middle-class neighborhood. During my last year of college I was a student teacher at an inner-city school in Denver where busing for integration was put into effect for the first time. Later I taught on a Navaho Reservation. I have taught at universities rich in ethnic diversity in the heart of Los Angeles, and I have taught at universities where ethnic students represent a small percentage of the population.

Over the years, I have learned that racism and discrimination are, on the one hand, complex phenomena caused by economic, social, political, historical, psychological, and spiritual factors. On the other hand, I see that racism and discrimination are very simple responses to fear and threat.

The more I teach about and learn from African Americans in the United States, the more I see that it's all about identity. We all want to feel good about ourselves, we all want to exert a certain amount of influence over our environment and other people, and we all want to have some hope for the future. The beating of Rodney King, an African American, by White police officers in Los Angeles, was captured on videotape for the world to see. The subsequent trial, acquittal of the police involved, and violence that followed in Los Angeles and throughout the United States show the results of such differences in identity avowal and ascription, ultimate hopelessness, and inevitable rage.

I continue to learn from my students and my friends about what it means to be African American, and I continue to learn about myself from their views of me. I believe that there is hope for understanding one another, for appreciating one another, for empowering one another. This book is one step in that direction. The path is long and difficult, but it is an essential journey for all of us.

Sidney A. Ribeau

Throughout my academic career I have attempted to explore areas of intellectual interest that posed challenging questions regarding human relationships. In graduate school I was initially interested in interpersonal communication but quickly came to realize that African Americans were not included in the literature that defined the field. Further research confirmed my experience in the interpersonal area—research studies on African American communication were almost nonexistent in the entire discipline.

At the same time, relationships between Black and White America had deteriorated to an all-time low. Throughout the country nonviolent social protests were rapidly becoming demands for Black power. In many cities frustration fermented and eventually exploded into urban rebellions. It seemed clear to me that something must be done to reopen the channels of dialogue and reduce the violence. Thus I became interested in what was then known as interracial communication. Time passed, and my interests were solidified in graduate study that included speech communication, anthropology, and sociology.

I completed graduate school armed with many ideas concerning the role of communication in race relations, yet aware that there was still limited information available that helped explicate ethnic communication. On one occasion, I was discussing these ideas with a friend who was also a communication professor. He seemed quite interested in the academic problems that I described and in the need for academics to study communication as it is lived in ethnic communities. An interethnic team was formed during those discussions that has authored a number of papers and published several articles. Our early work has evolved into this book. Along the way much has changed in our personal lives, America, and the world. All of these events reaffirm for me the need for human dialogue. I believe that our work provides insight into an important communication phenomenon and ethnic culture that helps us better understand our humanity.

CHAPTER ONE

Introduction

This is a book about African American identity and communication. Our goal is to articulate how African Americans define themselves and membership in their group and how they perceive intra- and interethnic communication. We work to portray the voices of African Americans as we have heard and experienced them in our research and read about them in the work of others. However, no claims are made to speak for members of the group or the group as a whole. We pursue our goal by interpreting this rich cultural system in order to understand the major patterns of thought and conduct and explicate the problematic elements of competent communication. We describe what is distinct about African American communication and then explain the emerging pattern of norms across situations. In doing so we emphasize ethnic identity and perceptions of communication, explaining which identities emerge, what they mean, and how they are enacted.

Communication is seen as a problematic part of cultural affiliation and not as caused or predicted by that affiliation. Communication and culture are not truly separable. Communication is meaningful because of the culture that frames it and culture must be expressed to exist. Thus the term *cultural communication* is a useful redundancy because all communication exists in a cultural context and all culture is communicated.

Communication is problematic because there are few "givens" or "taken-for-granteds." In writing these sentences the authors cannot assume that the reader interprets meanings as we would. In meeting a stranger one cannot assume a shared understanding of the nature of the encounter (e.g., is this friendship or romance,

1

business or pleasure?). Within a relationship one cannot assume that a conflict will be resolved as previous ones have.

Cultural affiliations are also problematic. There is no single and correct way to be "African American." These identities are negotiated in context and situationally emergent. As identities emerge they present problems for the interactants, problems managing individual identities and jointly negotiating conversations.

These problems are part of communication and cultural affiliation. In other words, the affiliation process and the expression of affiliation are problematic. Problems may be a cause or consequent of affiliation but are always a characteristic of affiliation and communication. As a result, our research seeks to understand the problematic elements of communication and cultural affiliation rather than predicting from one to the other.

Ethnicity plays a major role in everyday life in a culturally diverse nation such as the United States. As R. Rosaldo (1989) reports:

> Cities throughout the world today increasingly include minorities defined by race, ethnicity, language, class, religion, and sexual orientation. Encounters with "difference" now pervade modern everyday life in urban settings. (p. 28)

Ethnic groups are difficult to define since there are no essential characteristics that are common to all groups so distinguished (De Vos, 1982). We define *ethnicity* as shared heritage. An ethnic group is a self-perceived community of people who hold a common set of traditions not shared by those with whom they are in contact (De Vos, 1982). Despite the importance of ethnicity, there is little research about the diversity within and between ethnic cultures and what makes interethnic contact effective or ineffective. Most studies of interethnic communication are binary, invoking comparisons between European Americans and one other group with the European American group as the assumed norm or point of comparison (Nakayama & Peñaloza, in press). Even less is known about how members of nonmainstream or disempowered ethnic groups perceive these interactions. We review this research in Chapter 4. Most of the research is Eurocentric, particularly Anglocentric, in theory, method, and focus (Asante, 1980, 1987; Delgado, 1984; Olivas, 1989; van Dijk, 1987). Eurocentric studies are derived from European

American theories, conducted by European Americans about European Americans, and the results are assumed to be culture general rather than culture-specific findings (Martin, in press).

This book attempts to give voice to an alternative view and experience of communication, that of African Americans. These voices expand the range of experiences that inform the communication discipline and provide a diversity on the levels of theory and practice. Perhaps this alternative worldview will broaden us and facilitate new and richer theories and explanations. Pragmatically, to feel included in a body of knowledge a group must feel heard. One implication of work on diverse groups is their inclusion in the social science literature.

A study of African Americans brings into focus the ethnocultural aspects of communication and provides a counterpoint to Eurocentric perspectives. Historically, politically, and socially, African Americans occupy a unique position within U.S. society. Their history includes slavery and segregation, the migration north, and the civil rights and Black Power movements. Their political past involves voter disenfranchisement and separation from formal channels of power (Lemann, 1991), and their economic life can be characterized as disadvantaged compared to European Americans of comparable skills and training (Dewart, 1989; Mincy, 1989). African American culture is also socially distinctive, including language/dialect, nonverbal and verbal style, and patterns of interaction (Hecht, Ribeau, & Alberts, 1989; Kochman, 1972, 1981; Labov, 1970, 1972). Structural, cultural, ethnic, and social distinctions define the African American experience and lead us to argue that African Americans constitute an ethnic culture.

The remainder of this chapter describes the context for the book. First we describe the African American experience in the United States. This section is not intended as a complete description of the social, political, historical, cultural, and economic conditions. Rather, we attempt to capture the essence of that experience by highlighting findings in each of these areas. Second, we attempt to articulate the basic assumptions that guide our work. These assumptions provide a starting point and help the reader understand the choices we have made. Finally, we provide an overview of the remaining chapters, which describe African American ethnic identity, communication style, and communication competencies.

The African American Experience

In this section we provide an overview of the African American experience in the United States. African American communication must be understood against this cultural backdrop in order to understand its grounding. No communication system exists in isolation. So here we paint the historical, political, economic, and social milieu in the United States as a way of describing the context within which African Americans grow and develop a communication system. First we will briefly describe some of the main historical events that shape the culture, explaining the Afrocentric approach. Next we will examine the African American experience in contemporary U.S. culture. Finally, we examine social structures and institutions that influence African American life.

Afrocentricity and the Historical and Social Roots of the African American Experience

The African American experience is the term often used to characterize the African diaspora that created African America. Forcibly removed from their native land, the Africans created a culture and way of life in America that blended the indigenous cultures of the past with the cruel reality of life in racially segregated America. Slavery and the life of African Americans in the United States for the past 300 years are a matter of historical record. While actual accounts differ in detail and point of view depending on the writer's perspective, the works of W. E. B. DuBois, Carter G. Woodson, and John Hope Franklin are particularly useful in understanding African American life and culture (DuBois, 1964; Franklin, 1988; Woodson, 1966).

These scholars employ what is currently labeled an Afrocentric approach (Asante, 1980, 1987) in their work, which emphasizes the holistic experience of the people in the explication of their social reality. The Afrocentric account is written from an African American frame of reference and includes early experiences on the African continent as the structural foundation for African American culture. Covin (1990) identifies five constructs that support the Afrocentric perspective:

(1) People of African descent share a common experience, struggle, and origin.

(2) Present in African culture is a nonmaterial element of resistance to the assault upon traditional values caused by the intrusion of European legal procedures, medicines, political processes, and religions into African culture.

(3) African culture takes the view that an Afrocentric modernization process would be based upon three traditional values: harmony with nature, humaneness, and rhythm.

(4) Afrocentricity involves the development of a theory of an African way of knowing and interpreting the world.

(5) Some form of communalism or socialism is an important component of the way wealth is produced, owned, and distributed.

These constructs provide the philosophical starting point for an analysis of African American culture. Not all African Americans today embrace these assumptions in their day-to-day life and others do not embrace them fully. However, the historical effect of these assumptions is unquestionable and, as such, they guide our discussion of African American communication.

A complex relationship exists between a theoretical consideration of the African American experience and the realities of daily existence. The glory of periods in early Africa (Diop, 1991; J. Williams, 1964) seem far removed from the world of the "truly disadvantaged" described by W. Wilson (1987). Few deny that African Americans can rightfully take pride in the achievements of their ancestors, yet the harsh reality of life for many African Americans often overshadows the study of history (R. Hill, 1989; Jacob, 1989). A brief discussion of life in modern African America provides a useful background for our discussion of African American communication and ethnic identity.

African American life, social structure, and identity have always reflected the complexity of a people caught in a cultural chasm. Before being brought to America, life in Africa was characterized by tribal affiliations that employed separate languages, rituals, and beliefs. Group similarities were at the deep structural level that accounted for a general orientation and worldview rather than culturally shared behaviors. Precolonial Africa consisted of tribal nations, not a homogenous group. The African continent housed a number of tribal nations as distinct as the countries that comprise Europe. When brought to this country these groups were forcibly thrust together and created an African American culture that was shaped by the African past and the cruel vicissitudes of slavery. This background has evolved into an African American society existing within the socially stratified matrix of America. Because it survives in a larger social structure, it shares many of its characteristics. However, it is separated by racism, discrimination, and prejudice, creating what Gunnar Myrdal (1944) referred to as *An American Dilemma* and the Kerner Commission (Kerner, 1969) warned could lead to a "racially-divided and unequal nation."

An accurate assessment of the current status of African America must consider both economic and sociocultural factors. A National Research Council study (Jaynes & Williams, 1989, p. 7) identifies four independent events that have significantly influenced contemporary African American life:

(1) Urbanization and northern movement of the African American population from 1940 to 1970.
(2) A civil rights movement that forced the nation to open its major institutions to African American participation during the same three decades.
(3) An unprecedented high and sustained rate of national economic growth for roughly the same period.
(4) A significant slowdown in the United States economy since the early 1970s.

The interaction of these events with institutional racism and the devastating psychological and material legacy of slavery has created a complex and diverse African American social reality that is captured in a statement by the National Research Council (Jaynes & Williams, 1989).

The status of Black Americans today can be characterized as a glass that is half full—if measured by the progress since 1939—or as a glass that is half empty—if measured by the persisting disparities between Black and White Americans since the early 1970's. Any assessment of the quality of life for Blacks is also complicated by the contrast between Blacks who have achieved middle-class status and those who have not.

We highlight salient aspects of this social world.

Social Structure

Significant changes in African American social structure have occurred in the past 50 years. Indicators of this are better jobs, increased income, and improved educational opportunities. A comparison of African American life from 1940 to 1980 illustrates these changes. In 1940 "one out of every two Black adults had no more than eight years of education, and 62 percent of working Black men and women were employed either in agriculture or in menial personal service jobs" (Jaynes & Williams, 1989, p. 164). In addition, one third of African American families had incomes of $3,000 or below (in 1974 constant dollars) while 1 of 50 exceeded $15,000, and only 13% of all African American workers were in white-collar occupations.

During the 1960s these figures were significantly changed. The percentage of African American white-collar workers increased from 13% to 26%, the median years of schooling was 10.5, and the types of employment became far more diversified. Overall, African Americans shared in the general prosperity of the country; however, these changes did not significantly close the gap between African Americans and European Americans.

Progress is evident when using in-group comparisons, but when compared to European Americans the marker of inequality becomes obvious. Using economic indicators as the basis for social stratification, African Americans are overrepresented in the lowest class in America. On all counts of economic indicators, African Americans rank drastically lower than European Americans and usually rank below other minority groups, except Puerto Ricans (Tienda, 1989). While weekly and hourly wages of African Americans have risen relative to other groups, their relative employment rates have decreased significantly (Jaynes & Williams, 1989). The overall effect of these changes has left a wider gap between African American and European American per capita incomes since 1964. In *The State of Black America: 1989* (Swinton, 1989), the disparities become obvious.

(1) Black per capita mean income was $7,499, compared to a White per capita mean income of $13,031.

(2) Black median family income was $18,098, compared to a White median family income of $32,274.

(3) The percentage of Blacks living below the poverty level was 33.2%, compared to a 10.5% poverty rate for Whites.

(4) More than half (53.8%) of the families headed by Black females were in poverty compared to 26.4% of families headed by White females.

(5) The unemployment rate for Blacks was 11.8% compared to 4.7% for Whites.

(6) The mean or per household net worth (i.e., property or investments) for Blacks was less than ¼ of the mean of White households.

(7) Blacks owned only 15% of the businesses it would be required for them to own if parity (proportionate equality with White business ownership) were to be achieved.

These figures indicate patterns of inequality that have worsened in recent years. They also suggest the growth of the African American underclass who occupy the bottom position in every indicator of social and economic disenfranchisement. In 1985 it was reported that 44% of African American children lived in poor households and the general poverty rate for the group was 31%; figures that compare to 16% and 11% for European Americans. Many of this group are the working poor whose low wages and vulnerability to economic trends have led to increased poverty.

Juxtaposed to this group are the African American elite composed of educators, medical doctors, lawyers, and other professionals, and a growing number of elected officials and corporate executives. It is estimated that business executives and government officials now comprise "12 and 11 percent respectively, of the Black elite as of 1978" (Jaynes & Williams, 1989, p. 171). These groups grew significantly in the 1970s and 1980s and have stabilized with some incremental growth.

Contrary to the belief of some social commentators (W. Wilson, 1978) the new African American middle class is "more predisposed to align itself politically with the Black lower class than was earlier the case" (Jaynes & Williams, 1989, p. 169). R. Smith (1982) suggests that what he calls "structural liberalism," shared political ideology, and group consciousness, might account for this (pp. 36-38).

The complexity of the social structure constituting African American life has significantly influenced ethnic identity and communication. This social structure is enacted in communication behaviors that respond to and define social reality.

Institutions

National organizations such as the National Association for the Advancement of Colored People, the Congress of Racial Equality, the Urban League, and a number of local community groups—which were often church affiliated—became the heart of the civil rights movement. They formed the nucleus for social change and remain significant social forces. Through their activism and the support of a number of White liberal organizations, the national status of African Americans changed as America was forced to confront the contradictions in its democracy. The premier institutions in African America from the early slavery period until the present are the Black church, educational institutions, and the family.

The Black Church. E. Franklin Frazier (1963) credits religious life for providing the means for a structured and organized social life among African Americans. The church established the moral fabric of the community and the organizational network for leadership training. Membership data suggest that church affiliation has grown in the past 50 years. From the 1940s through 1988 the National Baptist Convention, the largest denomination, has increased its rolls from 4,022,000 to 6,300,000, and the Church of God in Christ has grown from 300,000 to 3,710,000. Current membership in African American denominations totals approximately 17,000,000, making them the largest independently funded African American institution in America.

The church has also contributed significantly to African American culture. Spirituals served as the precursor of gospel music (Baraka, 1963), which spawned rhythm and blues and rock and roll. The African American oral tradition that originated in the African experience and is enacted weekly in pulpits across the country has produced orators such as Dr. Martin Luther King, Jr., Jesse Jackson, and former House Whip Bill Gray, to name only a few. The church, through its outreach programs, continues to feed the homeless, provide youth support groups, and advocate for the community. Through organizations such as the Congress of National Black Churches, a coalition of seven major African American denominations (the three major Baptist conventions, the three major Methodist churches, and the Church of God in Christ) the church has pursued six broad priorities: theological education, employment, economic development, the media, evangelism, and human services (Lincoln, 1984).

It is estimated that African American church supporters contribute $1 billion a year to their parishes, and total assets are believed to exceed $10 billion. The African American church remains a purveyor of the culture and spiritual cornerstone of the community. It is central to any analysis of the people's social reality.

Education. Education is the primary vehicle for improving the social and economic status of African Americans. The traditionally Black colleges pioneered this role, starting with Cheyney University (1837) in Pennsylvania and expanding to 121 institutions by 1936 (S. Hill, 1984).

Black colleges were a response to racial segregation. Since African Americans were not allowed to attend school with European Americans, private charities, churches, and freedman's societies started these alternative institutions. Many of the colleges began offering secondary-level course work and eventually added college-level work. Integration of predominantly European American institutions began on a large scale in the 1960s and 1970s, yet S. Hill (1984) reports the majority of "Black lawyers, dentists, and teachers in the United States today received their degrees from Black institutions of higher learning."

Elementary and secondary education for the majority of African Americans is a public enterprise. There are some African American private alternative schools, but the overwhelming majority of African American youth are educated in public institutions. Since the 1954 *Brown v. the Board of Education* decision and the Civil Rights Act of 1964, school desegregation has been mandated. Yet many of the nation's school districts remain segregated as a result of European American abandonment of urban centers (Kozol, 1991). While several districts, then, serve an African American population, they usually suffer from deterioration of the physical plant and severe underfunding based on an eroding tax base and other problems associated with socioeconomic deprivation.

The schools are where African Americans enact cultural rituals that forge ethnic identity. Predominantly African American public institutions provide fertile ground for the creation and maintenance of cultural behaviors that remain group specific because of geographic isolation. Most African American students will not attend college (R. Wilson, 1989) so they will have little opportunity to join the ranks of the African American middle class. There has been a decline in college enrollment during the 1970s and early 1980s from 33.4% to 28.6% (R. Wilson, 1989), but between 1985 and 1990 enrollments increased from 26.1% to 33% ("Minority College Attendance," 1992). For the past 50 years, African Americans collectively have demonstrated improvements in the area of educational achievement; but recent trends suggest a widening of the gap between African Americans and European Americans, an indicator that further clouds the future.

Family. Any discussion of African American life and culture is incomplete without consideration of the family. Franklin suggests that the family is the primary and most important tradition in the African American community (Franklin, 1988). Pioneering work in this area was done by W. E. B. DuBois (1969) and E. Franklin Frazier (1962). After these writers, a number of scholars have studied the traditions of this extremely important African American institution (Gutman, 1976; Nobles, 1979; Staples, 1971; Sudarkasa, 1980, 1988).

Research in the area is characterized by what Harriet Pipes McAdoo (1988) calls the "Africanist" and "Empiricist" perspectives. The former, which was initiated by the work of DuBois, studies the African American family in relation to its African roots and assumes that the enslaved Africans brought with them societal codes that governed family life in Africa (Sudarkasa, 1988). The Empiricist view focuses on the experiences of the African American family during slavery and since Reconstruction, emphasizing the role of poverty and social adaptation in determining family values and structure. Excellent research has been conducted by scholars in both schools; however, a comprehensive theory of the African American family has not yet been developed.

Two factors seem important in the study of the contemporary African American family: (1) Enslaved Africans utilized their cultural backgrounds and experiences in creating family life in America; (2) Economic, geographic, and public policy changes affected the development of family traditions. Most ethnic populations in America maintain group-specific traditions for a number of reasons while adapting to mainstream society. The African American family is a product of this same dynamic process.

In the past 30 years there have been significant changes in American families, which have established patterns that directly influenced mothers and children by weakening the economic base of the family. Higher divorce rates and lower marriage rates have led to a higher percentage of children living in female-headed families, which often accounts for a higher percentage of children living in poverty. While these changes have affected all families, they have been more pronounced for African Americans than European Americans. Recent statistics show that 86% of African American children will spend some time in a female-only or other single-parent household (Bumpass, 1984). This high percentage indicates a trend that differs from previous years. In 1940, 76% of African American families consisted of a husband and wife, a percentage that remained relatively constant until the 1960s. From 1960 to 1985 the percentage had dropped to 56. A number of factors account for this change. Among the most important are "differences in social class and economic position, family assistance benefits, changes in men's and women's economic status, scarcity of men, and a culture of poverty" (Jaynes & Williams, 1989, p. 527). It should be noted that more than half of African American families remain husband and wife units. The change of 20% from 1940 to 1985 does not include the national trend of unmarried couples living together. When adjusted for this population, the statistics might show slight variations.

The factor that most clearly distinguishes two-parent households from single-parent groups headed by females is actual income. The gap between African American single- and dual-parent families has also increased. An African American family with husband and wife will generate 3 times the median income of their mother-only counterpart. In real terms, this means that in female-headed households there are fewer economic and human resources to meet the challenges of raising a family.

There are a number of explanations for the economic conditions of single-parent families.

A single-parent family is more likely to be poor simply because there is usually only one earner. Second, women on the average earn much less than men; so even among single-parent families, those with a female head are much more likely to be poor than those with a male head. Third, young Black women who form single-parent households predominantly come from poor households and often lack the requisite skills for high earnings. Fourth, in the absence of relatively inexpensive day care, many single mothers of young children cannot earn enough from outside employment to justify working. (Jaynes & Williams, 1989, p. 525)

Consequently, we find that 67% of African American children in female-headed households live in poverty (Jaynes & Williams, 1989). For these children, health problems and limited educational opportunities lead to an uncertain future.

Significant changes have occurred in the African American family during the past 30 years. These changes followed years of relative stability in which descendants of slaves created a family life consisting of traditional African societal codes adapted to the "peculiar institution" of slavery, Reconstruction, and the migration north. A recent national study compared African American and European American differences in family structure and came to the following conclusion:

The most powerful hypothesis is that the economic situation in the black community together with residential segregation not only affect the immediate living conditions of blacks, but also strongly influence family structures and thereby alter the social and economic prospects for the next generation. (Jaynes & Williams, 1989, p. 545)

The family is one of the primary conduits of ethnic identity and cultural codes. It is here that the young begin to define and negotiate their worlds. Language acquisition and the identification of significant group symbols are *essentials* of this process. For

African Americans, we see the ethnic aspects of this expressed in Black English, contemporary music, and other expressive forms that are discussed in other chapters. Ethnic identity for this group becomes an amalgamation of cultural traditions and social realities that are fused by racial isolation and class distinctions. The study of communication in the African American family, then, becomes an opportunity to experience the lives of a significant ethnic co-population as they live it.

African American Culture and Communication

An Afrocentric perspective on African American social reality starts with recognition of an African past and considers the complexities of life in a segregated America and the elements that fundamentally shape people's lives. The assessment provided is not exhaustive, yet it strives to highlight dynamics that constitute a struggle to balance culture and class in the context of an environment replete with institutional racism and discrimination. This racism is communicated in subtle and overt ways (van Dijk, 1987), while the African American community negotiates the challenges of daily life.

The intersection of the psychology of the individual and the larger societal structures that shape this culture is found most richly represented in interaction (Haines, 1988). Pettigrew (1985) has stated that our most sophisticated understanding of ethnic group conditions can be found at the intersection of the macro and micro levels of analysis. He suggests that the dynamics of many of the social problems cannot be understood from only one level of analysis, but that these must be combined for a complete picture. For example, the continued patterns of occupational segregation of women and many ethnic groups in the lowest levels of organizations must be viewed as a web of interacting forces of individual attitudes, interactive behavior, and numerous societal/structural factors. Ethnic identity, as expressed through interaction, is a critical point at which the macro and micro levels merge in African American life. Communication becomes the vehicle for the creation and maintenance of culture and the mechanism to "deal with" European America. In the next section we explain our approach to studying identity and communication.

An Interpretive Approach

We describe the communication system of this ethnic culture from the perspective of its actors by focusing on how African Americans conceptualize their ethnic identity and their intra- and interethnic interactions. Although we incorporate objective descriptions of behavior, particularly in Chapter 3, our primary approach is *interpretive* as we explore the members' taken-for-granted, in-group assumptions about identity and communication. We do not derogate the importance of other research approaches including those that are Eurocentric. To the contrary, we feel these traditions complement our research, which eventually may incorporate some of these alternative methods in an attempt to triangulate (Denzin, 1978) our knowledge claims. Rather than constituting an end point, the book is meant as a beginning. Our secondary objective, then, is to explicate in the pages that follow the approach we have used so that it might be extended to other ethnic cultures and prove useful in describing culture-specific patterns of communication.

Communication is a complex and multidimensional process, and African American communication is no exception. In order to make sense of this process and, in particular, to understand the actor's social constructions, we adopted an interpretive perspective. This perspective distinguishes African Americans as a group and, by focusing on reports or descriptions of their own experiences, informs us about the creation and enactment of identity (Collier & Thomas, 1988; Geertz, 1973, 1983; Gumperz & Cook-Gumperz, 1982).

Ethnicity and culture become the frames through which we view African American communication to understand their experience of social reality and articulate their perspective on appropriate and effective communication. We define *culture*, whether national, ethnic, professional, organizational, or gender based, as a social organization. By this we mean that a culture is the common patterns of interaction and perception shared by a group of people (Collier, 1992). *Ethnic groups*, as we have defined them, have origins that are external to or precede existing nation-states and are constituted through a shared sense of tradition, peoplehood, heritage, orientation to the past, religion, language, ancestry, social-psychologies (e.g., values), economics, and aesthetics (S. Banks, 1987; Collier, 1989; De Vos, 1982; De Vos & Romanucci-Ross, 1982a, 1982b; Horowitz, 1975; Isajiw, 1974; Kim, 1986; Obidinsky, 1978). Ethnicity is defined psychologically and historically through shared symbols, meanings, and norms rather than being defined territorially or geographically. Ethnicity includes traditions such as "folk" religious beliefs and practices, language, a sense of historical continuity, and common ancestry or place of origin (De Vos, 1982). Finally, ethnicity and culture may be differentiated from race, which is a biological grouping (Michaels, 1982; Vora & Asante, 1978).

These groupings are not meant to be mutually exclusive. A group can have elements of all three, as the South African ruling class and government attempted to create by defining full membership in their society racially (Caucasian), ethnically (Afrikaans), and culturally (apartheid). Ethnic communities may be racial as well (e.g., American Indians), but they need not be so defined (e.g., Jews). One might consider culture to be a combination of the characteristics listed for both culture and ethnicity, and limit ethnicity to cultural groups that share a common racial characteristic. However, we use the tripartite definitional system and study African Americans as an *ethnic culture,* which revolves at least in part around race.

Ethnic culture connotes the social or communicative system shared by a group with similar heritage. These groups are constituted by membership in a system with common patterns of interaction and perception and a historically transmitted system of symbols, meanings, and norms (Collier, 1992; Geertz, 1973, 1983; Schneider, 1976). Thus ethnic cultures are characterized by a shared orientation to the past as well as toward current group identity.

Depending on one's viewpoint, ethnic culture can be said to be an individual, social, or societal construct (Middleton & Edwards, 1990). On the individual level, ethnic culture is a characteristic of a personal worldview that is at least partially shared in common with other group members. Here *membership* is defined as a sense of belonging to a social group and adopting its perspective on the world. The focus is on how the individual relates to the group. On the social level, ethnic culture is enacted and maintained in conversation among group members (Giles & Johnson, 1987). Thus ethnic culture is a patterned social network with shared history, traditions, and so forth. Finally, on a societal level, ethnic culture is a structural variable that characterizes large groups of people. This is, perhaps, the most common view of ethnic culture and connotes attention to the social organization as an entity, including its practices, power dynamics, rituals, and institutions.

We are interested in the group members' interpretations of the social processes through which members interact with others who have similar and different identities and, in the process, define, co-create, interpret, and evaluate those identities and messages. By collecting and analyzing African American descriptions and evaluations of identity and communication we understand these social processes. Interviews, open-ended questionnaires, and surveys have been used to interpret members' perceptions as reflections of ethnocultural patterns.

Our focus on communication is distinct from but complementary to anthropological, sociological, psychological, historical, political, and other perspectives. Communication provides a unique focus by emphasizing the points of interaction through which ethnic culture is created and confirmed, yet these interactions must be understood in the context of cognate disciplines. For example, one cannot fully understand power as it is communicated in African American ethnic culture without placing it in the historical context of victimization and discrimination derived from historical, political, anthropological, and sociological studies. Similarly, knowledge of individual personality and style derived from anthropology, psychology, and sociology is needed to interpret the symbols used to express identity in interethnic relationships. Our goal is to incorporate and acknowledge previous literature from these disciplines and approaches to the extent that such research speaks to our understanding of an African American perspective on communication.

Communication as a Cultural Process: A Perspective

Our objective in this section is to outline our assumptions about communication as an ethnocultural process. This will help the reader understand the bases for our research programs and judge the appropriateness and utility of our approach. Ultimately, this information will prove useful in placing our work within the nexus of cultural research (Geertz, 1973, 1983; Hymes, 1972) and intercultural interaction, integrating our work with that of other scholars and applying our approaches to other ethnic groups.

Several assumptions underlie our conceptualization of ethnic culture:

(1) ethnic culture is historically and socially emergent,
(2) people co-create and maintain ethnic culture as a function of identity,
(3) memberships in ethnic cultures are pluralistic and overlapping,
(4) ethnic culture is a system of interdependent patterns of conduct and interpretations, and
(5) perceptions provide a rich source of interpretive data.

These assumptions provided the basis for our research.

Ethnic Culture Is Historically Emergent. Ethnic culture is historically and socially emergent. Ethnic culture emerges intergenerationally and in social interaction. This means that ethnic culture is an historically transmitted system of symbols, meanings, and norms (Collier & Thomas, 1988; Geertz, 1973; Schneider, 1976). The attribute of shared history that is transferred intergenerationally or to new members distinguishes ethnic cultures from task or social groups who may have a system of shared symbols, meanings, and norms but do not have a shared and transmitted culture. Conquergood (1991) and R. Rosaldo (1989) stress the temporal aspects of culture, extending the concept to a theory and method that examine the unfolding of human conduct through time. Ethnic culture is a process, never static and always changing. Thus a cultural perspective examines the structures and processes that emerge and change over time and are handed down to new members, thereby creating "history."

This chapter provides an overview of the historical factors influencing African American life in the United States. This history is present in other sections as well. Our discussion of African American language, for example, examines assumptions about the language acquisition of slaves and our analysis of identity considers changes in ethnic labels and meanings throughout U.S. history.

Further, we believe that ethnic culture is most effectively studied as it emerges in behavior and cognition. Ethnic culture is enacted in feelings, thoughts, and social behaviors of group members and in interactions with the out-group. This assumption led us to examine the interactional style in Chapter 3 and communication effectiveness in Chapter 4. African American culture is constituted through communicative forms such as the use of code switching from Black English to Mainstream American English, an assertive, stylized communication manner, and rituals such as "playing the dozens" and "jiving." We believe that communication is an essential aspect of culture.

People Co-Create and Maintain Ethnic Culture as a Function of Identity. Our second assumption is that persons co-create and maintain (Deetz & Kersten, 1983) ethnic culture as a function of identity. In this view reality is socially constructed (P. Berger & Luckmann, 1966) through identity. Social constructions are not just something "out there" that get built through sense-making, but rather at the very heart of these constructions are the expressions of self and group identity so needed for the continued emergence of cultural character. African Americans observe their social world and learn from it. They also discuss this social world with others and test their constructions through interaction. For example, an African American student may decide that certain teachers are prejudiced and others are not. The student may try out this conclusion by suggesting African American authors for assignments.

Identity plays an important role in this sense-making process. By figuring out who you think you are, you decide how you want to be treated by others, whom you want to interact with, and how you will treat others. For example, I make these decisions based on who I think I am (identity) and derive this identity from my culture. Again, these decision do not exist in social isolation. They must be socially constructed to have force. If my identity requires me to interact with intellectuals but intellectuals will not interact with me, my identity is presented with a dilemma that requires redefinition or renegotiation with others. In this process of negotiation, the creation and maintenance of ethnic culture interacts with the establishment and expression of ethnocultural identity.

This assumption is clearly manifested in Chapter 2, which deals with ethnic identity and Chapter 5 in which our conclusions are presented. In Chapter 2 ethnic identity is tied to social interaction, while in Chapter 5 a new Communication Theory of Identity is articulated. In both of these places we stress the interdependence of cocreation and maintenance of identity and culture.

Cultural Memberships Are Pluralistic and Overlapping. Our third assumption is that memberships in cultures are pluralistic and overlapping. People typically assume multiple, overlapping identities in any situation. The reader might simultaneously be enacting gender, ethnicity, and occupational identities as these words are read. Our approach to Chapter 2 is based on this assumption. There we attempt to ground our study of ethnic identity in a more general discussion of self and identity. Ethnic identity is then framed as one identity and understood within the larger system. The intersection of gender and ethnicity is discussed in Chapter 2 where we focus on Black Feminism. This discussion also considers social class as an additional identity that combines with gender and ethnicity to produce "triple jeopardy."

But even a single ethnic community is pluralistic. Just as it is impractical to define a single American cultural identity (though generalizations may produce such a definition), so is it an oversimplification to define a single African American identity. Identity itself is both an individual and group phenomenon and therefore can be defined at any point in the range from micro (individual) to macro (societal) levels of analysis. Ethnic identity—or perceived membership in an ethnic culture—requires a group definition, but almost any boundary around a group leaves us open to missing the differentiation of groups within. Therefore, we take into consideration the larger African American ethnic identity as well as the differences within this group as defined by different labels (Black, Black American, African American) and foci (political and social). The memberships subsumed within the African American ethnic culture are discussed in Chapter 2.

Ethnic Culture Is a System of Interdependent Patterns of Conduct and Interpretations. We conceptualize ethnic culture as a system of interdependent patterns of conduct and interpretations. Ethnic culture describes communication patterns of action and meaning that are deeply felt, commonly intelligible, and widely accessible in the process of creating, defining, and communicating identity or personhood (Carbaugh, 1988). Ethnic culture is thus constituted and created through systematic and patterned communication that is interpreted through a shared code.

This assumption is played out in our examination of the interpretations of ethnic identity (Chapter 2) and interethnic interaction (Chapters 3 and 4). This work examines the meanings African Americans ascribe to their identity and the communication that enacts it. Studies of interethnic communication focus on patterns of conduct and interpretations of these patterns. Through this work a code of identity is articulated and an agenda for effective interaction is described.

Perceptions Provide a Rich Source of Interpretive Data. Our interpretive perspective diverges from some others within this general frame on methodological grounds. Most "interpretivists" would concur that the perspective of the cultural members provides a rich source of knowledge about ethnic culture (Carbaugh, 1988) and that it is critical to understand the in-group members' personal process of coming to know and define self, community, and membership. This process traditionally has been accessed through observation of actors in situ and through conversational texts. These are not necessarily the only sources or even the primary source of data (cf. Carbaugh, 1988). In particular, when these conversations are disembodied or separated from the actors, additional data are needed to capture fully the actors' social construction of reality.

Accordingly, the members' perspective communicates a great deal about the ethnic culture. In particular, their definitions of key terms and descriptions of social interaction tell us how they create, maintain, enact, and interpret ethnic culture, and it is these definitions we consider the primary data for our research. Group members' descriptions of effective and ineffective communication, for example, may not "accurately" reconstruct the text of the event but, instead, provide a representation of how those events are interpreted. Recalled conversations tell us how members construct their identity and social world in the symbols and frameworks they can articulate. We agree that "recall data and reconstructed acts . . . cannot substitute for data gathered in situ" (Carbaugh, 1988, p. 39). However, the obverse, that text and observation cannot substitute for the actors' interpretations, is equally true. Contextually grounded description from respondents' perspectives is a different type of data but no less useful than "expert" textual analysis of conduct (sometimes by out-group members). Based on this assumption we pursued our research through interviews and written descriptions of recalled conversations and interpretations of identities, messages, and relationships.

Sensitizing Constructs

Having articulated these primary assumptions, we approach the study of African American communication by focusing on sensitizing constructs that point out the means by which persons create ethnic culture and identity and reinforce their commonality. Sensitizing constructs point the researcher in a direction toward a general area or topic without specifying operational definitions (Denzin, 1978). These constructs tell us where to look without telling us what we might find. For example, the sensitizing construct of "privacy" might be used to study families. This tells us that privacy is likely to be an issue in these relationships and alerts us to these practices so we can recognize them when they appear. The construct sensitizes us to privacy issues and interpretations and guides us to observe relevant behaviors. In our research the sensitizing constructs are:

- core symbols
- prescriptions
- communication as problematic
- code
- conversation
- community
- ethnic identity

Core Symbols and Prescriptions. The first two constructs are called *core symbols* (Collier, 1992; Schneider, 1976) and *prescriptions* (Geertz, 1973; Hymes, 1972). People define themselves, their ethnic cultures, and their experiences through their beliefs and understandings as expressed in core symbols, and through prescriptions about appropriate and effective behavior. Together, core symbols and prescriptions tell us what it takes to be a competent and accepted member of an ethnic culture.

It is often difficult to separate core symbols from prescriptions and, in fact, these are not meant to be distinct constructs. For example, the institution of marriage may revolve around the core symbol of "permanence" and prescribe commitment and staying together. Core symbols and prescriptions are overlapping frameworks for exploring and understanding ethnic culture that, together, sensitize us to salient aspects of the actors' interpretations of interaction. Epistemologically, this information explains what one needs to know to identify with or claim membership in a cultural group.

Core symbols are the central features of the code used to interpret the social world. Schneider (1976) claims that cultures can be defined through the identification of clusters of symbols and meanings into analytic galaxies with central, unifying, and epitomizing core symbols. Geertz (1973) notes that there are sets of beliefs that can be called "worldviews" consisting of concepts of self and society as well as descriptions of the "ways things are." Core symbols tell us about the definitions, premises, and propositions regarding the universe and the place of humans. They sensitize us to cultural beliefs about the management of nature and technology and to views of the institutions of marriage, education, and politics. The symbols point us toward the central ideas and concepts of the ethnic culture and the everyday behaviors that characterize membership as expressed in the patterned use and interpretation of messages. These symbols, then, reference the central beliefs of an ethnic culture and answer questions such as: "How do you make sense of your world?" "What do you believe and why?" "Who are you/we as a people?" "What are the institutions, artistic forms, and organized frameworks that are used to establish contacts with one another?" "What do you do?" "What symbols are significant?" "What do these symbols mean?"

The symbols are identified through recurrent patterns of message use, repeating categories of verbal and nonverbal conduct, and shared interpretations of these messages and categories. These messages convey both a symbolic category and the meanings associated with the symbol. For example, Philipsen (1975) conducted an ethnography in a south Chicago neighborhood and identified in the speech of male community members the symbolic category of *"talking like a man."* Collier (1989) analyzed intensive interviews and found that communication among African American friends reflects the core symbol of *respect for the individual* and Carbaugh (1989) analyzed transcripts of the popular television talk show, *The Donahue Show,* and identified *self-expression* as a core symbol of mainstream U.S. identity.

The meanings of these symbols are also evident in the structures of co-occurring and repetitive messages. A culture's use of metaphors, stories, and myths (Philipsen, 1987) reveals themes and dimensions that identify the key symbols and tell us how social life is interpreted. Katriel and Philipsen (1981) examined "real communication" as a core symbol co-occurring with the symbolic categories of "self" and "relationship" in U.S. culture. They noted that the meaning of the "real communication" (for European Americans) is "close, supportive, and flexible" speech that pays ritual homage to the individuals in the relationship.

Meanings are also evident in the definition of and participation in such institutions as government, media, education, and religion, and in the creation and interpretation of art in all of its forms. For example, members of an ethnic culture may believe that government is a means of social control or believe that the people must control the government. Each belief system implies something very different about the nature of society. In the former, people are seen as weak and in need of control in order to maintain social order. Here the people are the potential source of evil. In the second view, government is seen as the corrupting force and the inherent good nature of the people must be used to keep this from actualizing. Similarly, professions, recreation, entertainment, and other valued activities provide information about the meanings and symbols in use, the behavioral patterns that emerge, and the notion of identity or personhood.

Core symbols provide our frame for understanding African American communication style in Chapter 3. After examining research describing this style we pose five core symbols as an organizing framework. Core symbols are also used to explain African American norms in Chapter 4.

In addition to understanding people's interpretations of "what is," we must also come to understand their notions of "what ought to be." Thus the *prescriptive* or evaluative aspect of ethnic culture also must be considered in order to gain a more complete picture. This framework focuses our view on the norms of appropriate and acceptable behavior, moral standards, expectations for conduct, and criteria of competence. One can say that the "ethos" of an ethnic culture is its moral, aesthetic, and evaluative patterns that establish attitudes toward individuals and environments as well as the quality of life (Geertz, 1973). Since norms are situated behaviors (Hymes, 1972), they prescribe appropriate behavior in particular contexts (Schneider, 1976).

The notion of prescription points us to the definitions of competent communication (in addition to other important cultural norms) that explicate an ethnic culture (Collier, Ribeau, & Hecht, 1986; Hecht, Ribeau, & Alberts, 1989). Hymes (1972), for example, defines *communication competence* as the knowledge of and demonstrable ability to carry out appropriate conduct in particular contexts. Similarly, Spitzberg and Cupach (1984) conceptualize *relational competence* as the knowledge, motivation, and skills needed to behave appropriately and effectively. From this perspective, competence includes conduct that is both appropriate and effective in particular contexts (Collier, 1989; Collier et al., 1986; Spitzberg & Hecht, 1984). Saville-Troike (1982) summarizes this notion:

> Interaction requires the perception, selection, and interpretation of salient features of the code used in actual communication situations, integrating these with other cultural knowledge and skills, and implementing appropriate strategies for achieving communication goals. (p. 24)

Cultural groups provide criteria for evaluating appropriate and effective communication. Inherent in a cultural system are notions of what it takes to "perform the culture" by following norms and interacting with in-group and out-group members (Collier et al., 1986; Hecht & Ribeau, 1984, 1987; Hecht, Ribeau, & Alberts, 1989;

Hecht, Ribeau, & Sedano, 1990). Since appropriate communication is rule following (Shimanoff, 1980), effective rule-following behavior results in positive outcomes such as self-concept reinforcement (Collier, 1988), desire to maintain the relationship (Collier, 1988) and goal attainment (Collier et al., 1986; Hecht et al., 1990).

This prescriptive component is the basis for much of Chapter 4. There we discuss African American perceptions of effective and ineffective intra- and interethnic communication. We attempt to articulate an agenda for appropriate and effective communication.

Communication as Problematic. The model presented thus far seems to imply that communication is easy and smooth when interactants are members of the same ethnic culture and share notions of appropriateness and effectiveness. Such is not the case. Communication is conceptualized as a *problematic event* during which persons assign meanings to messages and jointly create identities and social reality. Ethnic cultures provide parameters within which interaction occurs but can never specify all of the emergent properties of social behavior, nor do individuals always fully intend to follow the parameters. Meanings and identities do not exist a priori. Instead they present interactants with a dilemma or puzzle that must be solved. The question of how to negotiate meanings and identities through discourse is a predicament because people do not share the same experiential space and, therefore, differ in their interpretations and uses of symbols and norms, their abilities to interact competently, and their communication styles. Interactants also must negotiate definitions of interaction, answering the "what are we doing" question and establishing the *communication episode* (Pearce & Cronen, 1980). They also must adjust and accommodate to each other, the situation, and the relationship (Gallois, Franklyn-Stokes, Giles, & Coupland, 1988). Even well-intentioned, skilled communicators must continually maneuver through the conversational turns in order to discover and negotiate the norms and maintain competent interaction. As a result, specific instances of communication even among those within the same cultural group membership are more often *problematic* than not (Coupland, Wiemann, & Giles, 1991).

This process is further obfuscated when ethnic and cultural factors are considered. Misunderstandings and other obstacles are likely when any two persons navigate the stream of differing symbols, norms, competencies, and styles, but when the persons are of diverse cultural and ethnic backgrounds this process can be even more difficult. In addition, people are simultaneously members of multiple identity groups that can be interpreted in a variety of different ways. The selection of the memberships salient to a particular time, place, relationship, and interaction is problematic in its own right.

We say, then, that communication is problematic because all interactions, no matter how smoothly they appear to flow, involve choices and dilemmas that challenge the interactants' abilities. When interactants do not share the same ethnic culture, appropriateness and effectiveness are even more problematic. For example, American and Japanese co-workers each make choices about language, nonverbal behaviors, dress, conflict management strategies, and level of disclosure and then relationally negotiate conversational choices such as turn taking, speaking time, topic, and intimacy.

This conceptualization changes the way competence is viewed. When communication is conceptualized as problematic, the focus moves away from global definitions of competence and incompetence. Instead we emphasize the ongoing management of conversations. The fundamental areas of interest move from lists of competence skills to identification of the problematic issues that emerge in conversations and the moment-by-moment strategies used to deal with these issues.

An example of this shift in emphasis is provided by the key communication skill, *Other Orientation* (Spitzberg & Hecht, 1984). Other Orientation might help one recognize that it is important to the other person to feel accepted and might be used as a guideline to provide this feeling. Other Orientation is treated as a communication competence skill and included on most complete lists of how to be a good communicator. However, this behavior may be interpreted by the other interactant as "overaccommodation" even when it is intended to be a culturally sensitive adjustment to a person perceived to be a member of a different cultural group. A person who feels others are overaccommodating may perceive them as stereotyping or patronizing (Giles, Coupland, & Coupland, 1991; Hecht, Ribeau, & Alberts, 1989). If Other Orientation is considered a skill in the traditional sense, one would deal with this perception of overaccommodation through increased efforts to focus on the other person's perceived interests and orientations. Our work suggests that this may be the wrong strategy. For example, if a European American has expressed Other Orientation through introduction of "Black topics" when talking to an African American and this has lead to the perception of stereotyping through overaccommodation, continued attempts to recognize cultural identity may only exacerbate the situation.

If the keys to competence are understanding the emerging issues in communication and developing and utilizing strategies for responding to these issues, what role do skills play? One can imagine a model in which skills are seen as contributing to both the creation or anticipation of issues, as well as providing a repertoire of responses to conversational problems. Such a model alters the emphases of the traditional views of competence to focus on the problematic issues that emerge, their anticipation, and the coping strategies for avoiding and/or adapting. Thus different sets of "skills" are needed: anticipating the issues, avoiding the issues, recognizing the issues, and responding.

This new emphasis guides our discussion of communication competence in Chapter 4. Through a series of studies, we identify the issues that African Americans find problematic in their interactions with other members of the group and with European Americans. We go on to examine a series of improvement strategies that can be used to overcome the problematic elements. Studies of these other competencies await future research.

Code, Conversation, and Community. Philipsen (1987) has proposed that cultural communication is composed of *conversation, code,* and *community.* This system provides us with three sensitizing constructs by shifting our attention to how symbols, meanings, and norms occur in conversations and become codes of conduct that create shared identities.

The three constructs are interrelated. Conversations express patterns of social interaction or discourse that evolve into codes of conduct for members of particular groups. These codes, in turn, guide conversational behavior in line with cultural indications. Conversation and code, then, are identifiable structures of communicative conduct that define and express membership in a community. Cultural communication is a system of interdependent patterns of conduct (conversation) and interpretations (code) that are used by a group of people to define their personhood and reinforce group identity (community).

Philipsen's tripartite system for defining culture is part of the Communication Theory of Identity presented in Chapter 5. We argue that communication can be used as a frame for understanding identity and utilize principles, including communication as code, conversation, and communication, to build the theory.

On one level cultural communication can be studied as *conversation*, a patterned representation of a people's experience. Conversations include ritual exchanges between persons in particular contexts. They enact core symbols and are guided by prescriptions for appropriate and effective communication. We think of conversation as answering questions such as, "What kind of contact are you having?" "What is your relationship?" "What kind of messages are you exchanging?" "What is being accomplished through social interaction?" Conversation is represented in Chapter 3, which describes African American communication style.

Code is a broad system of beliefs, values, and images of the ideal that is reflected in language patterns. A code is a set of symbols and meanings that is based upon sets of cognitive and moral constraints and results in a worldview. Codes can be epitomized by core symbols and thought of as a set of consensual norms and conduct that is expected, valued, prohibited, or predicted. When shared by a community of persons, codes serve social ordering and coordinating functions, guiding language choices and patterns through which people come to know their place in the world. In this manner codes prescribe effective and appropriate behavior. According to Philipsen (1987), "Cultural communication is the process by which a code is realized and negotiated in a communal conversation" (p. 249). Codes answer questions such as, "Who are you as a people?" "What do you mean?" "Who do you want to be?" We examine the identity codes that are marked by ethnic labels in Chapter 2 and the communication codes for interpreting interaction in Chapters 3 and 4.

Philipsen's (1987) third sensitizing construct, *community*, is a grouping of persons whose commonality is derived from shared identity and setting. A sense of membership stems from shared symbol use, meanings, norms, prescriptions, and history. This bonding creates an in-group/out-group distinction that guides social relationships (Tajfel, 1981).

Our discussion has identified three types of communities: racial, ethnic, and cultural communities. The essence of community is a sense of belonging, loyalty, or membership (De Vos & Romanucci-Ross, 1982b; Philipsen, 1987). Membership in communities is seen as central because it provides a reference point for interpreting codes and conversations. It is the enactment of identification within a community that is most salient. We believe that members of the African American community identify with an ethnic culture, a social organization with a common sense of ancestry, tradition, aesthetics, and values that coalesces around racial characteristics. For ease of terminology we will call the sense of belonging to an ethnic culture, *ethnic identity*. This focus on communities permeates our discussion of identity in Chapter 2 and guides our assumption of identity as a central feature of social interaction. In the next section we provide an overview of ethnic identity.

Ethnic Identity. Ethnic identity is defined as perceived membership in an ethnic culture that is enacted in the appropriate and effective use of symbols and cultural narratives, similar interpretations and meanings, and common ancestry and traditions. *Identity* implies a sense of self or personhood and ethnic identity is the subjective sense of belonging to or membership in an ethnic culture. Ethnic identities such as African American, French, Hindu move in and through time and space and are composed of diverse elements such as geography, politics, economics, sociology, psychology, and history. At any moment, identity is what it was, currently is, and is becoming and exists on individual, social, and societal levels across time and space.

Identity creates and is created by the people, interactions, and environments in which it has, does, or will exist. Identity is defined by the individual and co-created as people come into contact with one another and the environment. As people align themselves with various groups, this cocreation process is negotiated, and boundaries, symbols, meanings, and norms are developed and modified. Thus identity is a characteristic of the individual, the interaction, the relationship, and the collectivity (Middleton & Edwards, 1990).

Our interest in this book is with those who belong to the African American ethnic culture. The book discusses how persons identifying themselves as African American in ethnicity and culture create a sense of shared community and codes in conversation through the use of symbols, meanings, and norms. In other words, we want to know how African Americans interpret the creation and enactment of their identity in everyday conversation.

It is clear that for any individual there may be more than one identity and, further, that each identity is in a continuous state of enactment and change. African Americans in the United States face a continuing series of dilemmas including the potential tensions between being African American and American, being an individual and a group member, and different ways of being African American. In addition, members of this group are faced with in-group conflict and out-group assimilationist pressure and discrimination. As a result, African American ethnic identity and cultural communication is a problematic, provocative, and important area of study.

Summary and Overview of Chapters

In this first chapter we explained our interpretive approach to communication. We view communication as a socially constructed process that revolves around membership in ethnic cultures. These memberships are formed out of interaction and frame our interpretations of interaction. Thus interpretation, membership, and interaction are privileged in this perspective and each is seen as emerging within an ethnocultural context.

It is from this perspective that we describe the emergent and problematic nature of ethnic culture as expressed in symbols, meanings, and norms. Communication is socially constructed and interpreted through these forms and is inherently problematic because it involves socially constructed and enacted interpretations. This focus shifts us from the objective study of skills to an understanding of how the actors interpret the challenges of social discourse.

While stressing the role of perceived identity, we have tried to emphasize the importance of the larger ethnic and cultural environment as well as in-group and out-group relationships. This led us to explicate Afrocentrism and the African American experience in the United States, thus providing a broader social context with which to interpret African American communication.

Further, we have explicated core symbols, prescriptions, problematic communication, code, conversation, community, and ethnic identity as sensitizing constructs. These constructs are derived from our theoretical perspective and point us to salient aspects of African American communication. This list is not exhaustive, but rather it represents the constructs we have found most useful in our work. They are laid out here to inform the reader of our theoretical basis, building upon the interpretive framework presenting earlier in the chapter.

In the remainder of the book we will apply this framework to African American communication. Sometimes the context, theory, assumptions, and sensitizing constructs are implicit in our writing. At other times we attempt to make explicit these assumptions as we explore the taken-for-granted everyday world of African Americans.

In the second chapter, "Self, Identity, Ethnic Identity, and African American Ethnic Identity," we discuss membership in African American ethnic culture. Information from social and psychological processes is synthesized in order to understand the notions of *self* and *identity* and to apply these notions to ethnic identity, particularly that of African Americans. Current research on African Americans' perceptions and identities is integrated. While we touch on the prescriptive aspects of identity (how appropriately and effectively to adopt a particular African American identity), the chapter focuses primarily on the symbols, meanings, codes, and communities (what are the identities and what do they mean?).

"African American Communication Style," the third chapter, summarizes information on African American language codes and communication style. This chapter is organized around five core symbols: Sharing, Uniqueness, Positivity, Realism, and Assertiveness. Understanding the linguistic and interaction styles illuminates the code and conversation of this group and helps us comprehend specific message preferences and adaptive strategies. These styles are those that typify African American conversation and focus us on the use of symbols.

The fourth chapter, "Communication Competence," focuses on appropriate and effective communication among African Americans as well as between in-group and out-group members. We examine the problematic nature of communication by examining the norms and issues that are salient to African Americans in their communication. These norms and issues constitute an agenda for effective communication and include core symbols as well as their interpretations and meanings. This discussion also considers the communicative strategies needed to overcome conversational obstacles and achieve positive outcomes. These competencies represent the prescriptive aspect of ethnic culture.

Chapter 5, "Conclusions," synthesizes ethnic identity, communication style, and competence and suggests applications and pragmatic issues in African American communication. The chapter presents a Communication Theory of Identity as a framework for interpreting previous research and guiding future endeavors. Research challenges are discussed with suggestions for future directions. This final chapter, like the entire book, is meant also as a beginning.

CHAPTER TWO

Self, Identity, Ethnic Identity, and African American Ethnic Identity

The approach to culture articulated in Chapter 1 emphasizes the role of cultural and ethnic identity. Culture is an interpretive process that manifests itself in code, conversation, and community as a framework for understanding the world (code), interacting with others (conversation), and aligning with groups of people (community). These central elements of code, conversation, and community are inherently entwined with a sense of identity.

Ethnic identity connotes the ethnic culture with which one associates oneself. As described in Chapter 1, this involves associations with one's ethnicity (traditions, peoplehood, heritage, orientation to the past, religion, language, ancestry, values, economics, and aesthetics) and culture (social organization). The process of identification is one of adopting the code, learning to "do the conversation," and associating within the community literally and/or symbolically. Identity means orienting self toward a particular ethnocultural framework.

Since there are imposed aspects to ethnic culture, identification does not fully define ethnocultural consciousness. Any person born into and socialized within a particular ethnic culture, for example mainstream U.S. culture, will be shaped by those experiences. These ethnocultural properties are likely to become part of that person's consciousness even if the person leaves the ethnic culture and lives as an "expatriate." In addition, we do not assume that people are always highly aware of even those aspects that an individual selects. Much of social life is processed mindlessly (C. Berger & Douglas,

1981; Folkes, 1985; Kitayama & Burnstein, 1988; Langer, 1978), and this includes identity. The role of identity, therefore, is to provide a selected orientation toward an ethnic culture. As the selection or choice of the individual, ethnic identity can be a powerful source of meaning and behavior. However, ethnic identity is only one aspect of the total self-concept. Thus there are many other sources of interpretation in any particular interaction, and we are not always aware of any or all of these.

This sense of identity is multifaceted and complex, with ethnic identity only a part of it. Therefore, in order to understand ethnic identity we first explicate the concepts of *self* and *identity*. We can then apply ethnic identity to the African American community. This approach also allows us to understand identity in its broadest sense and fit ethnic identity into this larger framework. In this way African American ethnic identity is contextualized as a part of an overall personal identity as well as characterized as a quality of the community. We ask the reader to bear with us as we weave our way through a discussion of self and identity before reaching our goal of discussing African American ethnic identity.

The purpose of the current chapter, then, is to articulate a conceptualization of ethnic identity that is derived from an understanding of the total self-concept and then apply that conceptualization to African American identity. Finally, the results of a series of studies focusing on African American ethnic identity will be described. While discussing the self in general terms, we focus on U.S. culture since, ultimately, it is the identities of an ethnic group within that national culture we wish to explicate.

Self-Concept and Identity

The notion of self, personhood, or personal identity seems to be universally held (Geertz, 1976; Hallowell, 1955), although culturally variant. Existing evidence indicates that most, perhaps all, cultures have a notion about something we can call "self," although the specific notions of self vary greatly across cultures. In addition, a number of perspectives on self have emerged as researchers attempt to explain the construct (Carbaugh, 1989).

We start by conceptualizing the self as both a psychological and a communication process. As a psychological construct the self is seen as an integrated, hierarchically organized set of self-attributes or components (Bugenthal & Zelen, 1950; P. Burke, 1980; Cheek & Hogan, 1983; Hoelter, 1985; Kuhn & McPartland, 1954) that defines how an individual perceives him- or herself and that influences perceptions and social behavior. The self, then, is constituted by "the meanings one attributes to oneself as an object" that are experienced in interaction with others (P. Burke & Tully, 1977). These meanings are constituted into identities and the identities into organized sets, each of which is associated with a situation or role and some of which cut across a wider range of situations and performances than others (P. Burke & Tully, 1977).

The self is also a communicative process. All social behavior has an aspect of enacted self. That is, a person's sense of self is part of that person's social behavior and the sense of self emerges and is defined and redefined in social interaction (Blumer, 1969; G. Fine & Kleinman, 1983).

From this perspective the self can been seen as a characteristic of the individual as well as of communication, of the communicator as well as the relationship, and of the mind as well as social behavior. Identities are part of the self and take on these same characteristics. We will briefly explicate some of the implications of this position for identity, and then apply this perspective to the study of ethnic identity.

Hierarchical Organization of Identity

Individual, internal, subjective identities are seen as organized *hierarchically*, with the more general, pervasive, encompassing, and influential identities on top and more situation-specific identities on the bottom (P. Burke & Tully, 1977; McCall & Simmons, 1978; Rosenberg, 1979/1986; Stryker, 1968). Hierarchically superordinate identities are more likely to be invoked in general and in more situations as well as more likely to be enacted in combination with other identities (P. Burke, 1980; P. Burke & Franzoi, 1988). Some may call these superordinate identities the "personality." This hierarchy has a degree of permanence, its parts are interrelated, and it exists on at least two levels of interpretation. Each of these aspects of hierarchy is discussed in turn.

Theorists disagree as to the permanence of the hierarchy. Some see the relative ordering of identities as more transient and situational (e.g., McCall & Simmons, 1978), while others see it as more enduring (Stryker, 1968; Stryker & Statham, 1984). However, R. Turner (1968) notes that the self has the contradictory properties of *constant change* and *temporal consistency*. Slugoski and Ginsburg (1989) call this "the paradox of personal identity—that at any moment we are the same as, yet different from, the persons we once were or ever will be" (p. 36). This paradox or duality is problematic for dimensional perspectives that see meaning as constructed of bipolar opposites. Emphasis is not placed on polarity nor the tension between the poles. Rather, the emphasis is on aligning a person or event at one point along a continuum. A dialectical perspective[1] however, integrates opposites. An event is both bad *and* good; it does not have to exist at one point along a bad-good continuum. The key to the dialectical view is the tension between the polarities and the movement along the continuum in response to changing and evolving pressures.

Utilizing the perspective derived from dialectical thought we conceptualize the identity hierarchy as both *enduring* and *situational/changing*. Fitzgerald (1974), for example, distinguishes between fixed (derived from group membership) and relative (situational) identity. One way to work through this apparent contradiction is to hypothesize that, depending on the maturity of the individual, the overall central image of the self is relatively enduring; specific manifestations in specific identities less enduring; and enactments in social interaction the least stable of all. In addition, the ordering and structuring of identities to form the overall self-concept may also change, with the gestalt experienced as stable. Another way to view the dialectic is to understand the competing pressures of maintaining self-consistency and conforming to social norms. How did persons who saw themselves as "Negro" handle a shift in identity to "Black" during the Black Power Movement of the 1960s?

Certain identities, then, tend to emerge more frequently across situations as hierarchically superordinate but there are situational variations in these processes and how they are enacted in social situations. Thus a hierarchically *super*ordinate construct on the individual level may be *sub*ordinate in an instantiation. Further, the superordinate construct may be enacted in different ways in different situations depending upon which other identities are salient and manifested in the situation. For example, one's gender identity may be enacted differently when linked with "employer" or with "friend," or when enacted in a situation calling for comforting (e.g., an employee's spouse dies) or discipline (e.g., an employee is consistently late for work).

This principle has important implications for African American ethnic identity. As indicated in Chapter 1, the Afrocentric position stresses the commonalities among African people over time and across space (Asante, 1980, 1987). As we shall see, however, identities have changed during historical periods. For the individual the implications are also profound. Later we will discuss code switching and other aspects of identity management. These can be seen as part of the enduring and changing nature of identity as African Americans retain a sense of self and adjust to competing situational demands. In addition, we can see that ethnic identity itself will be more or less salient for particular people and in particular situations. Thus an African American may be troubled by behavior that stresses ethnic identity in a situation in which this identity is not particularly salient. As we shall see in Chapter 4, such treatment may be seen as an indirect form of stereotyping.

A second quality of the hierarchy is the interrelationship among its elements as well as between elements and the environment. Roles and identities are always viewed in relation to *counteridentities* and *co-identities* (P. Burke & Tully, 1977; Lindesmith & Strauss, 1956). Counteridentities are those enacted to complement an identity. Just as one's role can only exist in relation to the counterroles played by others in the social environment (e.g., teacher/student; buyer/seller), identities exist in relation to counteridentities within the hierarchy. Co-identities refer to the multiple identities enacted in any instantiation. For example, while discussing a film at a party, you may enact gender, occupational, and personality identities. Each of these may be seen as co-identities.

Counteridentities can be of two types. First, there is the complementary identity enacted by others to allow smooth social interaction (e.g., speaker/listener). Second there are the identities not chosen. For example, choosing the identity of buyer often pre-cludes the role of seller. And, in some situations, there are many counterroles/-identities (e.g., ethnicity) (P. Burke & Tully, 1977). In a group discussion there may be coalition members, opposition, and group facilitators. The commercial marketplace may consist of buyer, seller, consumer advocate, and government regulator.

Most behavior enacts multiple identities. It is rare for a single identity to overwhelm all others. It is more common for multiple co-identities to be enacted. As Nakayama and Peñaloza (in press) note, identity is fluid with an instantiation expressing a number of positions. Like counteridentities, these co-identities can be com-plementary or impose competing demands. It is, in part, for this reason that we begin this chapter with a discussion of self and identity before focusing on ethnic identity. African American ethnic identity is but a part of an individual's overall identity. The organization of this chapter stresses this framing. However, in a racialized society such as the United States we often focus nar-rowly on racial identity. As we shall see later in the chapter, ethnic identities are often salient.

Both of these relational properties—identities in relation to counteridentities and in relation to other identities in the hierar-chy—have *ethnocultural properties*. This is a third quality of hierar-chy. The reference points and relational juxtapositions are defined by ethnocultural standards, thus allowing for social interaction based on shared meanings and consensus on role expectations (P. Burke, 1980). P. Burke (1980) suggests that identities must always be studied relationally and never in isolation. The salient issues are the similarities with a class of similarly situated people and the differences from other classes (McGuire, McGuire, Child, & Fujioka, 1978; Stone, 1962). This property of identity has impor-tant implications for social categorization as we shall see later in this chapter.

Fourth, identities exist on different levels of interpretation. Like other social and cultural constructs, identity has both *content* and relational aspects (Watzlawick, Beavin, & Jackson, 1967). Watzlawick et al. point out that specific messages have a content (the topic and manifest meaning) and imply something about the relationship between people. For example, saying "pick that up" means that you want something lifted up (content) at the same time it implies power or control over the other person (relationship). Identities also have a content or meaning to people (both self-perceived and other ascribed) and imply a relationship.

The content or meaning of the identity is largely invested in self-labeling and its associations. Thus one may label an identity "teacher" and this label will have personal meaning. The relationship aspect implies a connection between and among various self-identities and with other people and positions in social life. As a "teacher" I need "students." The identity "minority" means that the person is a member of a group that is numerically less than 50% (content), but implies an inferior relationship that has led many to question the usefulness of the term (Fairchild, 1985). This has led some to use the terms co-culture or co-population instead.

Expressions of identity also have content (i.e., the messages that enact it) and relationship (i.e., the implications about the relationships between people) levels of interpretation. For example, African Americanism can be expressed through African metaphors that constitute part of the content of the enactment of the identity. But the enactment also implies a relationship to other members of the group and to members of other groups. This relational element may manifest itself in code switching to reflect in-group/out-group distinctions and power relationships.

In addition to the components articulated above, the self-concept hierarchy also includes an *affective* dimension. Zajonc (1984) argues that emotional reactions are hierarchically prior to rational analyses. Interactionists view an *affective self-identity* as one in which the self is seen as a person who operates on affect or emotion rather than action (Mutran, 1987). Others would label this construct *"self-esteem"* and define it as a person's affective reaction to self-attributes and roles (Jenkins, 1982). This emotional component is one of the more frequently examined aspects of self (P. Burke & Tully, 1977). Greenwald, Bellezza, and Banaji (1988) have shown "that self-esteem is a pervasive component of measured self-concept, even for measures that lack manifest esteem-related content" (p. 34). Although self-esteem is not stressed in the work of identity conducted under the rubric of symbolic interaction, one may apply the previous analysis to the affective dimension of self.

Studies have repeatedly shown African American self-esteem to be equal to or greater than that of European Americans, in apparent contraction to expectations based on status differentials in U.S. culture (Hughes & Demo, 1989). Recent analyses have separated personal and racial self-esteem and personal self-efficacy (Hughes & Demo, 1989; McCombs, 1985; Wright, 1985). Only personal self-efficacy seems vulnerable to racial inequality and this may explain differential achievement levels (Hughes & Demo, 1989).

From this discussion we conclude that identities are parts of a hierarchically arranged self-concept that is both enduring and changing and consists of identities and their counter- and co-identities, content and relationship dimensions, and affect. We continue our discussion by considering the types of identities that constitute the hierarchy.

Types of Identities

A number of systems have been proposed to delineate the types of identities. Many writers divide identity into social roles and individual attributes, although they provide different labels or terms for each (Brittan, 1973; P. Burke & Tully, 1977; C. Gordon, 1968; Kuhn & McPartland, 1954). All these approaches share in common the distinction that the self consists of identities associated with roles, groups, and categories (e.g., group memberships) on the one hand, and personal or individual characteristics (e.g., personality characteristics) on the other, or both. In U.S. culture the locus of identity has increasingly emphasized the individual rather than society, thereby rendering the development of a sense of self more problematic (Bellah, Madsen, Sullivan, Swidler, & Tipson, 1985; Philipsen, 1987) and situationally emergent.

Some writers limit identity to group memberships (e.g., Barth, 1969; Isaacs, 1975; Lian, 1982). Others argue that identity should not be vested in objective group membership. Collier and Thomas (1988) maintain that a priori predictions from ethnic or racial memberships are an oversimplification because the identity may not be salient to a particular situation or may have different meanings to various group members. Instead, Lian (1982) and Collier and Thomas (1988) believe that identity is established and reestablished in interaction and, therefore, has an *emergent* quality. From this emergent perspective identity is situationally problematic, not static and ascribed based on a priori group membership (S. Banks, 1987;

G. Fine & Kleinman, 1983), and persons are continually negotiating their identity (Brown & Levinson, 1978). Thus the language or discourse of a community, particularly that which is about its identity, is an important component of identity.

Even emergent identity may be located in group memberships. One's membership in an academic group may emerge as a salient identity when discussing occupations at a party or when interacting with other academics. How are we to know which group memberships are salient in any one interaction? It has been suggested that this is dealt with by the *networks* approach that incorporates the notion that people choose among social groupings and constitute them through their actions (Geertz, 1973).

Hoelter (1985) argues that social categories (e.g., gender, age, ethnicity) are relevant to identity when they manifest themselves in the social networks within which people interact. *Networks* are membership groups with shifting compositions and meanings that are enacted in social life. Networks are created and enacted into being; groups exist a priori. Networks may enact existing groups, but the concept of network stresses the social bonds and lines of communication between and among people rather than the a priori existence of the group. At issue are the actual social relationships among people. With whom does an individual interact?

Within the African American community this issue is salient in a number of areas. What sort of identity is communicated by membership in Black community churches? A Pentecostal or an Episcopalian church? Whose children participate in the Jack and Jill Clubs? Date only European American partners? Within the community, what of associations with lighter or darker skinned people? Which individuals and groups speak the language of the "hood" (i.e., neighborhood) and which do not? These questions are emotionally charged and speak to central issues in the role of social networks in African American identity. They also are reflected in artistic expressions such as Spike Lee and John Singleton movies and permeate the legal structure of society. For example, a judge recently ruled that discrimination suits may be predicated on distinctions among African American skin colors ("Color Bias," 1989).

The question of group membership and network involvement also highlights the distinction between identities that are *internally defined* (subjective, perceived, or private identity) and those that are *externally imposed* (objective, actual, or public identity) (Barth, 1969; P. Berger, 1966; Erikson, 1968; Hofman, 1985; Lian, 1982). Lian (1982, p. 44) argues that "in an ethnically plural society where there are several competing universes, identity is highly problematic because individuals and groups have to adapt to a situation of competing universes." As an individual moves through and among various networks, identities are subjectively perceived and externally attributed. Again, it is the dialectical tension between internal and external definitions that gives vitality to the lived experience. We feel that self-concept consists of both individual and social elements such that both *objective* (imposed from the outside) and *subjective* (self-perceived) group memberships are salient and the dialectical tension between the two is often more salient than either individually.

Objective group membership, which is ascribed to an individual by others (Sachdev & Bourhis, 1990), may directly influence the development of identity through socialization and stereotyping (McCall & Simmons, 1978). Objective membership also may indirectly affect interaction through its influence on situated self-labeling (McCall & Simmons, 1978) and how the ascriber interacts with the person (Collier & Thomas, 1988; De Vos, 1982). Certain objective memberships are more overt because they are difficult to hide (e.g., language, race, gender), while others are more covert (e.g., occupation, mental abilities) and therefore more easily hidden or selectively revealed. For example, the fact that people racially categorize makes it difficult for African American ethnic identity not to be salient in interethnic interaction. However, African Americans may label this Stereotyping when ethnic identity is not germane to the situation (Hecht, Ribeau, & Alberts, 1989). Thus the clash between objective, externally imposed, or ascribed identities and subjective or internally selected identities is an important one.

While we retain objective group memberships as part of the overall model of self and identity, we emphasize subjective group membership based on our belief in the symbolic dimension of culture and the social construction of identity (P. Berger & Luckmann, 1966). K. Burke (1954) asserts that the name we give to things and people (e.g., identities) is a way of categorizing our experience of them, and Schneider (1976) argues that cultures are constituted by "symbolic galaxies" or clusters that form around "core symbols." More politicized groups may be more consciously aware of these symbolic galaxies.

Thus identities may be symbolic in nature and core symbols are the most central of these symbols. As discussed in Chapter 1, core symbols are unifying and dominating and orient people to their social world (Carbaugh, 1989; Collier, 1992; Katriel, 1987; Mechling, 1980; Philipsen, 1987; Schneider, 1976; Shuman, 1986). Cultural and ethnic groups differentiate themselves through symbolic emblems (De Vos, 1982), and these symbols unite communities (Taylor, 1977). This symbolic notion consists of selves that people would like to become, might become, or are afraid of becoming.

The importance of verbal and nonverbal symbols can be seen in Cultural Nationalism movements (Asante, 1980, 1987; Karenga, 1982). These movements frequently seek to change names, key labels, dress, celebrations, and other emblems and symbols. However, it is important to keep in mind that while ethnic identity may now be considered symbolic, historically it has been a racial ascription (Goldberg, 1990).

Gans (1979) argues that the ethnic identity of third and fourth generation European Americans is voluntary and largely symbolic. He claims that the functions of such groups have disappeared along with ethnic neighborhoods and occupational stratification by culture and, as a result, membership is primarily a symbolic activity with expressive rather than instrumental functions. These symbols must be visible and clear and easily expressed and felt. Examples of these symbols might include the "holocaust" for members of the Jewish religion and the "diaspora" for descendants of Africa and Palestine. He terms this phenomenon *symbolic identity* and utilizes the concept of "core symbols" to refer to the key features. Thus identities function symbolically to convey the meaning of the ethnic group and to establish uniqueness. Identity does not require actually functioning groups or networks for its maintenance since the allegiance is to the symbol and not to the actual collectivity (Gans, 1979).

In an insightful analysis, Krizek and Stempien (1990) demonstrate the geographic and cultural influences on symbolic identity maintenance. They argue that in areas of the United States where established ethnic communities exist, Gans's formulations have greater applicability. There, ethnic identities can be maintained symbolically since membership in those groups has a long and established history. However, in areas such as the southwestern United States where ethnic groups are reconstituting themselves through second-wave migratory patterns, face-to-face interaction ("ethnic revivals") are being evidenced. Thus it would seem that both subjective/symbolic identity and actual group/network membership approaches are needed to encompass all aspects of identity.

Dimensions and Dialectics

While identities may be classified within typological systems, they also may be aligned along dimensions of meaning or constructed as dialectical clashes between polar opposites. Semantic dimensions and dialectics may be conceived of as codified rules or norms (Carbaugh, 1987; Sigman, 1980). In the present analysis dimensions are cast as polarities reflective of rules and norms, with stress on the tension between the poles as well as temporally framed placement along the dimension. For example, we might be concerned with how active or passive an identity is perceived to be as well as how the individual manages the activity *and* passivity in the identity.

Numerous dimensional systems have been proposed. Research shows that a great deal of information is lost when a global model of identity, which ignores dimensional distinctions, is applied to the data (Hoelter, 1985). Examples of these dimensional systems are included in Table 2.1. Most dimensional systems include the concept of salience or potency. Salient identities have greater impact on social behavior (Hoelter, 1985).

A different type of dimensional system is offered by Carbaugh (1989). The dimensions of independence/dependence, communicative/closed and aware/unaware are derived from an analysis of talk on the Donahue show. The "U.S. self" is described as normatively independent, aware of self and others, and communicative (i.e., expressive).

The actual naming and numbering of dimensions is probably situationally variant. What is important here is the identification of normative categories and the understanding that in any situation,

Table 2.1 Dimensions of Ethnic Identity

Dimensions	Source
Evaluation	Burke & Tully, 1977; Heise, 1977a, 1977b, 1979; Hoelter, 1983, 1985; Hofman, 1985
Activity	Burke & Tully, 1977; Heise, 1977a, 1977b, 1979; Hoelter, 1983, 1985
Potency	Burke & Tully, 1977; Heise, 1977a, 1977b, 1979; Hoelter, 1983, 1985; Hofman, 1985
Stability	Hoelter, 1983, 1985
Affect-General	Hoelter, 1983, 1985
Affect-Depression	Hoelter, 1983, 1985
Anxiety	Hoelter, 1983, 1985
Salience	Collier & Thomas, 1988; Giles & Johnson, 1981, 1986, 1987; Hoelter, 1983, 1985; Stryker, 1968, 1980, 1981; Stryker & Serpe, 1983
Intensity	Collier & Thomas, 1988
Scope	Collier & Thomas, 1988
Centrality	Hofman, 1985

individual and social identities are dimensionally situated by social actors. The process is fluid and dynamic, reflecting the dialectic tension inherent in polarities. For example, a social identity such as "relational partner" may be situated along an intensity dimension. At various points in time the relationship has the competing pressures of intensity and passivity, is experienced as more or less intense, and the intensity with which one identifies as a relational partner emerges and recedes as an issue as the dialectic is resolved and remanifested. The dynamic tension between the individual and social levels and the poles of the dimensions (e.g., conflicting needs for intensity and passivity) are played out in social life.

Identity and Social Interaction

Thus far we have attempted to clarify the essential nature of identity. We noted in Chapter 1 that one of our primary assumptions is that interaction is constituted and interpreted through identity. Thus interaction is central to the notion of identity and vice versa. Identity is formed, maintained, and modified through social interaction. Identity then begins to influence interaction through shaping expectations and motivating behavior. Identity is also enacted in social interaction, and the conditions of that interaction influences the enactments. Finally, identity is both an individual and a social event. These processes will be discussed in the section that follows.

The self can be thought of as an organized system of meanings created through social interaction (P. Burke & Tully, 1977). People perform certain roles and are influenced by the reactions of others to their role performance (Erikson, 1959, 1960; Ganiere & Enright, 1989). Meanings are attributed by others and attributions internalized as, over time, a person's actions are assigned meanings through and in social interaction (Mead, 1934). Gradually, some of these meanings are generalized across time and form the more core identities in the self. Significant symbols become attached to self and the self-concept is experienced through these symbols (Mead, 1934).

Identities also are formed through naming or locating the self in socially recognizable categories (P. Burke & Reitzes, 1981; Foote, 1951; Stryker, 1968). We create an identity through applying these categorical labels to ourselves (e.g., woman, middle class, yuppie), and these identities are confirmed and validated (or disconfirmed and invalidated) through social interaction (P. Burke & Reitzes, 1981; Goffman, 1959; Weinstein, 1969).

Thus identity is formed and shaped through social interaction. Once formed, identity influences the flow of social behavior and continues to be influenced by social interaction. The influences on interaction may be seen in expectations and motivations, while the enactment of identity in interaction exemplifies the mutually caus-ative process discussed in Chapter 1.

Identities provide expectations about society. Tajfel (1978) ar-gues that belief systems about the nature of society are a part of identity that influences relations between groups. From these beliefs and experiences in the ethnic culture, social actors form expectations about social roles, conversations, situations, and re-lationships. For example, gender identity influences the ways that women and men are expected to behave in reference to each other (Maltz & Borker, 1982; Weedon, 1987) and certain variants of African American identities imply differential power relationships with European Americans (Hecht & Ribeau, 1991). Finally, certain identities are linked to personality traits. Stereotypes of ethnic terms or labels are based on rigid use of these links (Fairchild, 1985).

Identity can also be seen as motivating behavior. P. Burke and Reitzes (1981) identify two ways this occurs. First, people seek to maximize self-esteem or think well of themselves (also see Jenkins, 1982). Second, people strive for self-consistency. We may add a third and perhaps overriding constraint emerging out of the interpretivist framework. Identity is a frame of reference for interpreting the social world and it is out of these interpretations that social behavior emerges. Identity schema also influence emotional reactions, further guiding interaction. The findings of P. Burke and Reitzes (1981) and P. Burke and Franzoi (1988) support this interpretation of the link between identity and social interaction.

As we have seen, identities provide expectations and motivation, thereby influencing interaction. On an even more intrinsic level, identity may be viewed as enacted in social behavior. Gans (1979) describes feelings, actions, and situations as enactments of identity, pointing to rites of passage, holidays, rituals, consumer goods (especially food), and political forms. Social interaction influences the enactment of identities in a number of ways. People monitor feedback to assess the effectiveness of *performances,* modifying their presentation of self to fit the situation (Goffman, 1959). Through a regulative process, the self assesses and modulates interaction in relation to identity (P. Burke, 1980).

The relationship between identity and social interaction raises important theoretical questions about the "location" of identity. Is it a property of the individual or the interaction? This theoretical distinction loosely mirrors the "theories in use" regarding self of participants in various world cultures. Carbaugh (1989) and Hofstede (1980) argue that views of self fall into two general camps: collectivist/holistic or individualistic notions. Holistic notions embed the self in the collectivity (social view of self) while individualistic notions view people as separate from society. Similarly, some social scientists have argued that interaction can best be studied at the individual level (Hewes & Planalp, 1987; Triandis et al., 1984), while others argue for the relational or social level (Montgomery, 1984), and still others seek to integrate the two (Harré, 1989; Kenny, 1988).

We believe that identity exists on each level (individual and interactional) and that the tension created between individual and social levels is part and parcel of that which constitutes the self. We conceptualize the self as a characteristic of both the individual and social interaction, the dialectic between the two, and the interpenetration of one in the other. Let us start with a discussion of the individual and social interaction before moving to the more complicated issues of dialectic and interpenetration.

Within mainstream U.S. folklore the self tends to be viewed as an individual entity (Carbaugh, 1987; Geertz, 1976). Carbaugh (1989) argues that for this culture "the symbolic self is considered something that the individual *has*" (italics in original) (p. 62), and mainstream members of U.S. culture use a "container" metaphor to "create a sense of self as a separate, or at least separable, entity" (p. 77). Finally, members of this culture see the self as existing within each person and accessible only to that person (Carbaugh, 1989). Thus any discussion of self in U.S. culture should include the individual level of analysis as well as the social. This is particularly salient to African American identity. As we have seen, group members' personal and racial identities are not affected by racial discrimination, but their sense of personal efficacy is (Hughes & Demo, 1989). Thus the distinction between the level of identity (individual or collectivity) and the type of identity (esteem or efficacy) allows us to understand how many African Americans process ethnic relations in the United States.

We ascribe meaning to our self and use our identities to interpret and respond to the social world. At this level identity is a property of the individual's interpretative or cognitive processing. Rosenberg (1979/1986) defines *self-concept* as all of a person's thoughts and feelings about the self as an object and argues that conceptualizing the self as a property of the individual is one of the major approaches to self-concept research. From the perspective of social cognition, self can be seen as a schema or overall perspective for viewing oneself, with identities as models or prototypes. These schema and prototypes are enacted in conversation through sequences of acts or scripts (Markus & Sentis, 1982).

Conversely, identities are lived in communication and have existence in the social world between and among people. As P. Burke and Reitzes (1981) note, identities are social processes.

Indeed, it has been argued that the very idea of an individual psychology is a social and historical construction (Sampson, 1989). Geertz (1976) notes that the view of the self as a unique, separated whole is a uniquely Western one not shared by many of the world's other cultures. Others have argued for the ontological primacy of relationships rather than individual entities (Bateson, 1972; Watzlawick et al., 1967). Deconstructionists have challenged any view built on the primacy of the subject, claiming that the individual approach is designed to serve the ideological purposes of capitalism (Sampson, 1989). Out of these recent perspectives emerges a new and changing conception of identity or "personhood" as relational (Shotter & Gergen, 1989).

Conceptualizing identity from a social perspective provides a very different set of assumptions. Identities are formed, changed, and negotiated through social interaction (Goffman, 1967; McCall & Simmons, 1978; Scotton, 1983), enacted or performed through communication and relationships (Goffman, 1967) and language (Weedon, 1987), and constitutive of social pattern (Shotter & Gergen, 1989). We develop and modify our identities through a process of contrasting self with others and in-group with out-group (De Vos, 1982; Tajfel, 1974, 1982; J. Turner, 1987).

From a social perspective self is not only created through and in social interaction, but interaction is an enactment of self (Carbaugh, 1987, 1989; Collier, 1991; Philipsen, 1987). All social life enacts or presents an identity. The most extreme version of this position holds that identities exist *only* in communication. Pearce (1989) argues that people "consist of a cluster of social conversations, and that these patterns of communication constitute the world as we know it." Shotter and Gergen (1989) claim that "persons are largely ascribed identities according to the manner of their embedding within discourse—in their own or in the discourse of others" and social structure may be seen as created through enactments of identity (Weedon, 1987).

Our position is between the extremes. We believe that identity is both an individual and a social construct, emerging in a dialectic between the two (Babad, Birnbaum, & Benne, 1983; P. Berger & Luckmann, 1966; Carbaugh, 1989; Cheek & Briggs, 1982; Lian, 1982; J. Turner, 1982). S. Banks (1987) argues that the locus of control over identity is switched from individual to social levels according to situational demands. In this manner, identity is a feature of participants that is created in interaction at both levels of meaning. Philipsen (1987) maintains that the tension between the competing communal and individual pulls is a dominant theme in human action and we can describe cultures by locating them along this axis. Thus it is important to understand how individual African Americans construct their identity, looking at their language for self-description, meanings, and affect. In addition, we must understand how African American ethnic identity is enacted in conversation. What is there about their communication rituals that characterizes identity? dress? How do language choices such as code switching and verbal games invoke an identity?

Analysis of the dialectic between the individual and social levels also produces useful information. Some of the fundamental questions of psychology concern the relationship between an individual's self-concept and the enacted self within the social world. Carbaugh's (1989) analysis of the individual nature of self emerges from a method that examines this dialectic. Other social and human scientists struggle with questions of the individual in society. Indeed, the dialectic between individualism and collectivism appears to be one of the core, cross-cultural dimensions of values (Hofstede, 1980) and nonverbal communication (Hecht, Andersen, & Ribeau, 1989). Harré (1989) notes that all concepts are embedded in an individual and a collective matrix.

As a result we find it useful to retain each perspective (individual and social identity) as well as the dialectic between each in order to explicate the self more fully. By retaining these three elements a fourth emerges: the *interpenetration* of society and the individual. Interpenetration means that the individual and society cannot be defined apart from each other. Rather, they are seen as constitutive of each other (Sampson, 1989). P. Burke and Reitzes (1981) argue that performance and identity are mutually causal because each is derived from a common frame of reference. One uses this frame of reference to simultaneously assess the situation and enact an identity through behavior. While not cast in dialectic terms, their view is reflective of interpenetration.

The interpenetration of individual and social levels can be seen in concepts such as collective memory (Middleton & Edwards, 1990) and cultural space (Rota, 1990). *Collective memory* refers to the body of knowledge that is held intersubjectively by a group of people and forms the basis for their culture. *Cultural space* is used by Rota to denote the fact that ethnocultural groups may not occupy a contiguous geographic space, but instead maintain a collective construction or interpretation of the world.

We depart from a strict critical theory interpretation that stresses social and institutional control and focuses heavily on the dialectic through which social control is manifested. Our view allows for both the individual and the social perspectives, the dialectic between the levels *and* the interpenetration of the social and individual levels with each other, and emphasizes the individual's interpretation of each level as well as structural properties of interactional and societal systems.

The Process of Identity

The establishment and maintenance of identity are problematic due to the competing forces in society that push and pull individuals toward a variety of identities. These forces are the process of identity and have become even more problematic in modern society (Klapp, 1969). While ethnically pluralistic societies are not new, pluralism and identity are more important now due to geographical and social mobility and the recording of social and cultural history that calls attention to ethnic groups (De Vos, 1982).

Through these processes an individual develops and maintains multiple and shifting identities (Collier & Thomas, 1989; G. Fine & Kleinman, 1983) that emerge out of social interaction and are enacted in conversation. The salience of various identities ebbs and rises contextually and relationally (P. Burke & Franzoi, 1988). Group/network memberships emerge and recede in importance depending on situational factors such as group status, demographics (e.g., proportional group size), institutional and societal support (e.g., mass media messages), distinctiveness of identity within the group, group boundary permeability, and multiple group membership (Giles, Bourhis, & Taylor, 1977; Giles & Johnson, 1981, 1987; McGuire et al., 1978; Sachdev & Bourhis, 1990). Brittan (1973) discusses multiple identity as a result of this type of fragmentation.

Individuals often switch or alter identities. This is particularly common among people who occupy two social worlds, such as ethnic minorities. Sometimes called biculturalism, the alteration between the identities occurs as people move between social worlds (Lian, 1982). The shifting and problematic nature of identity may result in fragmentation (Brittan, 1973) and produce an ongoing tension.

These pressures, in turn, can lead to changes in identity as well as dysfunction. When the management of identities interferes with successful social functioning an individual may experience *identity diffusion* in which there is conflict between inconsistent values, *defensive narrowness,* in which barriers are erected, and *identity flexibility,* in which identities are minimized and diffused (De Vos, 1980; Erikson, 1968).

Others have criticized Erikson's position for its inappropriateness to nonmainstream groups. Attempting to correct for this problem, Marcia (1966) developed an alternative system for resolving identity crises:

> *Identity Achievement:* crisis has been resolved in commitment to occupation and ideology.
> *Moratorium:* crisis with vague commitments.
> *Foreclosure:* externally imposed commitments formed without crisis.
> *Identity Diffusion:* no set commitments, no crisis.

However, identity change is not the only outcome of tensions and crises. Musgrove's (1977) study of marginalized groups shows that people can make fundamental changes in behavior while maintaining identity. The groups in this study (blind people, gays, Hare Krishnas) often understood and adapted to the dominant group's definition of social reality and made significant changes in behavior without altering values and basic identity. Lian (1982) extends this analysis to members of "minority" groups who have to operate within the limitations of the dominant, mainstream culture. These people can maintain their own values and beliefs through interaction within group boundaries, and their marginalization may serve to strengthen group identity. Similar analyses have been drawn in the case of ethnic minority students who attend dominant culture schools. Bernal, Saenz, and Knight (1991), for example, suggest that those students who identify closely with nondominant ethnic groups can accommodate without assimilating the dominant culture. On the other hand, Blau (1977) argues that membership in more than one minority group may lead to increasing isolation. Thus the flowing and changing nature of identity is problematic but not necessarily dysfunctional.

Sachdev and Bourhis (1990) identify both individual and group strategies for dealing with pressures on language identity (identification with a language group) that involve both identity management and identity change. Individual strategies include *situational techniques* such as style or code switching, which occurs when members of a language group adapt their language use to the situation (Jenkins, 1982; Seymour & Seymour, 1979), and *language mobility*, which occurs when individuals switch to another language almost exclusively. Group strategies are aimed at changing perceptions of the entire language community and may be seen in recent events in Quebec, Canada (Sachdev & Bourhis, 1990).

Clearly, one potential outcome of identity pressures is *group mobility*. A number of related constructs have been developed to account for mobility in group membership. One of these is the construct of *near-group* memberships (G. Fine & Kleinman, 1983; Yablonsky, 1959) that involves participation in only a portion of the network based on self-interest (Strauss, 1976). Similarly, Mayer (1966) discussed *quasi-groups* or collections of people who have interacted in the past and will interact again if the situation calls forth these linkages.

The study of assimilation processes may also be relevant. Alba (1985) notes that most assimilation theories assume a motivation on the part of low-power groups to merge with high-power groups. Assimilation of identity, therefore, is assumed to be unidimensional. As a result, assimilation depends on the willingness to become part of the majority and is linked to identity and identity salience. Alba (1985) suggests reconceptualizing assimilation as a boundary control process emphasizing criteria for membership and methods of signaling membership. More akin to a cultural diversity or pluralism position, this process mirrors the construct of multiple shifting identities and identity diffusion and does not assume a unidirectional movement toward assimilation into the mainstream culture.

One way that shifting identities is managed is through a *boundary control* process (I. Altman, Vinsel, & Brown, 1981; Petronio,

1990, 1991). The flow of information about self is managed and the private self regulated. Various conditions (e.g., predicted outcomes, prerequisite conditions, threats) influence boundary conditions and ownership of information (Petronio, 1990, 1991).

These processes make it difficult to get a "fix" on identity. There are many different types of identities, hierarchically aligned along various dimensions such as salience. These hierarchies, while somewhat enduring, are also changing. Thus it is important to understand how these identities are created, chosen, and altered. Social categorization plays a key role in these processes.

Social Categorization

Without privileging any type of identity at the expense of the others, it is clear that many identities are tied to group memberships. Due to their salience in human experience certain perceived group memberships achieve a life of their own that almost transcends situational constraints. Thus while identity is often tied to individual self-perceptions and emergent relationships or group roles, evidence suggests that certain group memberships are superordinate constructs for many communicators (e.g., Aries & Moorehead, 1989; Emmison & Western, 1990; M. Fine & Bowers, 1984). For example, while marital status may be an important identity for many people, gender is often a hierarchically superordinate identity.

The problem lies in attempting to articulate a fixed hierarchy of identities that cuts across communicators and encounters. Research suggests that gender may override or interact with ethnicity among European Americans, while ethnicity emerges as the predominant factor among other U.S. ethnic groups (Gudykunst & Hammer, 1988; Ickes, 1984). This distinction is particularly salient to our discussion of Black Feminism later in the chapter. Similarly, the role of spouse may override group memberships (e.g., gender, family) in certain settings (e.g., anniversaries among couples with equal and non-gender-based relationships). What is clear in all of these discussions is that social groups often play a major role in identification. The next section of this chapter discusses social categorization and identity.

J. Turner (1982) defines a social group as two or more people who share a common social identification or perceive themselves as belonging in the same social category. *Social categorization* occurs when people organize their perceptions of the world around perceived memberships in these groups. Categorization is a natural cognitive process whose more salient categories include gender, socioeconomic groups, family, political organizations, nations, and ethnic groups. De Vos (1982) argues that a sense of common origin and survival has bound humans into groups throughout time. Thus social groupings have a historical origin and the classification of people based on these groupings seems a natural outgrowth.

These memberships provide a means of self-categorization. Tajfel (1982) claimed that people use the cognitive tool of social categorization to define themselves. He defined social categorization as "that part of an individual's self-concept which derives from his knowledge of his membership in a social group (or groups) together with the emotional significance attached to that membership" (1974, p. 69). Social categories are used to determine memberships and memberships guide perceptions of people and choices of interaction. However, the importance of membership as a factor varies with the value attached to the group, positive in-group image, imagined out-group image of in-group, importance of group membership, and group security (Bond & Hewstone, 1986).

Social categories also provide a means for differentiating people. One of the most common of these differentiations is that between in-group and out-group membership. Behavior may be conceptualized along a continuum from interindividual to intergroup (G. Miller & Steinberg, 1975; Sherif, 1966; Tajfel, 1982). Others (Giles & Hewstone, 1982; Stephenson, 1981) argue that interpersonal and intergroup factors are present in all interactions, with emphases shifting. Interindividual behavior is that in which memberships are less salient and people are responded to on a one-to-one, personalized basis. Intergroup behavior occurs when membership is salient and differential, and people are responded to based on group attributes. Treating another on an idiosyncratic basis characterizes the former category, while treatment as a group member characterizes the latter.

Membership is both self-perceived and ascribed (Garza & Herringer, 1987). As discussed earlier, there is an a priori or objective nature to group membership that is ascribed by the culture. However, membership is also subjective and because of this, actual membership may not be the key factor. Interaction with people who may objectively be classified as out-group members may be defined by participants in in-group terms and interaction with "in-group members" may be defined as intergroup.

Across a wide range of situations people tend to exaggerate intergroup differences and minimize in-group differences (Tajfel, 1981). Group differences tend to be more salient when there are convergent boundaries—categories based on a number of distinctions (e.g., gender, race, SES together) (Campbell, 1967). Tajfel (1978, 1981) argues that people try to perceive their own group in positive terms, and Brewer (1979) and Gudykunst and Hammer (1988) argue that in-group bias is based on assumed in-group superiority. When this superiority is challenged people restore positive identity by leaving the group, making group identity more positive, joining other positive groups to provide balance, or reinterpreting the negativity to martyr the group (Tajfel & Turner, 1979).

However, this analysis may not apply to all groups. Some groups may internalize their low power position (De Vos, 1982), and there are also many other perceptual bases for differentiating groups including common language, customs, and values; shared neighborhoods and occupational opportunities; and a common history of oppression. Positivity may be one of the bases for intergroup comparison but its relationship to other criteria must be subject to empirical scrutiny situated in the lived experience of group members. Bond and Hewstone (1986) report that intergroup differentiation in general was more salient to British respondents than Chinese respondents in their Hong Kong sample. Thus group differentiation itself may be a culturally variant phenomenon.

Social categories, however, do not subsume all of the self-concept. As indicated previously, identities have both an individual and a social component. As Garza and Herringer (1987) note, "The social categories used to group people (e.g., gender, ethnicity, religion, club memberships) are an important source of 'social self-identity' —the identity that guides social interactions." The importance of these social identities is demonstrated in research using the 20 Statements Test to measure self-concept. The task requires participants to complete the sentence stem "I am" 20 times in order to define their identity. Social identity is a major category in self-concept when measured this way (Garza & Herringer, 1987; C. Gordon, 1968; Kuhn, 1960).

Social identities may be further broken down into types or categories. Tajfel's (1974, 1978, 1981, 1982) model describes three essential aspects of social identity: knowledge (salience), value (evaluation and importance), and emotional significance. Garza and Herringer (1987) found three general categories of college students' social identities: (1) gender, religion, ethnicity; (2) school major and student status; and (3) hobbies and athletics.

Among these our interest here is focused the knowledge, value, and emotional significance of *ethnic identity*. M. Gordon (1978) argues that ethnic identity is a social category that develops during early socialization and constitutes a core status within the self. Others also present empirical and theoretical evidence of the superordinancy of ethnic identity (e.g., Aries & Moorehead, 1989; J. Banks, 1984; Emmison & Western, 1990; M. Fine & Bowers, 1984; Garza & Herringer, 1987), and ethnic identity appears to be more salient to African Americans, Hispanic Americans, and Asian Americans than to European Americans (Espinoza & Garza, 1985; Garza & Herringer, 1987; Gudykunst & Hammer, 1988; Larkey & Hecht, 1991; McGuire et al., 1978).

The ethnic identity of European American members of U.S. culture is relatively more stable but less important to them because they are society's "in-group," whereas the ethnic identity of "out-groups" such as African Americans and Hispanic Americans is relatively more important because they lack social status and use membership in their ethnic group as a source of social categorization (Garza & Herringer, 1987). For example, a decade ago a nationwide survey reported that 6 times as many African Americans as European Americans felt closest to their own group, and ethnic identity was strongest among low-power African Americans (Gurin, Miller, & Gurin, 1980). Although we have continued evidence of strong African American identity, this imbalance may be shifting. Recently, we have observed that the rhetoric of "White supremacists" in the United States attempts to raise the consciousness of European American ethnic identity and to increase its salience. In other areas (e.g., San Francisco) European American ethnic awareness may be increasing as a result of their numerical minority position.

We can see that for many U.S. residents ethnicity is a salient social identity. In the next section we will define ethnic identity, explore its problematic nature, and consider its linguistic features.

Ethnic Identity

Ethnicity is a complex experience, involving cultural, political, and economic factors (Lian, 1982). The notion of ethnic identity has important implications for intercultural communication. *Interethnic communication* may be defined as contact between people who identify themselves as ethnically distinct from one another (Collier & Thomas, 1988) or interaction in which differing ethnic identities are enacted by participants. Another way of looking at intercultural interaction is to view it as a social encounter in which ethnic identity is salient to one or both interactants and these identities are perceived as different and/or enacted differently in conversation. Similarly, *intercultural competence* may be defined in terms of the match between ascribed and avowed ethnic identity (Collier & Thomas, 1988). One way in which an interaction is considered competent is when the behavior of one interactant confirms the enacted ethnic identity of the other interactant.

Regardless of the overall importance of ethnicity, ethnic identity increases and decreases in salience depending on the situation (S. Banks, 1987). Ethnic identity is more salient when group identity is threatened (Bourhis & Giles, 1977), comparisons are made (Tajfel, 1978), or the person is perceived as more typical of his or her social group (Gudykunst & Hammer, 1988; Pettigrew, 1979). People use linguistic distinctiveness strategies when they identify strongly with their own group and are insecure about other groups (Giles & Johnson, 1981).

Thus ethnic identity is problematic, receding and emerging in importance as people seek to define and redefine group memberships.

For members of nonmainstream groups this process often involves consideration of the mainstream culture.

People not only adjust their own identities and identity performances, but adjust their perceptions of the identities of others. The "typicality" of a group representative influences membership interpretation. People will "subtype" information that differs from the stereotype (R. Weber & Crocker, 1983), and typical group members are perceived as better predictors of other group members (Wilder, 1984). Atypical members are perceived with more individualized or person-centered cognitive structures, while typical people activate category-based structures (Hewstone & Brown, 1986). People will individuate or treat a person as out of the group category after attempts to place the person within the category have failed (Fiske & Neuberg, 1990). When someone violates the stereotype this may also disrupt the view of the group as homogeneous (Wilder, 1986). Other studies indicate that people treat more intimate relational partners idiosyncratically and not through cultural stereotypes (I. Altman & Taylor, 1973; Honeycutt, Knapp, & Powers, 1983; Knapp, Ellis, & Williams, 1980; G. Miller & Steinberg, 1975; Won-Doornink, 1985).

Language plays an important role in the shifting nature of ethnic identity. Harré (1989) argues that self is linguistically constructed and Rota (1990) maintains that language explains and binds the identity of self through its surface and deep structures. Giles and Johnson (1981) contend that language is vital to any group's identity and is particularly salient for ethnic groups.

The issue of language and identity has been dealt with in a number of ways. Giles and colleagues have derived ethnolinguistic identity theory as an explanation for the relationship between language and ethnic identity. More generally, specific language and dialect have been related to identities (e.g., Jenkins, 1982; Smitherman-Donaldson, 1988). Finally, others have examined the semantic properties of labels (e.g., Hecht & Ribeau, 1991; Smitherman, 1977) under the assumption that the names we apply to people, places, and things influence how we behave toward them (K. Burke, 1954, 1959) and reflect how people give meaning to and organize their experiences (Hymes, 1972; Katriel & Philipsen, 1981). In the next section we will discuss ethnolinguistic identity theory. We will address the dialect and semantic labeling approaches when we deal with African American identity.

Ethnolinguistic Identity

Drawing on social identity theory (Tajfel, 1981, 1982; J. Turner, 1987), Giles and colleagues developed ethnolinguistic identity theory to explain how members of language communities maintain their linguistic distinctiveness, and how and when language strategies are used (Giles, Bourhis, & Taylor, 1977). The basic tenets of the theory revolve around techniques and processes for maintaining distinctiveness that include a variety of speech and nonverbal markers (e.g., vocabulary, slang, posture, gesture, discourse styles, accent) that create "psycholinguistic distinctiveness" (Giles & Coupland, 1991). One aspect of this distinctiveness is *vitality*, the ability of the group to survive as a unique and active collectivity in intergroup settings (Sachdev & Bourhis, 1990). Vitality depends on three sets of factors: status, demographics, and institutional support/control. Less vital groups are more likely to linguistically assimilate (Sachdev, Bourhis, Phang, & D'Eye, 1987).

While the original vitality factors were objectively assessed, more recent formulations take into account subjective elements (Bourhis, Giles, & Rosenthal, 1981; Giles & Johnson, 1981) and the factors of perceived group boundaries and multiple group memberships (Giles & Johnson, 1981, 1987). In addition, research suggests that subtractive identity, the difference between identification with one's own language group and the dominant group, is a better predictor than group identification alone (Ros, Cano, & Huici, 1987). Finally, recent research differentiates internal and external group factors (Allard & Landry, in press).

The theory also predicts convergence and divergence of communication styles (Gallois et al., 1988; Giles, Mulac, Bradac, & Johnson, 1987). Communicators use group status (in-group/out-group) to decide how and when to adjust to the other person. These adjustments or accommodations take the form of divergence and convergence in style. Early formulations of the theory predicted communication is more likely to diverge when the encounter is defined in intergroup terms and there is a strong desire for group identity or when there is the desire to disassociate self from other (Beebe & Giles, 1984; Bourhis, 1985). More recent work has identified a series of factors that constitute a model of accommodation. The factors include the individual's focus (what is being attended to), listener attributes, dependence on the group and available options (i.e., out-group contact), group solidarity (identification and satisfaction with group membership), power and dominance relationships, situational constraints (i.e., rules and norms), individual and group motivations, communicator's repertoires and abilities, and expectations (i.e., match between conversations and expectations) (Gallois et al., 1988).

The theory plays particular attention to the conditions under which ethnolinguistic identity is most salient. Giles and Johnson (1981) specify the boundary conditions as when people: (1) identify with a group that emphasizes its language, (2) are insecure in their comparisons to other groups, (3) have high perceived group vitality, (4) have closed and hard intergroup boundaries, (5) strongly identify with only one group, (6) perceive the other person as a member of a different group, and (7) perceive their status as higher within their social group than within any other group. If these conditions are met, people will tend to support the distinctiveness of their language group. Sachdev and Bourhis (1990) identified individual (e.g., change groups) and group (e.g., change evaluations) responses to negative identity when the comparison between one's own group and other groups is not favorable.

Research has not, as yet, linked ethnolinguistic identity theory to African Americans. There are clear linguistic (Black English) and nonverbal markers of distinctiveness and research on code switching that speaks to how group members manage the boundary process. These and other aspects of African American language use are presented in Chapter 3. Further, the analysis of the African American experience presented in Chapter 1 forms a basis for a vitality analysis. However, it would be informative to learn how and when African Americans identify with their group as a language community, manage issues of distinctiveness, and process the subjective vitality of their group.

African American Ethnic Identity

In this section we apply our analysis of self and identity to African Americans. As we have proceeded through the chapter we have attempted to foreshadow this move by using extensive examples from African American ethnic culture. Next we will provide a more detailed analysis of this identity group.

Studies of African American ethnic identity are not well advanced. Research is just beginning to explore the identities of this group and link them to social interaction. Existing work has largely focused on the labels used to connote identities and has been conducted from dimensional and semantic approaches. Others have discussed the role of language, focusing on Black English, a creole language form common to many African Americans (Smitherman-Donaldson, 1988). Finally, and only recently, researchers have begun to explore how African American identity is enacted in conversation (Hecht & Ribeau, 1987, 1991; Hecht, Ribeau, & Alberts, 1989).

In this section we will explore each of these areas of research. It should be apparent, however, that a great need exists for identity research within this population. Specifically, we would be informed by the application of ethnolinguistic identity theory; descriptions of identity crisis and maintenance in U.S. society; an understanding of how members of this group manage the dialectic forces of identity management both psychologically and through everyday talk; and a focus on the interplay among gender, class, and ethnic identity. In addition, African American identity has rarely been examined in terms of social roles or the objective and symbolic participation in social networks, and an understanding of these processes would be useful.

African American ethnic identity has emerged within a history of oppression (Bergman, 1969) and slavery (Comer, 1980) that has had a profound effect on emerging identities (Bolling, 1974; Jenkins, 1982; Wildeson, 1985). Our review of the social, political, and economic milieu for African Americans in the United States during the 1980s and into the 1990s presented in Chapter 1 indicates that the environment is still not conducive to a strong, positive identity.

The media often reinforce these negative identities and certainly reflect them. Early studies reveal that African American females were typically portrayed as aggressive and domineering, males as submissive, docile, and nonproductive, and families as matriarchal and pathological (Bogel, 1973; Hyman & Reed, 1969; Jewell, 1985; Staples, 1971). More recent research finds a bifurcation of images into the middle-class success story (e.g., Cosby/Huxtables) versus the drug and crime menace (e.g., police shows) (Gray, 1989). Unfortunately, Gray argues that these competing identities communicate the message, "you can make it if you try," which perpetuates the myth that the United States is a land of equal opportunity and those who do not make it did not try hard enough.

The competing pressures and duality of African American identity has a historical basis. This is consistent with our assumption that ethnic culture is historically emergent. W. E. B. DuBois establishes the conceptual foundation for African American identity when suggesting that he was both American—by citizenship, political ideals, language, and religion—and African, as a member of a "vast historic race of separate origin from the rest of America. In spite of their citizenship, the destiny of African Americans was not absorption into a servile imitation of Anglo-Saxon culture, but a stalwart originality which shall unswervingly follow Negro ideals" (quoted in Rampersad, 1976). The tension between these two realities has sparked the push for both integration and Pan-Africanism. Integrationists have worked to create expressive forms, educational philosophies, and political strategies that accentuate the American aspects of the equation (Frazier, 1962). Pan-Africanist and nationalist groups strive to strengthen the ties to Africa and develop traditions and rituals that grow from the philosophical and cultural roots of the "motherland" (Karenga, 1982).

As we argued in Chapter 1, African American identity must be viewed in the context of the larger ethnocultural system of the United States. Acknowledgment of African American duality is a prerequisite for the study of African Americans and African American/European American relations (Jaynes & Williams, 1989). For African Americans the pursuit of one or the other extreme on the continuum of consciousness (separatism/assimilation) can be problematic. R. Jones (1980) discusses the social isolation and adjustment problems that can arise from the emersion of an African American into a White middle-class world, and the decline of the Nation of Islam indicates the perils of separatism.

Glaser (1958) and Stanbeck and Pearce (1981) locate identities in relation to mainstream, European American culture using a model they claim is applicable to all status-defined group relationships. Glaser (1958) distinguishes four ways that groups adapt to the definitions of social reality defined by the mainstream culture. Some *segregate,* valuing their own identity as an end in itself even when this process disadvantages themselves. Others are *marginal* in that they shift between self-identities and are insecure in their definitions of themselves. A third type is called *desegregating.* These people seek to avoid an ethnic identity. Finally, there are those who *assimilate,* reacting only on an individual and nonethnic basis.

Stanbeck and Pearce (1981) describe four strategies for dealing with mainstream culture and define four corresponding identities: "tomming" (accepting lower status position), "passing" (acting as a member of the higher status group), "shucking" (conforming to the stereotype while rejecting the meanings), and "disassembling" (conforming to the stereotype while redefining the meanings).

While we applaud these attempts to relate identity to mainstream culture and to link identity and enactment, it is unfortunate the analyses do not include more positive strategies for identity management and maintenance. Neither Glaser nor Stanbeck and Pearce provide a means for functional and positive identity among African Americans that does not either separate entirely or assimilate.

Others describe the developmental stages of African American identity responses to mainstream U.S. culture. One system focuses on the conversion during the 1960s and 1970s from the label "Negro" to that of "Black" and the attendant meanings associated with the terms (Cross, 1978; Helms, 1990). Five stages were conceptualized. In the first stage thinking is dominated by European American determinants, denying African American elements of identity. Stage Two is the "Encounter" stage. Here Stage One thinking is disrupted by a new view of ethnic group membership. Usually this disruption involves a specific event that ends in the decision to "become Black." Next comes "Immersion-Emersion" in which the individual tries to rid the self of Stage One views and seek out a "Black self." This third stage has characteristics of "conversion." In Stage Four the new views are "Internalized," and in Stage Five they are reinforced and ritualized through participation in activities and networks. The final stage is therefore labeled "Internalization-Commitment." The implication is clearly that the end state is the desirable one toward which all African Americans should strive.

Jenkins (1982) argues that this view is limited since there is no single developmental path and no single desirable end state. Jenkins argues that all styles have both positive and negative consequences. Drawing on the work of Harrell (1979), Jenkins identifies six styles and their consequences: *Continued Apathy* (passive style), *Seeking a Piece of the Action, Counter Culture* (e.g., art, religion, drugs), *Black Nationalism, Authoritarian Identification,* and *Cognitive Flexibility.*

The Black social movement of the 1960s may be seen as a response to these negative identities. This movement sought to discard images and labels that communicate inferiority (Jewell, 1985), transform the identities from passive to active (Asante, 1978, 1980; Karenga, 1982), and promote pride and activism (Broom & Selznick, 1977). The attempt to move from subordinate status emphasized ethnic identity (M. Berry & Blassingame, 1982; Broom & Selznick, 1977).

These historical factors impact the age cohort that experiences them most directly during the formative years. The life experiences of these age cohorts probably are a more important force in explaining identity and interethnic relationships than their stage in the life cycle (MacLaury & Hecht, in press). Attitudes and behaviors, once established, tend to remain stable across the life span (Barresi, 1990). Shifts in identity are more likely to come about through new age cohorts than in changes in existing cohorts.

As a result, the history of African American rhetoric has been characterized by a continuing search for identity (Hope, 1975). This rhetoric is often played out in linguistic devices. As discussed in Chapter 3, Black English, a creole language created by slaves out of merging native African language with English, is characteristic of some African American talk (Jenkins, 1982; Seymour & Seymour, 1979; Smitherman-Donaldson, 1988). However, as Jenkins (1982) notes, African Americans are a pluralistic language community, with variations by geographic region and social class. As a result it is difficult to apply a consistent language or ethno-linguistic identity analysis.

Language clearly does play a role in African American ethnic identity. Within the African American community there are linguistic markers of identity and members of the group are often catalogued by their language characteristics (Jenkins, 1982). Many European Americans have negative attitudes toward speakers of any form of Black English (Seymour & Seymour, 1979) that are particularly salient when the topic is abstract or intellectual (F. Johnson & Buttny, 1982). Thus speakers of Black English may be disadvantaged in situations requiring expertise.

Many African Americans are ambivalent toward their own speech (Jenkins, 1982), calling it "slang" and treating it as substandard (Hecht & Ribeau, 1991). This makes it difficult for them to form and maintain a positive identity (Jenkins, 1982). This ambivalence may play itself out in many forms, prominent among which is code or style switching (Jenkins, 1982; Seymour & Seymour, 1979). Some have suggested that the African American who speaks both Mainstream American English and some form of Black English is the prototype for success (Jenkins, 1982; Seymour & Seymour, 1979). Thus language stylistics have important implications for African American ethnic identity.

Other studies examined the semantic associations for African American identity. The National Survey of Black Americans (see Table 2.2) measured the traits and qualities that characterize group membership. They asked a question regarding "the things about Black people that make you feel most proud." The majority of the responses fell into three categories: 28% concerned with socioeconomic and scholastic achievement; 24% concerned with group pride and mutual support shown by Blacks; 22% concerned with qualities of endurance, striving, and group progress.

These responses do not reflect an emphasis on communication and language. This may be explained by the question, which asked about Black people and thus focused the respondents on personal and group factors, and the fact that communication is often an implicit part of identity that must be either directly addressed (e.g., ask about their communication and identity) or measured separately and related (e.g., through statistical methods).

Table 2.2 Reasons for Feeling a Sense of Black Group Pride: What Are the Things About Black People That Make You Feel Most Proud? ($N = 2,107$)

Responses	Percentage
Socioeconomic or scholastic achievements	28
Group pride, identity, togetherness, and mutual support	24
Endurance, striving, progress made	22
Impact on mass cultures or athletics	5
Black cultural heritage	4
Morality and religiosity	4
Nothing or no difference	3
Miscellaneous	6
Not ascertained or inapplicable	4

SOURCE: Data from the 1970-1980 National Survey of Black Americans (National Opinion Research Center, 1991).

Ethnic labels are one aspect of language that is related to identity maintenance and evolution. Due to social categorization and stereotyping processes within U.S. culture, ethnic identity seems particularly focused on labels that provide a frame or anchor for naming identities and are thus useful for identity maintenance and management (Bosmajian, 1978; K. Burke, 1954, 1959). Labels and their associated meanings provide a useful measure of ethnic identity (Rosenberg, 1979/1986, 1989). The labels used for African American self-identification and the traits attributed to their group are revealing of social realities (Hecht & Ribeau, 1991; Jackson & Gurin, 1987; Jaynes & Williams, 1989; Lampe, 1982), and changing semantic designations reflect shifts in consciousness and a sensitivity to the sociopolitical milieu (Smitherman, 1977).

Labels or names fulfill two functions (Lampe, 1982). The *manifest function* is to denote similarities and differences, while the *latent function* is to provide expectations and guide behavior. Thus the labels assigned to identities are reflective of a confluence of meanings and associations and, as such, ethnic labels become representative of ethnic identities.

Earlier in U.S. history, African American identity labels were derived from Europeans (Fairchild, 1985). The label Negro is derived from the Latin *niger*, which translates to *negro* in Spanish and Portuguese, and the English language translation for *negro* is *black* (Fairchild, 1985). Thus the movement from Negro to Black as identity labels represents a movement from one European-based language to another.

Similarly, the grouping of African Americans and other ethnic groups of color into categories such as minority and non-White may reflect an inferior and negative image. The word *minority* is derived from *minor,* which connotes an inferior role and importance (Gettone, 1981) and "non-White" asserts that "White" is the relevant frame of reference for understanding and defining other groups.

The European influence on African American identity may have been greater in the 18th century South. Lavender (1989) argues that northern free African Americans of that era established identities that were more separate from European American citizens and that this is reflected in name choices. Examining historical records, Lavender (1989) shows that northern free African Americans used fewer European-based names than southern free African Americans.

The movement in identity is reflected in the shift of labels from Negro to Black to African American (Jewell, 1985). An attempt was made to substitute the label Black for Negro in the belief that the newer term would reflect self-improvement and unity (Carmichael & Hamilton, 1967). The predominant identities were expressed first in the labels Black, Black American, Afro American, and Black Afro American (Hecht & Ribeau, 1991), and most recently Black, Black American, and African American (Hecht & Ribeau, 1987; Hecht, Ribeau, & Alberts, 1989). Overall, Black is still the most frequently self-selected label although its use may be decreasing in favor of the label African American (Hecht & Ribeau, 1987, 1991; Hecht, Ribeau, & Alberts, 1989; Jewell, 1985; Lampe, 1982).

Much of the earlier work on African American ethnic identity looks at how European Americans and African Americans perceive various labels along prescribed dimensions. These studies grew out of interest in stereotyping and racism and, as a result, focused on perceptions of these labels without delving deeply into the gestalt of identity formation and maintenance.

In general, these studies show that overall the terms *African American* and *Negro* are viewed more positively than *Black* (Fairchild, 1985; Lampe, 1982), although this is truer of European Americans' and

Mexican Americans' perceptions than it is for African Americans' perceptions (Lampe, 1982). In particular, Lampe (1982) found that European Americans and Mexican Americans both rated Black as more threatening than Negro. Fairchild (1985) reports that European Americans associate the label Black with being loud, lazy and rude, and associate African American with talkative. Similarly, C. White (1989) and C. White and Burke (1987) found that hardworking, liberal, uneducated, follower, loud, musical, sensitive, neat, nonmaterialistic, struggling, and powerless are more likely to be associated with the term *Black* than the term *White*, and that European American and African American students do not differ significantly in their perceptions of these labels. Further, C. White (1989) reports that the profile African Americans provide for themselves is very similar to the profile provided for the general label Black, and there are fewer African Americans who associate with "White terms" (7%) than there are European Americans who identify with "Black terms" (19%).

C. White (1989) concludes that many of the terms associated with the label Black fit the typical stereotypes of this ethnic group (A. Miller, 1982; Stephen & Rosenfeld, 1982). For example, a recent survey found that African Americans were perceived to be less hard working, more violence-prone, less intelligent, and less patriotic than European Americans (National Opinion Research Center, 1991).

Haskins (1984) argues that these perceptions are consistent with the traditional associations for these labels. The argument is presented that "black" has long been synonymous with evil, sin, and sorcery, while "white" is associated with goodness. Further, Haskins points out that the color black is absolute, there being no real shades of it. While the term *black* traditionally evokes negative reactions, the term *Negro* has a more forgiving history. For example, Negro is traced to the Greek *Piper Nigrum*, which was used as a medicine. Thus findings that the term *Negro* is perceived more positively than *Black* is, for Haskins, consistent with the etiology of the terms. Further, the same study reveals that when compared with White, Black is associated with physical traits, rendering athleticism a cultural stigma. In contrast White is rated as more intellectual. These findings are consistent with the dialect perceptions (Black English/Mainstream American English) reported in Chapter 3.

African American identity may coalesce along a limited number of dimensions. C. White (1989) argues that these dimensions are *political* (African Americans are more liberal, struggling, powerless, and following than European Americans) and *social-cultural* (African Americans are more musical, neat, sensitive, hard working, loud, and less educated than European Americans). Similarly, Staiano (1980) argues that African American identity may be reduced to two major elements: power or action orientation and soul or emotion orientation. Hofman (1985), however, reports that ethnic identity is part of social identity for both African Americans and European Americans.

Our own preliminary analysis of a measure that sought to separate ethnic identity into political and social identity does not unequivocally support this view (Larkey & Hecht, 1991). From the descriptions provided in the literature we constructed a measure of the strength or degree of ethnic identification tapping both political (e.g., importance of participation by one's ethnic group in politics, education, the media, and business) and social/personal (e.g., centrality of being a member of the group, importance for self-definition, importance of group membership) dimensions. We administered this instrument to 129 African American and 95 European American student and nonstudent respondents and conducted a confirmatory factor analysis using the program PACKAGE.

Findings do not support the notion that there are two separate factors for identity for European Americans. Instead, identity appeared to be unidimensional (overall identity) for this group. Among African Americans, however, clear support was found for the two-factor solution (political and social identity). These findings suggest that ethnic identity operates very differently in the two groups. When interpreted more broadly, the implications are that ethnic identity may, conceptually, mean very different things in mainstream and nonmainstream groups. If validated in future studies these findings would suggest that ethnic identity theory must develop an explanatory mechanism to account for the differing dimensionality within each group.

Regardless of whether identity breaks down into political and social components one would expect that African Americans would experience problems developing and maintaining an identity given the cultural pressures and interpretations of the labels summarized above. This is one of the assumptions behind increased attention to counseling/psychotherapy issues specific to African Americans (e.g., Jenkins, 1990). However, research shows that African Americans have stronger (Hofman, 1985; Larkey & Hecht, 1991) and more positive (L. Smith & Millham, 1979) racial, ethnic, and national identities than European Americans. In fact, C. White and Burke (1987) report a negative relationship between self-esteem and commitment to ethnic identity among European Americans as compared to a positive relationship among these variables among African American college students. Similarly, Larkey and Hecht (1991) found a negative correlation between the degree of European American identity and the intimacy of their interethnic relationships. Thus stronger identity seems to be an inhibiting factor for European American interethnic relationships, but not for African Americans.

C. White and Burke conclude that African Americans do not internalize the negative images presented of them. But research also shows that European Americans have a more integrated personal identity structure than African Americans (Hofman, 1985), and higher socioeconomic status is associated with self-perceptions that include more "White traits" than "Black traits" (C. White & Burke, 1987). While racial inequality may not directly influence personal or racial esteem, it does impact feelings of personal efficacy or the belief that one can accomplish goals and be successful (Hughes & Demo, 1989). Thus there is a basis to conclude that for many individual African Americans, identity is indeed a problematic issue.

Our own work in this area shares an emphasis on ethnic labels as representative of identity. Identity types seem to coalesce around group labels or names. This work has identified the prevalence of the labels Black, Black American, and African American (as evolved from Afro American) as the most frequent labels and has examined related elements of identity salience. However, the primary focus of our studies has been the meanings associated with these labels as manifested in verbal descriptions instead of ratings, and the enactment of ethnic identity in social interaction.

We have used open-ended questions to understand the actor's ethnic identity. We do not devalue scalar methods of measuring meaning. However, open-ended or free-response descriptions provide a different view of the actor's perspective that is not restricted by providing anchors. The adjective descriptors in the C. White (1989) and C. White and Burke (1987) studies, for example, are meant to describe any ethnic identity. Research shows that checklists provide different information than free response formats (Burleson et al., 1988; R. Clark, 1979). In view of our emphasis on the interpretive and symbolic function of identity we chose to obtain the actor's own words and descriptions. Scales can be useful when derived from the perspective of the ethnic group. Therefore, prior to the construction of a scale we have attempted to capture the unique ethnocultural views of the designated group in their own language and then translate those descriptions into survey items.

We also believe that no single identity describes the variation within this community (J. Banks, 1981). Instead there exist many complicated and changing identities. While one label or identity may be used by the majority of the people (e.g., Black) or used in more situations, other labels provide a reflection of the diversity within the group and across situations. Additional definitions or meanings associated with any one label also may vary. Unfortunately, not enough research has been conducted to examine how identity is adjusted to situational demands nor how individuals change identity situationally and across the life span in response to the enduring/changing dialectic presented earlier.

With these issues and the view of identity articulated in this chapter in mind, we have been studying the identities that are used by African Americans, what these identities mean to members of the community, and how these identities are enacted.

In answer to the first question, we have consistently found three labels provided by African Americans to name their ethnic identity. In our data collected in the early 1980s among college students in California *(N* = 43) and Arizona *(N* = 26)[2] (Hecht & Ribeau, 1991) we initially found four labels: Black (46%), Black American (22%), Afro American (16%), and Black Afro American (11%). More recent studies (Hecht, Larkey, Johnson, & Reinard, 1991; Hecht & Ribeau, 1987; Hecht, Ribeau, & Alberts, 1989; Larkey

& Hecht, 1991; Larkey, Hecht, & Martin, 1991) identified Black, Black American, and African American as the primary labels,[3] with the most recent study in Arizona (Larkey et al., 1991) reflecting the following distribution:

    Black = 39%
    African American = 34%
    Black American = 10%

Earlier studies suggest that even larger numbers (52% and 72%) may have preferred the term *Black* (Jaynes & Williams, 1989). Since our own work is based on small, nonrandom samples in a limited geographic region, conclusions about these trends must be tempered. Labels such as Negro and Colored appear infrequently in all of these studies, and it would be informative to find out the characteristics of those retaining these labels.

We have also been interested in what these labels mean to those using them. To this end we have asked respondents, "Why do you use this label?" (Hecht & Ribeau, 1991) and "What does this term mean to you?" (Larkey et al., 1991). For purposes of analysis we will combine the Black Afro American and Afro American groups since they are the smallest groups and their responses are conceptually similar and use the more current, African American label.

Those choosing the label Black justify their selection by saying that it is the right label, generally accepted, reflective of their skin color, and the label they were taught. These answers reflect use based on social acceptability and consensus, as well as an aspect of external ascription. Their answers also reflect a mild patriotism and an almost unconscious acceptance of the status quo. Our more recent study (Larkey et al., 1991) indicates that this label is described as a racial identity, although there also appears to be a growing emphasis on ethnic pride, ancestry, and heritage among those selecting Black to label their ethnicity. While these people felt the label communicated race to other African Americans, they also believe it communicates pride, rights, and kinship. In fact, some feel that the label sends mixed or varied messages to other members of the ethnic community. Users of the term believe that "Black" communicates a wide variety of meanings to European Americans. Some feel that European Americans react to it in a racist fashion, others feel it is a racial identifier, while others take a different view, saying it reflects equality or sameness and is acceptable. Thus the label Black is taken as a racial identifier whose choice is predicated on skin color and social acceptability and whose use communicates race, pride, rights, and equality.

Respondents selecting Black American explain that the label means being both Black and American. Their answers express both patriotism and ethnic pride and reflect a place of origin and heritage. This is exemplified by statements such as, "my people built this country," and "we were here from the beginning." They also express the need to assimilate and "make it" in America. Finally, the group is similar to those using Black alone in their belief that the label is socially acceptable. Their answers, however, reflect a developing sense of ethnic consciousness not found among those using Black as a label and a recognition of cultural differences in "ways of thinking and behaving" that exemplifies their awareness of the duality of their existence.

Ethnic heritage is the key for those using the label African American. This is reflected in statements such as, "our roots are not in America." In addition, this group seems sensitive to the need to function in mainstream culture as reflected in the perceived "necessity to succeed in the system," while expressing an ambivalence toward what they describe as "dominant group values." They are aware of their ethnic past and pragmatic about their present situation. This is in contrast to Black Americans who do not seem to have resolved the dialectic between these competing pressures. In a more recent study (Larkey et al., 1991) users of this label stressed a blended heritage from both Africa and the United States, with an awareness of the label as an ethnic rather than racial identifier. In addition, they felt that the label communicated this heritage to other African Americans along with a sense of ethnic pride and kinship. Users of this label feel that European Americans do not understand its use or react in a racist fashion.

This research has produced a pattern in which Black respondents are the most conservative and accepting of the status quo while African Americans are the least conservative. Further, Black Americans, as indicated by the name, seem caught between the two extremes. Future research should delve more deeply into the meanings and explore how members of one identity group (e.g.,

Blacks) perceive the other labels, how they believe European Americans perceive these labels, and when these identities change.

Next we developed three bipolar, 7-step scalar items to measure the degree or extent of identification (totally/not at all) and two comparisons to mainstream, European American culture (superior/inferior, totally different/totally similar). All groups exhibited relatively high levels of identification (means of 5.76-6.08 with 7 being the highest score), with no significant group differences. Scores for the amount of difference were relatively neutral (4.57-4.71) and did not differ across the groups. Finally, results for superiority approached statistical significance ($p < .09$) and indicated that the African American group had the strongest feelings of superiority (mean = 5.69), followed by the Black group (5.19) and the Black Americans (4.50).

Correlations were also computed between the scales. These indicated a moderate relationship between the level of identification and superiority ($r = .54$; $p < .05$), such that the stronger the identification with the ethnic group the more likely were members to see their group as superior to mainstream culture. Small relationships also existed between similarity and level of identification ($r = .24$; $p < .05$) and between similarity and superiority ($r = .27$; $p < .05$).

In a follow-up to this study Larkey and Hecht (1991) compared the degree of political and social/personal identity of those using the labels Black and African American (there were too few using Black American for comparison purposes). While there were no significant differences for social/personal identity, those using African American reported higher levels of political identity.

When demographic indicators were examined, additional trends emerged (Hecht & Ribeau, 1991). There was a slight tendency for males to use Black more than other labels. African American tends to be used more frequently by older people (within a range of 18 to 40), and Black American is reported more frequently among those with lower family incomes.

Finally, we are interested in how these identities are enacted in conversations and conducted three studies to address this question. In Hecht and Ribeau (1991) we asked respondents, "What is there about your communication that reflects each label?" In Hecht and Ribeau (1987) and Hecht, Ribeau, and Alberts (1989) we asked respondents to provide us with the label they use to describe their ethnic identity and then describe either a satisfying or dissatisfying conversation they had engaged in during the past week with a White person. Next we linked the identity to the enactment. We will summarize the results of these three studies below. We believe, however, that future research is needed to observe ongoing conversations and link linguistic devices (conversational analysis), nonverbal and verbal message types (interaction analysis), and communication strategies (discourse analysis) with identity types.

Blacks characterize their communication by the use of slang, verbal aggressiveness, and a willingness to talk. This group is moderately concerned about negative Stereotyping and Understanding as issues in their communication with European Americans, place great emphasis on Other Orientation, and are the least likely to use Assertiveness to overcome problems.

People who label themselves Black Americans describe their communication characteristics as "speaking an acceptable code," "code switching," and recognizing "dialect differences." This group is also the most likely to feel negatively stereotyped and to feel that a lack of understanding inhibits interethnic communication. Consistent with their dual ethnocultural affiliation and their recognition of both ethnocultural uniqueness and assimilation, they are the only group to report with any frequency trying to improve conversations with both Other Orientation and Assertiveness.

Finally, African Americans believe that their communication is marked by nonverbal factors such as unique touch and space norms and awareness of dialect differences. Members of this identity group are least likely to feel stereotyped and only moderately likely to see Understanding as an issue in their relationship with European Americans. They are highly likely to suggest Assertiveness as a strategy for dealing with interethnic communication problems, but the least likely to try Other Orientation when such problems occur.

From these studies a picture of African American ethnic identities is beginning to emerge. These identities represent gradients of differences along certain dimensions (e.g., concern with social acceptance), while reflecting differences of type in other domains (e.g., whether identity is linked to skin coloring). Further, the labels are meaningful to in-group and out-group members, and preferences exist for certain labels over others. Finally, evidence has been presented that these identities are differentially enacted.

Ethnic Identity and Gender

One of the areas of African American identity that merits particular attention is its relationship to gender. As discussed previously, identity is multifaceted with gender and ethnicity frequently emerging as hierarchically superordinate. Further, the interplay of factors such as gender and ethnicity may create a double jeopardy for female African Americans.

For this reason, many recent studies approach the African American community from a feminist point of view and call for the study of African American women as a separate ethnocultural group (Collins, 1990; Hooks, 1984; D. King, 1988). Feminist scholars such as Collins (1990) point out that women share a history of gender oppression and such experiences transcend divisions created by race, social class, religion and ethnicity (Hartsock, 1983; Jaggar, 1983; M. Rosaldo, 1974; D. Smith, 1987). Collins (1990) points out that African American women have access to both Afrocentric and feminist traditions. This alternative epistemology is used by African American women to reflect the intersection of values and ideas that Africanist scholars identify as characteristically "Black" and those described by feminist scholars as characteristically "female." She argues that the parallels in the conceptual schemes ought to be included in scholarship about African Americans.

African American women, Collins (1990) argues, have dual memberships as members of their in-group and members of the oppressed out-group of women. African American women are sometimes more closely aligned with African American men, sometimes more closely aligned with Euroamerican women, and sometimes aligned with neither group. African American women are called upon to negotiate these contradictions, and hence, for African American women another particular dialectic of identity emerges.

D. King (1988) describes identity dialectics for African American women as more than double jeopardy, as "multiple jeopardy." She notes that there are several simultaneous oppressions occurring in the form of racism, sexism, and classism. The relationships among these forms of oppression for women are multiplicative; in other words, racism can be multiplied by sexism, and so forth.

In managing this dialectic of identity, African American women share an epistemological frame of which researchers of identity need to be aware. One characteristic is an emphasis on experience as a criterion of meaning. In addition, African American women use dialogue to assess knowledge claims and are committed to an ethic of caring and an ethic of personal accountability (Collins, 1990). An Afrocentric feminist perspective to the study of African American women taps the experience of African American women and acknowledges the context of oppression in which they live. Therefore, such a frame is a better representation of the African American female experience.

We have just begun to appreciate the differences between male and female African American ethnic identities. Collier (1991) found that there were similarities and differences in the way that African American males and females managed conflict. Future research is necessary to begin to understand how women and men come to know who they are as African American men and women, and what they think are appropriate norms and positive outcomes in their contact with one another.

Conclusion

In this chapter we sought to ground ethnic identity in a more general discussion of self and identity and then explore the ethnic identities of African Americans. One of our original research foci was on the labels people use to describe their own ethnic identity. These studies examined the meanings of these labels and their expressions through verbal and nonverbal communication. An illustration of this point is a self-identified African American who assumes an African name and wears a kafi and dashiki. Here ethnic identity is captured in a label and enacted nonverbally through attire.

Certain areas remain for exploration. First, while these and other studies establish the meanings the labels have for people who use them and to European Americans, we do not know what these labels communicate to African Americans who do not use them. How is the label Black interpreted by someone who uses the label African American? In addition, we do not know what African Americans think these labels communicate to European Americans. Both of these will tell us more about why people choose their labels and provide information about intersubjective meanings.

Second, we do not know if there is a hierarchically superordinate label that can subsume most members of the larger group. There are indications, for example, that Spanish-origin people use the terms *Hispanic* or *Latino/Latina* as cover terms to communicate with out-group members (Padilla, Ruiz, & Alvarez, 1983). Is there a similar term for African Americans? Will most members accept the label Black, the most frequently used label in most surveys, for their ethnic identifier, even if they prefer either Black American or African American personally? If so, should we consider Black the label for identity of the community? If a hierarchically superordinate identity exists does this explain why there are fewer than expected differences in the communication issues associated with various labels in interethnic communication? Perhaps in intergroup situations the superordinate identity, Black, is more salient while the more specific label (e.g., African American, Black American, Black) is more important in in-group situations and intergroup situations with groups other than European Americans. Context might well elicit the appropriate aspects of ethnic identity as defined by ethno-cultural expectations and expressed through communication.

The relationship between ethnic identity and other identities must also be explored. In this chapter, we suggested the importance of gender and class. Age may also combine with ethnicity. Coupland, Coupland, and Giles (1991) point out that discourse reflects age identity, and facework and "troubles-telling" are primary ways in which older persons negotiate their identity. W. Edwards (1992) found gender differences in linguistic style among African Americans in a Detroit community who were over 40 years of age. It may be that the older the person the higher the ethnolinguistic vitality as well. Thus future research should examine how other aspects of identity interact with ethnic identity.

Clearly greater progress has been made in conceptual areas and in comparative work. Less is known about the interpretations of these identities and their enactments in social interaction, and no single theory of identity integrates the diverse elements discussed in this chapter. In some ways the chapter poses a challenge to expand the scope of research in this area. The promise is a recognition of the differences within this ethnic community and a greater understanding of certain trends or commonalities in how members of the group interpret themselves and their communication. In Chapter 5 we present the preliminary workings of a new theory of identity derived from the conclusions regarding self and identity presented in this chapter.

We have attempted to describe African American identity as we know it. This quote from W. E. B. DuBois poignantly captures the character of African American identity (quoted in Jaynes & Williams, 1989):

> One ever feels his twoness—an American, a Negro; two souls, two thoughts, two unreconciled strivings; two warring ideals in one dark body. . . . The history of the American Negro is the history of this strife—this longing to attain self-conscious manhood, to merge his double self into a better and truer self. . . . He would not Africanize America, for America has too much to teach the world and Africa. He would not bleach his Negro soul in a flood of white Americanism; for he knows that Negro blood has a message for the world. He simply wishes to make it possible for a man to be both a Negro and an American, without being cursed and spit upon.

Notes

1. The concept of dialectic derives from critical theory and is often used to describe the tensions between polarities in everyday life (K. Altman & Nakayama, 1991). For example, relationships are seen as constructed upon the dialectical tension between polarities such as openness and closedness (Baxter, 1988; Rawlins, 1983). Here we use dialectic to describe not only social processes, but theoretical processes as well. On the theoretical plane we can understand the dialectic between two positions and then utilize that abstract dialectic to understand the social dialectics. In this manner theories can be constituted and reconstituted in the clash between individual and social levels of analysis just as relationships are constituted and reconstituted through the dialectics of social processes such as openness/closedness.

2. Although students, this sample was older than typical college participants, averaging 28.5 years of age in California and 27.4 in Arizona, with an average income of $23,526 and $35,909 for these states respectively.

3. In these studies, both student and nonstudent samples were utilized ranging from a low of 61 respondents to a high of 204, and drawn from California, Arizona, and New York. The average age ranged from 25 to 31.3, with average incomes in the low to upper $20,000s.

CHAPTER THREE

African American Communication Style

In Chapter 1 we argued that culture is socially emergent and is co-created and maintained as a function of identity. We also defined ethnic culture as a system of interdependent patterns of conduct and interpretation. We began the process of explicating this system in Chapter 2, in which we described African American ethnic identity. However, we also argued that *conversation* is one of the key aspects of culture (Philipsen, 1987). In this chapter we focus on characteristic patterns of African American conversation. African American ethnic culture emerges through these social patterns that also co-created and maintained the culture.

These patterns also express ethnic identities. Communication is multifunctioned, accomplishing such goals as providing information, regulating conversational flow, and exercising social control (Patterson, 1983, 1987). One of its more important functions is to express identities, one of which is ethnic identity. Some of the communicative properties of identity were discussed in the previous chapter. However, conversational behaviors do more than express identity, and our goal is to describe all of these conversational patterns.

The conversational style of African American ethnic culture is characterized in a variety of studies. These studies reflect a unique cultural mode of conversing that is expressed in language, relationships, and verbal and nonverbal messages. In analyzing these studies we identified common themes and inferred their functional properties and the underlying core symbols.

Caution must be urged in interpreting these research findings. First, most of these studies describe language, verbal messages, and nonverbal messages. They rarely examine the message meanings or functions, although at times these can be inferred.

Second, most of these studies use race as a variable, not ethnicity or culture, and do not consider a sense of self-identity. That is, respondents in these studies are classified by biology and not factors such as traditions, membership, and social organization. These studies also do not consider the degree or type of identification with the group.

Third, African American/European American differences are likely to be mediated by variables such as in-group/out-group status, gender, or socioeconomic status as well as contextual and regional factors, and these often are not incorporated into research designs. For example, kinesic (body movement) behavior is influenced by both race and gender, with body lean and eye gaze differences more pronounced for females than males (A. Smith, 1983). Black females look at the conversational partner less and lean toward each other more than White females (A. Smith, 1983). Researchers have also observed gender and race differences in other aspects of male/female relationships (Cazenave, 1983; M. Clark, 1985; Cromwell & Cromwell, 1978; Dejarnett & Raven, 1981; Ericksen, Yancey, & Ericksen, 1979; Gray-Little, 1982; Mack, 1974; Peretti, 1976; Ransford & Miller, 1983; C. Robinson, 1983), suggesting that African American males are more negatively stereotyped by females of their race and are more traditional about heterosexual, intimate relationships (particularly African American males who are middle class) than other race and gender groups. J. White and Parham (1990) provide an excellent summary of many of these issues. Our discussion of Black Feminism (see Chapter 2) highlights the ideology of these differences.

As a result, the findings of these studies do not fit neatly into our system. This is not a criticism of the studies, which are conducted within their own research traditions, but an explanation of the difficulty of integrating findings with those from our perspective. Our discussion of these studies will consider language style, core symbols of communication style, and other aspects of communication style.

Language Style

Cultural groups define themselves in part through language, and members establish identity through language use. African Americans are a pluralistic speech communication community in which regional and social class differences are apparent (Jenkins, 1982). Even linguistic behavior in socioeconomically homogeneous inner-city Black neighborhoods is not necessarily homogeneous (W. Edwards, 1992). Physical isolation, sociocultural orientation, and age-group affiliations affect social networking and linguistic style. Gender variations were apparent only in the older group members. However, within this diversity a creole language or dialect, *Black English,* has been identified as a distinctive language characteristic of African American ethnic culture (Dillard, 1972; Harrison & Trabasso, 1976; Jenkins, 1982; N. King & James, 1983; Labov, 1982; Moulton, 1976; Stewart, 1970; Wolfram, 1971). As a result of this language difference and other linguistic markers, African Americans often feel the need to switch between their own cultural language code and that of the more dominant European American society. In the pages that follow we describe Black English, code or style switching, and the oral tradition.

Black English

Black English is a distinctive language code. Some treat it as a dialect of Mainstream American English under the assumption that Africans came to the United States with no knowledge of English and developed the dialect while learning the mainstream language (S. Weber, 1991). Others argue that it is a creole language formed out of Mainstream American English and native African languages (Jenkins, 1982; Labov, 1982; Smitherman-Donaldson, 1988; Stewart, 1970; S. Weber, 1991), evolving from largely West African pidgin forms (Stewart, 1970; Traugott, 1976). Some of those in this latter group have argued that the dialect position demeans the language system and the African slaves by assuming that their native language disappeared rather than merging with that spoken by slave owners (S. Weber, 1991). From this perspective the study of Black English has been highly politicized because of the tendency to describe the language as a deviant or deficient form of Mainstream or Standard American English (Smitherman, 1977; Smitherman-Donaldson, 1988). Viewing Black English as a dialect stems from a Eurocentric vision that only describes what is "missing" and what is grammatically "incorrect." For this reason we will use Black English rather than Black Dialect to denote the language form. Seymour and Seymour (1979) suggest the use of the label Ebonics, a term derived from the words ebony and phonics, as an alternative and more positive label.

Like other language forms, Black English is governed by rules with specific historical derivations; it has been passed on through socialization. Black English is now recognized as a legitimate language form with a unique and logical syntax, semantic system, and grammar (Jenkins, 1982; Smitherman, 1977; Smitherman-Donaldson, 1988; Stewart, 1970) that varies in its forms depending upon which African language influenced it and in which region it was developed (Smitherman, 1977).

Early forms of Black English are scantily and irregularly recorded, but there is strong evidence of the African influence in both early and current forms (Smitherman, 1977). These influences are seen most in sentence structure and in semantics. Sentence structures have been influenced profoundly by the rules of the African languages. Although the vocabularies of the enslaved members of multiple tribes were different, most of these languages shared the same structural patterns. For example, subject nouns are followed by a repeated pronoun ("my father, he . . ."), questions omit *do* ("what it come to?") and verbs do not vary form to indicate tense, but context clarifiers are used instead ("I know it good when he ask me") (Smitherman, 1977).

The language and its various forms originally developed in a context with no language teachers, little encouragement to learn more than a simple form of English, and strict segregation (Smitherman, 1977). It is no surprise that African language patterns and meanings survived and that language structure and new words were improvised to create a unique cultural form. Some of these structures and words are often misunderstood as "wrong" when, in fact, special meanings are communicated by the created forms. For example, the use of *be* or *bees* and the omission of the verb form *to be* are both done strategically to communicate a particular meaning. Using *be* or *bees*, as in "it bees dat way" indicates a recurring or habitual pattern, while "it dat way" implies a one-time occurrence.

Other unique grammatical usages include the more recent use of "steady" and "come" that, like the "be" form, are often considered to be incorrectly used. Baugh (1983) suggests looking beyond the camouflage (since they are used similarly to standard forms) to find their creole nature. They should be understood as meaningful terms used in systematic ways. For example, the word *steady* is used to clarify the durative or habitual nature of a verb and probably reflects an African derived construction. Support for the creole origin of this usage is that Caribbean English also uses this form to modify verbs. Phrases such as "we be steady running" or "he be steady sleeping" demonstrate the function of the term *steady*, not to be confused with misuse of the adverb "steadily" of standard dialect. Baugh shows that cases in which the nature of the verb is already clear would not employ the term—"They be steady knowing the truth" is not used.

Baugh's (1983) study of African American street speech also identified a number of other lexical forms. Lexical items include syllable contractions (e.g., suppose = spoze), variable forestressing of bisyllabic words (e.g., Po-lice, de-tain), and hypercorrection (e.g., picked = pickted).

Semantics of Black English have also been influenced by the African languages. Words have been directly borrowed (e.g., gorilla, okra, jazz), and many phrases or metaphors have been translated, but with a change in the meaning of the English word. For example, reversal of the meaning of *bad* derives from a Mandingo idiom that also uses a negative word to connote a positive meaning. The use of *skin* (as in "give me some skin") is also a direct translation of a Mandingo phrase used during a handshake.

Other creations emerged from the life and experiences of a segregated culture and include language concerning a life of oppression, expressions indicative of a strong Christian orientation, and phrases that are coded to mean something other than what they would mean to a non-Black listener (Smitherman, 1977). Such double-meaning expressions are used only until those outside the culture discover the true meaning; then new alternate-meaning words and phrases are created.

Research has identified at least two main modern forms of Black English, or standard form and nonstandard vernacular (Jenkins, 1982). Standard form is characterized by its own phonetic (sound) (Moulton, 1976), semantic (Traugott, 1976), and syntactic (Jenkins, 1982) system. Speakers of this form tend to weaken final consonants, simplify consonant clusters, and exhibit general *l*-lessness and *r*-lessness (Hoover, 1978; Jenkins, 1982). Final consonants will not be weakened (e.g., lack of possessive *s* or past tense *ed*), however, when such action affects grammar (Hoover, 1978; Jenkins, 1982). In the nonstandard, vernacular form of Black English, Mainstream American English syntax is used with vocabulary, phonetic, and intonation variations that resemble standard Ebonic usage (Jenkins, 1982). Despite these distinctions, it is possible to see not only the borrowed structural rules of the original African languages represented in modern-day Black English, but the translated words, created phrases, and co-opted words provide clues to a cultural heritage fraught with oppression.

There are also variants in Black English usage. Some Black English forms were not as salient nor as commonly used as others (W. Edwards, 1992). Older African Americans (over 40 years) use Black English variants more often than younger respondents; African Americans having strong ties to their neighborhoods, and the social networks there are more likely to use vernacular linguistic variants (W. Edwards, 1992).

The distinctiveness of African American speech style has been problematic for group members. On the one hand, speech that marks the individual as a member of the group can be important for in-group acceptance. Here the use of African American language markers promotes identity and may be reinforced by group members. This is true for Blacks in countries other than the United States as well. For example, in London, England, Black teenagers' use of creole tokens and formulaic expressions is embedded in standard London dialect to mark and represent group language in certain contexts (Hewitt, 1986). In this way creole use is equated with Black group identity and teenagers may feel the need to display some facility with the socially marked forms. Hewitt suggests that for this reason self-reports of language may over-report use of this language form.

The double bind emerges when one examines the socialization of children growing up in neighborhoods where the speech dominates on the street. Although many parents want their children to learn standard dialect so that they will be able to assimilate and demonstrate marketable skills in mainstream society, children and especially teens reinforce each other for maintaining the nonstandard dialect. The standard speech style that is fiercely ostracized in Black street teen culture is, of course, the same style that is rewarded by mainstream members, producing a conflict within as each speaker has to make moment by moment choices in style.

The stigma attached by dominant culture to nonstandard dialects and forms may prove costly for African American speech style. The dominant culture has selected Mainstream American English as preferred usage and relegated other forms, Black English among them, to nonstandard, lower prestige status (Jenkins, 1982; Seymour & Seymour, 1979). This rejection of Black English as a legitimate linguistic style has harmed the development of child speakers (Seymour & Seymour, 1979). Some children who speak Black English have been inaccurately diagnosed as communicatively handicapped, mentally retarded, or learning disabled (Seymour & Seymour, 1979). These children were diagnosed using tests written in Mainstream American English and standardized with its native speakers. The poor performance of Black English-speaking African American children may result from the nature of the tests rather than inherent deficiencies.

These problems continue into adulthood. Speech style is one of the dimensions on which African Americans experience conflict about their ethnic identity and self-concept. They often react to the stigma attached to their dialect and speech style with ambivalence, having received messages from their in-group *supporting* its use and from mainstream culture *rejecting* Black English as incorrect and deviant speech.

Recent tests of European American perceptions of "sounding Black" indicate that negative evaluations do not pervade all judgments. F. Johnson and Buttny (1982) reported that, contrary to predictions, European American listeners did not respond more negatively on all dimensions to speakers who "sounded Black" than to speakers who "sounded White." The effects depended on the content of the speech. When the content was narrative or experiential there were no differences attributable to speech style. However, when the topic was abstract and intellectual, "sounding Black" produced lower ratings from European Americans. Respondents were both more aware and more critical of African American speech characteristics when the topic was intellectual. These findings indicate that European Americans do not have uniformly negative global predispositions toward African American speech, but selectively bias their evaluations to be consistent with cultural stereotypes.

Code or Style Switching

African Americans may react to this stigma by *language mobility* (changing language groups) (Sachdev & Bourhis, 1990) or by *code or style switching* (selective use of Black English and Mainstream American English depending on the situation) (Giles et al., 1977; P. Robinson, 1978; Seymour & Seymour, 1979). While in the former, Mainstream American English is used instead of Black English, in code or style switching African Americans learn to identify what is acceptable in different situations and modify their speech to the appropriate style.[1]

Three types of style or code switchers have been identified (Seymour & Seymour, 1979), and each type varies in its facility with Black English and Mainstream American English. The first group consists of African Americans who are less formally educated and have difficulty using Mainstream American English. This group has trouble when Mainstream American English usage is situationally sanctioned. The second group is formally educated, fluent in Mainstream American English but has difficulty expressing themselves in Black English, and therefore experiences problems when Black English is preferred. The final group is educated and able to use both language systems. Seymour and Seymour (1979) suggest that this third group is a prototype of pluralistic language use and should be encouraged in educational settings. However, when this pluralism becomes *biculturalism* (real or pseudo-membership in two cultures often with no real attachments to either) (Lian, 1982), the result is some of the same deficits associated with exclusive Black English use (De Vos, 1980; Erikson, 1968).

Code switching also appears in cultures other than the United States. In London, topic and function trigger switches from Black creole forms to standard English dialect (Hewitt, 1986). Creole is used to establish in-group identity and to act aggressively. For example, among some groups arguments produce increased use of Jamaican pronunciations. Teenagers seem to equate strength and dauntless assertiveness with creole and use it strategically with authority figures such as police, teachers, and youth workers. Where there is a power differential, creole use takes on political and cultural significance because it denotes assertiveness and group identity. On the other hand, the standard Black English is associated with respect and is likely to be manifested when this is strategically desirable.

Style switching is more general and involves more than just language choices. While effective communicators adapt their style to fit the situation regardless of their ethnicity, the power dynamics of U.S. society and the history of African American oppression imbue this type of switching with a political meaning. African Americans change their behavior to fit the racial and gender composition of the dyad (Shuter, 1982). For example, African American males asked fewer questions in interracial dyads and African American females asked more questions of European American females than of other African American females (Shuter, 1982). In conversations among Black acquaintances opposite-sex partners are asked more questions than same sex partners.

African Americans adjust their general communication style in other ways as well. African Americans talk with each other to relax, to maintain or develop the friendship, and out of mutual interest, but talk with European Americans to negotiate status or get position, to obtain favorable future evaluations, to be seen as capable of getting along, and for mutual interest (Cheek, 1976). These motivations are reflected in style switching. Conversations with other African Americans are likely to include the use of slang, lots of laughter, in-group gestures, Black English, and assumed intimacy; in Black-White conversations there is restraint and an awareness of grammar (Cheek, 1976).

While these choices or style switches are only partially conscious or intentional, there are several systematic situational factors that influence the switching and these factors may combine in various ways (Baugh, 1983). Individuals do not just use one style or another. The full range of style choices, from deep slang and full stylistic manner, to toned-down versions of Black street speech, to increasing the amount of standard forms—all are used in different situations.

Major factors influencing style choice, then, include the frequency of contact with conversants, the familiarity of the contact, and the perceptions of the other as a member or nonmember of Black street culture. Other minor factors that may influence style on a moment-by-moment basis include the presence of females, the topic being discussed, and the intensity of emotion concerning the topic; however, it is not always possible to predict which way such factors will send the switch.

Some forms of situationally appropriate style switching are preferred by African Americans. Selectively adopting Mainstream American English while associating it with being educated and professional is preferred to adopting a form of Black English that resembles Mainstream American English but does not fully utilize its rules and forms (Garner & Rubin, 1986). Conversely, African Americans perceived Black English to be of high linguistic vitality and used it in casual settings with African Americans and European Americans (Garner & Rubin, 1986). Linguistic competency requires the use of both language systems. Persons who do not know when to use "slang," "image," and "street vernacular" for effect rather than as the major form of communication and who do not use Mainstream American English appropriately for the context are held in low regard and viewed as uneducated or just plain funny (Garner & Rubin, 1986).

The importance of code switching is apparent in a study of successful and unsuccessful African American job interviewees (Akinnaso & Ajirotutu, 1982). African American interviewees who were able to adopt more culture-general discourse strategies were perceived more positively. The African American interviewees who appropriately opened and closed their narratives and demonstrated the ability to stylistically signal talk as interview talk were perceived more positively. These candidates assumed a problem-solving mode and used a narrative form to illustrate their strengths as candidates. The less successful candidates, on the other hand, exemplified a more traditional stylistic form: the telling of stories that seemed to be an end in themselves rather than a way to illustrate qualifications for the job. Also, unsuccessful candidates used more back channel cuing *(um hum, um um, yeah,* and *OK)* and vowel lengthening.

African Americans may style switch while embedding an "in-group" message. This accomplishes the purpose of situationally appropriate use of Mainstream American English while signaling ethnic identity. For example, during interviews African Americans were observed to use culturally specific, contextualization cues that are typically understood by persons familiar with African American cultural traditions but misunderstood or missed by middle-class European American interviewers (Hansell & Ajirotutu, 1982). In addition, the strategies used to maintain and control the flow of conversation are also cues of the point of view and the relationship between speaker's intent and meaning.

The two observed, embedded stylistic features were prosodic features of Black English: rhythmical stress placement and marked intonation patterns and formulaic speech such as the use of metaphor or a "quotational style" (Hansell & Ajirotutu, 1982). African Americans shifted pitch, assumed the style of some other character who was being quoted, and used other nonmainstream paralinguistic features. Such signals were used to negotiate conversational agendas and meanings and can be used for one group to gain conversational control or "run a game" on the mainstream White interviewer.

Oral Tradition

Many researchers have taken a sociolinguistic approach to studying the codes used by African Americans in particular contexts. A common thread that characterizes these studies is the emphasis on use of language as a means of promoting and maintaining group identity. Much of the work has been influenced by Hymes's ethnography of speaking framework with its primary focus on norms of contextually appropriate conduct (Hymes, 1972, 1974).

Oral traditions and performance are long-standing traditions among African Americans (V. Edwards & Seinkewicz, 1990). African American culture values verbal skills, particularly those couched in interactive and narrative frameworks.

One conversational form that exemplifies this tradition is African American preaching style (V. Edwards & Seinkewicz, 1990). As we have seen in Chapter 1, the church plays an important role in African American ethnoculture. Likewise, the conversational style of the church's central character, the preacher, is representative of the community.

Preachers use tonal semantics (elongated articulation, lengthy pauses, interjections of expressions like *aha* and *uh huh)* to emphasize their message. The themes in African American sermons serve to reinforce the values of the community and rules of appropriate behavior. In many cases such themes call the members of the congregation to repent and take responsibility for their future actions. The role of the preacher is to involve the members of the congregation emotionally, nonverbally, and verbally.

There are also parallels between other forms of communication in church and the larger community. It is important to note the participative nature of performance in religious and other contexts and the differences in African American and European American norms for expressing approval and disapproval. A. Williams (1972) observed that African American audiences are likely to check out the "haps" (happenings) all around the audience even as they listen attentively and approve of the performance, which may signal inattentiveness to an European American speaker for instance.

The verbal skills and language competence of this oral tradition are learned at early ages in the African American community. Erickson (1984) describes the development of "stylin" or "show time" in which African American children take a comment from a parent telling them not to do something and gradually intensify their threats to do it. As the threats become more and more drastic, the adults reinforce the verbal prowess of the child by saying things like "he so bad" and laughing approvingly and making other comments that positively reinforce the child.

V. Edwards and Seinkewicz (1990) note the tendency of African Americans to transfer this style to the multiethnic classroom and to use narrative form and a style that includes a "topic associating" organizational frame typically not understood by the White teachers. Kochman (1981) also notes that African Americans tend to apply to the classroom the same rules used for personal interaction in the African American community. Individuals with better speaking abilities dominate the conversation, and African Americans do not simply debate an idea—they debate the person debating the idea.

Foster (1989) combines folklore and performance theories with an ethnography-of-speaking focus on norms in her investigation of classroom conduct of African Americans at the college level. Modeling her design after Piestrup's (1973) study of the Oakland, California, public school system, Foster focuses on two primary speech events, "It's cookin' now" and metaphors, used by an African American instructor to incorporate familiar ways of speaking and performance norms in the classroom.

"It's cookin' now" is the phrase that a student used to describe the performance mode of the instructor and participation by class members. Performances were participatory, spontaneous, interactive events, and the tone was perceived to be humorous. Foster (1989) notes that performances by the instructor were stylistically embellished and incorporated figurative language and gestures. There was a shift from Mainstream American Language to Black English, and although the talk resembled play, the function was instruction.

Metaphors were a second significant speech event used in this classroom. The instructor divided the management class into groups named after three local Black businesses. Foster (1989) points out that the metaphors surrounding successful African American businesses allow participants to develop figurative language and interpretations frequently found in African American communities (Mitchell-Kernan, 1971; Smitherman, 1977). In addition, the metaphor created an atmosphere of what Foster calls "dynamic opposition," in which competition has a cooperative function. Such a dialectic force is common in African American communities, compelling individuals to give their best performances (Abrahams, 1976; Kochman, 1981).

Performance and narrative are aspects of the African American oral tradition that serve the functions of extolling unique verbal skills, showcasing the ability to be assertive. They also link speaker to audience and reinforce shared identity, norms, and values. Involvement with audience members is critical and this involvement occurs through the use of prosodic features and metaphors and verbal/nonverbal response patterns. The way in which conversations are organized, particularly when using a narrative form, may be associational rather than logical, which presumes some predetermined knowledge of the cultural identity of the speaker. In addition, a dialectic of cooperation and competition may be reinforced, because appropriate competition reinforces cooperation and African American ethnic identity. Finally, African Americans' perceptions of style shifting may indicate a realistic appraisal of professional context requirement, while use of Black English demonstrates a continued pride and positive regard for their own cultural identity. These functions of the oral tradition foreshadow the core symbols of African American communication code that are presented in the next section.

African American language use, then, is marked by a speech style influenced by Black English and oral traditions, and manifested in code switching. While many African Americans speak Mainstream American English, the speech associated with group membership is marked in other ways. Language use, however, is only part of communication style. In the next section we will discuss these broader issues of stylistics.

Core Symbols and Communication Style

Communication is more than just language. People use language to create messages that involve topics, strategies, meanings, and verbal and nonverbal styles of expression. Communication style expresses the core symbols of the ethnic culture and enacted identities. Conversely, the core symbols represent stylistic nodes or tendencies in African American culture.

A basic constellation of these symbols can be derived from previous research. Rose (1982/1983) reviews work on African American psychology and literature and suggests that there are four basic values in African American culture:

(1) *sharing* one's life with family and close relationships,
(2) *uniqueness* or individual style,
(3) *affective humanism* or positive attitudes, and

(4) *diunital orientation*, which views things as both good and evil rather than either/or.

J. White and Parham (1990) provide a similar list from their review:

(1) *emotional vitality,*
(2) *realness,*
(3) *resilience,*
(4) *interrelatedness,*
(5) *the value of direct experience, and*
(6) *distrust and deception.*

These systems are derived from an analysis of existing literature and neither system has been empirically tested. However, there is a great deal of overlap between these two independently derived systems and this supports their validity. Similarities exist between sharing and interrelatedness, and among positivity, resilience, and emotional vitality. In addition, we find evidence in the literature on communication style to support uniqueness and realism. Direct experience and diunital processing describe a cognitive style, and distrust is more closely related to the problematic nature of interethnic communication that will be explored in Chapter 4. Our reading of the style literature suggests a fifth core symbol, assertiveness.

We will consider the communication styles associated with the core symbols of *Sharing, Uniqueness, Positivity, Realism,* and *Assertiveness.* Communication styles are seen as expressing these symbols and, conversely, shaping and recreating them. Future research may profit from considering the dialectical tensions between Uniqueness and Sharing, which may reflect competing or dialectic pressures between individualism and collectivism (Hofstede, 1980; Triandis, McCusker, & Hui, 1990), and between Realism and Positiveness. African Americans seem to face the competing pressures of sharing both a common identity with the group and a strong drive for individual style. Similarly, they are presented with the reality of life in the United States but are oriented by cultural style toward a positive outlook.

Sharing

The core symbol of *Sharing* or *endorsing the group* reflects collectivism (Hofstede, 1980; Triandis et al., 1990) and is characterized in a number of different aspects of African American style. This is exemplified by the call-response pattern in which a speakers' statements are affirmed through messages such as "amen," "right-on," and "yes sir" (J. White & Parham, 1990). The sharing of self and material possessions characterizes the African American family (Rose, 1982/1983). Interconnectedness, interrelatedness, sharing, and interdependence are viewed as central and unifying concepts.

Sharing is played out in a variety of communicative forms. These include touch, distance, relationship intimacy, and rituals. While these are considered separately, each enacts the symbol and we would expect them to be used together (e.g., touching at close distances while talking about intimate topics and enacting rituals).

Touch. African Americans touch members of their group more than they touch European Americans, and this is even more pronounced after successes such as those in athletics (Halberstadt, 1985; D. Smith, Willis, & Gier, 1980). This pattern is particularly true of lower socioeconomic class African Americans. In addition, interracial dyads are observed to touch less than intraracial dyads among both European Americans and African Americans (Willis, Reeves, & Buchanan, 1976). Interracial touching is less highly valued and not required by the Sharing value (Blubaugh & Pennington, 1976).

Distance. Distance preferences also enact this core symbol. Close distances signal connectedness and bonding. Across a variety of studies Halberstadt (1985) found that African Americans establish closer distances than European Americans. These close distances begin in childhood when African American children establish closer distances in play and other activities (Aiello & Jones, 1971; Duncan, 1978b, 1978c).

Relationship Intimacy. The nonverbal behaviors of touch and distance signal involvement, connection, and intimacy. It is not surprising, then, that African Americans develop closer, more intimate friendships than European Americans (Hammer & Gudykunst, 1987b). African American friendships involve deeper, more intimate contact in general (Hecht & Ribeau, 1984) and across the topics of religion, school and work, interest and hobbies, and physical condition (Hammer & Gudykunst, 1987b). Conversely, European Americans tend to develop more intimacy regarding love, dating, sex, emotions, and feelings (Hammer & Gudykunst, 1987b).

African Americans do not seem to carry this core symbol into the out-group relationships with European Americans. African Americans may appear to be indifferent or uninvolved in their interactions with European American acquaintances and strangers (Asante & Noor-Aldeen, 1984; Ickes, 1984). European Americans are more likely to experience such interactions as somewhat difficult and burdensome and they thus tend to talk, look at the other, and smile more (Ickes, 1984). Ickes (1984) concludes that compared to African Americans, European Americans either anticipate or perceive greater difficulty and awkwardness in these initial interracial interactions and feel a particular responsibility and concern for making the interaction work. These patterns may reflect overaccommodation on the part of European Americans (Giles & Coupland, 1991).

Eye contact patterns may account for some of these disparities in level of involvement in interethnic conversations. When European Americans speak they tend to look at their partner less than they do while listening (Atkinson, Morten, & Sue, 1979; Kendon, 1967; LaFrance & Mayo, 1976; Vontress, 1973). For African Americans this pattern is reversed, with listeners looking less and speakers looking more (LaFrance & Mayo, 1976). Thus while speaking, European Americans look less and African Americans look more, and while listening, European Americans look more and African Americans look less. When these patterns are combined we can anticipate that when a European American is speaking the interactants will not be looking at each other frequently. This may be interpreted as boredom, lack of interest, and low involvement. When an African American is speaking, there is more mutual eye contact than either would expect (LaFrance & Mayo, 1976) and this may be interpreted as intensity, hostility, or power.

Rituals. Communication rituals help tie a group together and affirm its members' interconnectedness. By engaging in rituals an individual is demonstrating allegiance to the group and communicating an identity. Further, the person is communicating a commitment to sharing with the group by participating in common activities. A number of rituals have been observed in African American culture. These include call-response sequences (described previously), various types of jiving, playing the dozens, boasting, and toasting.

Jiving is a style developed by African Americans based upon improvisation and accentuation of behaviors that are believed to be highly acceptable. African Americans used these behaviors before both European American and African American audiences with varying forms of recognition and positive reward (Cogdell & Wilson, 1980). Jiving developed out of a particular historical context; however, the current categories are important to the extent that they may have influenced more contemporary African American communication style.

Six groups of jivers are identified by Cogdell and Wilson (1980). These groups use jive for different purposes and in different ways. The first group is comprised of Black entertainers, professional and nonprofessional, who perpetuate the European American myth that all Blacks have rhythm, can sing and dance, and act uncouth. This group amuses both European American and African American audiences via song, dance, joke, and acting. The consequences of this type of jiving are the perpetuation of myths and the reduction of the status of African Americans.

The second group utilizes slang as a form of jive. Here, persons compose an idiosyncratic, informal, nonstandard vocabulary. Although the vocabulary is arbitrary in manner and extravagance, it is also forceful and laden with facetious figures of speech reflecting Black English codes. This type of jive may gain immediate and positive feedback from other African Americans.

A third type is comprised of those who use foolish talk as a means of gaining and holding a reputation for not being serious. For an African American to adopt a serious stance may be seen as comedic by many African Americans as well as European Americans. The most common form of foolish talk is slapstick comedy stressing farce and horse play. Sometimes foolish talk results in an easing of tension that under normal circumstances would erupt into an expression of overt hostility.

The hipster, fourth type, is a highly resourceful and creative jiver. The hipster is highly intelligent and remains peripherally inside the law while engaging in "shady activity." The hipster can think, act, and talk circles around the average person.

The fifth group uses the overt tease jive. The person who uses this form is capricious without being malicious. Pleasure is derived from playing tricks on other African Americans in order to evoke laughter and to make a fool of the victim. The goal is momentary discomfort resulting from skullduggery and resulting in laughter.

The sixth form of jive is the swing. African Americans who are professional and nonassuming in a professional environment become vigorous, vibrant, ostentatious, and often graceful in a nonserious environment. Swinging is consistent with a need to congregate and party together and relieve stress experienced in professional settings dominated by European Americans.

Another ritual is the folkloric speech event known as *playing the dozens* (Garner, 1983). The game is an aggressive contest often using obscene language in which the goal is to ridicule and demean the opponent's family members, notably the mother. Garner (1983) notes:

> The game is an important rhetorical device which promotes community stability and cooperation by regulating social and personal conflicts. This expressive game influences, controls, guides or directs human actions in ways consistent with community norms. (p. 47)

Abrahams (1963) argues that the dozens is a rhetorical event, an argument that uses a strategy or method of attack. Garner (1983) identifies several strategic forms including persuasion, legislation, justification, social pressure, play, and instruction. Playing the dozens is also a means of socialization and learning to compete with other males.

Boasting is a ritualized speech act reflecting the oral nature of African American communication. Garner (1983) posited that boasting occurs as play and entertainment and functions to enable the speaker to gain recognition within a group. African American boasting often contains humorous exaggeration (V. Edwards & Seinkewicz, 1990). Boasting is instrumental in conflicts in order to bring harmony and cohesiveness to the group. In addition, African American audience members accompany the performance with verbal and physical reactions, shouts, laughter, applause, and catcalls, and audience members often serve as referee or even judge of the performers. The performance cannot succeed without an audience psychologically prepared and able to participate in the event (V. Edwards & Seinkewicz, 1990).

A final ritual is the *toast* or *epic poem,* an exclusively African American speech event (V. Edwards & Seinkewicz, 1990). Features of the toast include sexual assertiveness, use of taboo four-letter words, and scorn for sentimental verbiage, all of which reinforce African American identity.

Uniqueness

Just as Sharing acknowledges and endorses the group, *Uniqueness* pays homage to the individual. Since both symbols are important, African Americans try to demonstrate both individuality and commonality in interactions with others (Rose, 1982/1983). Ritualized behaviors provide one important arena where these two competing forces may combine. For example, hand slapping has become a stylized, communal activity in which individuals have developed their own, unique style of "slapping five" (Cooke, 1980). Similarly, both communal (Sharing) and individual (Uniqueness) values can be seen in dance styles that combine the basic steps or forms with improvisation (Rose, 1982/1983).

This dual function (i.e., Uniqueness and Sharing) can be seen in ritualized boasting. As indicated above, boasting serves to promote group harmony and cohesiveness and often involves the group in the performance. Conversely boasting calls attention to the individual by making claims about abilities (V. Edwards & Seinkewicz, 1990). However, the same people who make extravagant claims about what they may do to an "opponent" also may use self-deprecating boasts about hunger or being tired.

The value of Uniqueness is inculcated in childhood, where children are taught to do their best and not compare themselves to others (Rose, 1982/1983). Throughout life, African Americans are encouraged to "be real" and express their true self through actions and style (J. White & Parham, 1990). This value is expressed through individual stylized nonverbal presentations (Cooke, 1980; Kochman, 1981).

To further illustrate this value, Kochman (1981) notes that African Americans have developed an important characteristic of flair that stresses individuality. He defines African American style as more self-conspicuous, more expressive, expansive, colorful, intense, assertive, aggressive, and more focused on the individual than the style of the majority society in the United States. The flair is captured in a style of walk that is used by African American males to attract attention and admiration, especially from females (Cooke, 1972; K. Johnson, 1971). The general form of the walk is slow and casual with the head elevated and tipped to one side, one arm swinging and the other held limply. The extent to which such a walk is generalizable to the bulk of young African American males is an empirical question not yet addressed sufficiently by the literature.

Kochman (1981) concluded that African American communication can be characterized as highly expressive and stylized as a means for signifying individuality and uniqueness. He describes expressive patterns such as the use of direct questions, public debate and argument, more active nonverbal expression, self-presentations through bragging, boasting, and emotional intensity. In support of these styles, Donohue (1985) observed that African Americans negotiate more loudly and intensely than European Americans, who tend to behave in a more solicitous and "friendly" manner.

Positivity and Emotionality

A high value is placed on being positive (Rose, 1982/1983), having a sense of aliveness, emotional vitality, and openness of feelings, and being resilient about this positivity (J. White & Parham, 1990). African American culture is infused with a spirit (a knowledge that there is more to life than sorrow, which will pass) and a renewal in sensuousness, joy, and laughter. This symbol has its roots in African culture and expresses the soul and rhythm of that culture in America (Rose, 1982/1983).

An expressive life-style is one of the basic survival strategies of African Americans (Rainwater, 1967; Wyne, White, & Coop, 1974). Some African Americans may use a strategy of making themselves as attractive and interesting as possible in order to control others in a manipulative fashion and satisfy immediate needs. This persuasive process also involves the development of smooth lines of patter to charm and disarm acquaintances and strangers alike. The strategy is sometimes called the "working game" (Rainwater, 1967; Wyne et al., 1974).

J. White and Parham (1990) call on examples of religion and art to support this category. They note the transcendent theme of gospel songs that teach that the sorrows will pass and a spiritual hope and joy will triumph. Rose (1982/1983) points to the vitality and variety of African American music and dance. J. White and Parham (1990) also discuss the use of humor as a means to confront hardships. Other writers have described the use of emotionality and "impulsivity" to manage life stresses actively (Jenkins, 1982). African American children are taught to "do it"—actively managing life's difficulties without signs of stress (Block, 1980).

The emotional content of the African American experience is of high importance, and, as a result, partying and "having a good time" have a compelling power (Cogdell & Wilson 1980). Expressions of positive emotionality serve the same cleansing function as religious rituals, and African American decisions often appear to be rooted in feelings and intuition rather than Eurocentric-type rationality (Cogdell & Wilson, 1980).

Realism

While African American culture stresses a positive and emotional outlook on life, this is juxtaposed with a strong grounding in reality (J. White & Parham, 1990). African American culture places a high value on "tellin' it like it is." Again, this realism is reflected in the lyrics of blues and gospel music that portray the difficulty of life and advise a cool, steady, and persistent toughness needed to overcome this difficulty (J. White & Parham, 1990).

In this sense the value of Realism is similar to the diunital perspective discussed by Rose (1982/1983). Rose argues that African Americans see both the good and bad in life and trust that, in the long run, good will triumph. This view requires a realism about the current state of affairs, a trust in fairness, and a positive outlook about the future.

The importance of genuineness or "being real" as a communication style is stressed in a number of studies. In research to be reviewed in the next chapter, genuineness is portrayed as a major issue in interethnic relationships (Hecht, Ribeau, & Alberts, 1989). Kochman (1981) argues that loudness is positively valued because it communicates sincerity and true conviction. It is unclear how the stylized forms of African American style, the importance of individual style, and the emphasis on genuineness or realness are worked out in cultural practices.

Assertiveness

Assertiveness can be described as behavior that stands up for and tries to achieve personal rights without damaging others. African American style is described as assertive by some, forceful by others, and aggressive by still others. Each is describing a style of communication that is intense, outspoken, challenging, and forward. Some would describe the same style as belligerent and hostile.

As a core symbol, Assertiveness means standing up for oneself in the face of oppression (Jenkins, 1982). It means taking charge of your own existence. African Americans are taught early in life that they must not only cope with the challenge of the task at hand, be it school or work, but also cope with racism. They learn that they must fight harder for limited resources and cannot afford to be merely good when anything less than excellence brings failure. From this emerges the assertive, determined, confrontational, "pushing" style that is often part of African American coping in a racist world.

Assertiveness is reflected in a variety of communicative behaviors including a loud strong voice, angry verbal disputes, threats, insults, manner of dress, and use of slang or "street talk" (Cheek, 1976; Kochman, 1981). The level of intensity may correspond to the type of activity, from calmly arguing for persuasion to more intensely ventilating anger (Kochman, 1981).

Assertiveness is acted out in a variety of cultural rituals. One, playing the dozens, has already been described. A second, called *woofing,* involves a type of threat that is not intended as imminent action (Kochman, 1981). Here, the African American communicator may challenge another to gain verbally the respect otherwise won through physical confrontation.

African Americans and European Americans differ in their interpretations of these actions (Cheek, 1976; Kochman, 1981). Many of the more assertive and aggressive African American behaviors (e.g., shouting, threatening) are not in the realm of typical public behavior for European Americans and signal impending physical violence when presented. European Americans may interpret African American behavior as signaling physical confrontation when none is intended, particularly when the behavior includes shouting, animated gesturing, and staring. Kochman (1981) argues that relative confidence in the ability to deal with anger is the basis for these divergent perceptions. European Americans, he argues, are less confident of their ability to control their anger and prevent verbal hostility from becoming physical. As a result they repress angry feelings as a form of self-control. African Americans have less need to repress these feelings and their expressions since they believe they can control the escalation of events.

A controversy over a rap music video in 1992 illustrates these differences. The video is called *By the Time I Get to Phoenix* by a group called Public Enemy. The song protests racism in Arizona, particularly the vote against a Martin Luther King holiday. The video depicts the car bombing and poisoning of Arizona politicians. An editorial in one local paper claimed that the group was embracing violence (Aleshire & Thomason, 1992), and a spokesperson for the Arizona Attorney General's Office also called the message violent ("A Rap on Arizona," 1992). However, Chuck D, the leader of Public Enemy, explained the video was "a trip into the fantasy world of Public Enemy" (Aleshire & Thomason, 1992) and the work has been described as a revenge fantasy. A spokesperson for the Arizona African American Political Action Committee argued that the video was neither violent nor did it advocate violence. Instead, Mr. Ealim stated that "you have to understand the symbolism of blowing up the governor's car. . . . We're advocating the symbolism of killing the idea (of racism)" (Coppola, 1992). In other words, European American audiences took the video as a literal expression of violence and violent intentions, while some African Americans argued that the message was just a style of presentation that was representational or metaphorical.

Other Communication Styles

Thus far this chapter has discussed communication styles expressive of five core symbols. Not all of the communication style literature fits neatly into these categories. The next section reviews the remaining literature, examining styles of coping with mainstream U.S. culture and interpersonal styles.

Coping Styles

It is clear that the history of African Americans in the United States has been one that has challenged the resources of group members. In response to their situation in mainstream society, group members have developed coping mechanisms for dealing with racism, discrimination, and prejudice. Six styles of coping have been identified. Each has both positive and negative possibilities for personal and social adjustment (Harding, 1975; Harrell, 1979; Jenkins, 1982). The styles are problematic in that there is no optimal end point or condition. These styles are called "continued apathy," "seeking a piece of the action," "obsession with counterculture alternative," "the Black nationalist alternative," "identification with an authoritarian solution," and "historically aware cognitive flexibility" and are described in greater detail in Table 3.1.

Interpersonal Styles

A number of researchers have examined African American interpersonal communication. This work, however, has not been systematic. We chose, therefore, to group these studies thematically into the categories of relationships, verbal messages, and nonverbal messages.

Relationships. A number of researchers have examined factors related to relationships and relationship development. Cross-ethnic comparisons of self-disclosure patterns show that European Americans are more disclosive than African Americans (Diamond & Hellcamp, 1969; Littlefield, 1974). Hammer and Gudykunst (1987a) studied ethnicity and uncertainty reduction processes in initial interactions in order to test the applicability of C. Berger and Calabrese's uncertainty reduction theory (C. Berger & Calabrese, 1975). The study indicated that the theory does not provide an accurate representation of relationship development in the African American community. Contrary to predictions, African Americans did not become more confident of their impressions when asking more questions and were not more attracted to people about whom they could make confident predictions (Hammer & Gudykunst, 1987a). This study demonstrates the difficulty of imposing Eurocentric theories as explanations of African American behavior.

African Americans and European Americans differ in other aspects of initial interaction. Kochman (1981) reported differences in the areas of direct questioning, modes of disagreements, negotiation, public debate, argument, and discussion. African Americans exhibit significantly more aggressive versus more passive styles of nonverbal expression, and more self-presentation talk such as boasting and bragging. Overall, African American speech had a higher emotional intensity.

Gray-Little (1982) investigated power, interaction patterns, and marital satisfaction among African Americans. She found that most couples were equal in the number of interruptions by husband and wife and more than half of the couples were classified as egalitarian with regard to assertiveness. More satisfied couples reported equality of talk time, positive regard, and fewer and equal interruptions.

Verbal Messages. African American ethnic culture can also be characterized by the type of messages that typify communication. The messages differ in both content and form. African Americans differ from European Americans in the topics they tend to discuss.

Table 3.1 African American Coping Styles

Style	Description
Continued Apathy	The person acknowledges the damaging effects of racism but manifests little or no coping strategy for responding to it. A positive consequence of this style is that the person is unlikely to succumb to some of the more damaging symptoms such as severe psychosomatic reactions (e.g., ulcers or hypertension). Conversely, the characteristic tendency of this style to blame "the man" for all troubles can lead to a strong dependency on an external source.
Seeking a Piece of the Action	The person is highly motivated toward achieving competence in certain skills in order to achieve success in mainstream society. The style may result in an improved personal situation with little attention to the effects his or her drive for personal gain has on other African Americans.
The Counterculture Alternative	This solution represents a mode of living outside both mainstream and African American ethnic cultures in an effort to transcend the struggle. Often, this alternative may include involvement in heavy drug usage, religious or art forms, or the frequent use of any number of consciousness altering techniques. The positive side to this choice can be creative and unorthodox activities with the potential drawback that the person may lose touch with the practical realities of racism.
The Black Nationalism Alternative	This style involves immersion in one of the movements stressing African American identity. This orientation promotes a positive view of African American people and African American culture but may be narrow and rigid in its approach to European American institutions.
Identification With an Authoritarian Solution	Identifying with an authoritarian solution involves dedication to one of any number of groups that require allegiance to a person or an idea. Groups such as Marxism or the Nation of Islam provide the individual with direction and discipline but that person may lose contact with personal perspectives in the overdependence on the authority.

| Aware Cognitive Flexibility | A person using this style is not as sharply defined as the others. It is a position in which the African American is aware of the ambiguities and complexities of the racial situation. This fits a humanistic definition of *awareness* and *orientation to life* that recognizes the need to struggle against racism. This person is conscious of alternatives but also realizes that there are presently no comforting or even familiar answers to the issues facing African Americans. This individual stands poised to accept new theory, practice, ideology, and, consequently, new hope. However, there is an ambiguity to such a position and the constant need to reassess and revise one's perspective. |

SOURCES: Harding, 1975; Harrell, 1979; Jenkins, 1982.

African Americans are more likely to talk with each other about European Americans and racism, social events, mutual friends, gossip, clothing, and making money and more likely to talk with European Americans about the weather, school, work, sports, news, current events, and activities of interest to European Americans (Cheek, 1976).

There is also a cultural distinctiveness to the strategies used to influence people. In marital relationships African Americans tend to be direct and "just tell" their mates their wishes rather than hinting, explaining the situation, offering tangible or personal rewards, or pleading helplessness (Dejarnett & Raven, 1981). Spouses tend to be more satisfied if their mates use reward or expert power than if the mates use coercive or legitimate power. Within the African American community, those in the middle class are more likely to ascribe informational power to their relational partners and to abide by their mates' requests because the mate gave good reasons and persuaded them with convincing information (DeJarnett & Raven, 1981).

Nonverbal Messages. The final area for consideration is nonverbal messages. African American style can be characterized by the structures and forms conveyed without words. While a number of these nonverbal characteristics have been directly or indirectly referred to already, some specific descriptions remain in the area of eye contact, body motion, time, and vocalics. These are summarized in Table 3.2.

Summary

Our discussion of communication style in this chapter was inhibited by the variable analytic and grounded frameworks used by researchers. What is needed now is a system for understanding these stylistic, cultural markers. Our five core symbols suggest such a framework. Are there other underlying consistencies within the communication style? Dimensions? Factors? How can we come to understand these as functions of the cultural system? For example, assertiveness seems to be a characteristic of the style. Are there others? How do these fit together? Why did they emerge from this cultural system? What does assertiveness mean to those who use it? What are the consequences of not being assertive?

Future research also should address the dialectics between the core symbols we identified. How are the competing pressures for sharing and individualism worked out? The pressures for realism and positivism? Is there an oppositional force to assertiveness or does it reflect the interpenetration of the other dialectics (i.e., uniqueness/sharing, realism/positivity)?

One characteristic of this style raises interesting questions about the enactment of identity. African American communication, particularly that of males, is often described as highly stylized (Hecht, Ribeau, & Alberts, 1989; Kochman, 1981). Questions have been raised about the genuineness of these stylized forms (Hecht, Ribeau, & Alberts, 1989). The suggestion was made by a respondent that if the style is seen as something natural to or part of the individual, then it is considered genuine. However, those who are perceived as "going along with the crowd" or "posing" in the style are perceived as less authentic. One may ask how an individual's performance comes to be seen as a genuine enactment of a personal identity rather than as a superficial or insincere behavior.

In this chapter we reviewed African American language and communication style. These are actions that typify African American interaction. They appear frequently and typically. This does not mean, however, that these behaviors are appropriate or effective. They may be effective or ineffective. An ethnic culture's style may contain dysfunctional elements and certainly contains behaviors not designed to obtain any specific outcome. In the next chapter we focus specifically on African American communication competence; those actions that are seen as normative (appropriate) and achieve desirable outcomes (effective).

Note

1. Baugh (1983) prefers the term *style switching*, reserving the term *code switching* for truly bilingual situations.

Table 3.2 Nonverbal Message Styles of African American Culture[1]

Nonverbal Code	Conclusion	Source
Eye Contact[2]	European Americans look at their conversational partner more frequently and for longer duration than do African Americans across a variety of situations and relationships. Certain types of questions (i.e., about racial topics) invoke longer gazes from both European Americans and African Americans. African American prefer authority figures who avert their gaze.	Aiello & Thompson, 1980; Dorch & Fontaine, 1978; Fugita, Wexley, & Hillery, 1974; Garrett, Baxter, & Rozelle, 1981; Marcelle, 1976
Body Movement[3]	African American children move around more than European American children and exhibit a greater variety of movements. African American children face each other less directly (indirect shoulder axis) than do European American children.	Duncan, 1978b, 1978c; Guttentag, 1982; K. Johnson, 1971
Time	African Americans are frequently late for scheduled occasions, especially social occasions. Lateness is a logical position within African American subjective reality. Understanding of "Colored People's Time" should be based upon an appreciation of history and economic circumstances. African Americans have not had much input into determining the structure of the system and may show defiance by arriving late. Concern, genuine regard, and respect were communicated by being early, prompt, or by taking the time to do something. Indifference, contempt, disrespect, and anger were communicated by being late, not showing up, or taking little time to do something.	Blubaugh & Pennington, 1976; Cogdell & Wilson, 1980; Horton, 1976; Pennington, 1979

| Vocal Behavior[4] | African American children speak to each other less than do European American children. European Americans tend to talk to males for longer periods, while African Americans spend more time talking to females. Both African Americans and European Americans pause longer in response to racially oriented questions. | Fugita et al., 1974; Shuter, 1982; Zimmerman & Brody, 1975 |

NOTES: 1. For reviews of ethnicity and nonverbal behavior see Halberstadt (1985) and Hecht, Andersen, and Ribeau (1989).

2. Some of the eye contact patterns have been reviewed earlier in the chapter while discussing involvement. These are not repeated here.

3. Much of the body movement research has been presented under discussions of individuality and flair. These will not be repeated here.

4. *Vocal behavior* (i.e., vocalics or paralinguistics) involves everything that is said other than the words themselves. These behaviors include the sound of the voice, rate of speech, pauses, and amount of talk. As with the other aspects of nonverbal communication, vocal behavior studies have been described previously in this chapter, particularly in regard to loud voices and assertiveness.

CHAPTER FOUR

Communication Competence

In Chapter 1 we introduced the idea that ethnic culture is enacted in conversation by a community that has knowledge of the code. Members of the community are said to act competently if they behave in an appropriate and effective fashion. In this chapter we explore African American communication competence in both intra- and interethnic settings. First, definitions and approaches to general communication competence are presented and adapted to an interpretive perspective. Then we develop the basis for an African American model of competence and examine how this code operates in both intra- and intercultural contexts. Our goal is to explain the code or system of symbols, meanings, and norms by which members of this community evaluate and enact competent conversation.

Competence is a particularly salient topic in today's world. Divorce rates, labor disputes, and domestic violence all speak, at least in part, to the breakdown of effective and jointly negotiated communication systems. In our increasingly intercultural world we find additional challenges. As we stated in Chapter 1, communication in general is problematic and interethnic communication is particularly so.

Most approaches to competence can be labeled Eurocentric in their focus on European American communication patterns (Martin, in press). While theories of communication competence (Spitzberg & Cupach, 1984; Spitzberg & Hecht, 1984; Wiemann, 1977) and, even more specifically, theories of interethnic communication effectiveness have been derived from a variety of approaches (for a review, see Martin, in press[1]), researchers have only recently begun to incorporate perspectives of participants from groups other than mainstream U.S. culture (e.g., Collier, 1989; Collier et al., 1986; Hecht, Ribeau, & Alberts, 1989[2]).

Eurocentric work informs our research but does not guide it. Rather, we believe in an emically derived approach (Cross, 1971) in which the specific culture is studied first in order to understand its construction and then, only after this culture-specific knowledge has emerged, are comparisons made across cultures in order to derive culture-general knowledge. We "emically" study African American culture and then compare those findings to other groups (e.g., European Americans, Mexican Americans) to test for generalizability and culture specificity. Our work examines how African Americans perceive themselves and their communication and then compares these perceptions to those of other ethnic cultures; this chapter reflects this orientation.

Current frameworks for communication competence point out the criteria for *judging* competence—effectiveness and appropriateness—and the requirements for *achieving* competence—skills, motivation, and knowledge. As we describe these more general models, it becomes obvious that the criteria and requirements are culturally based.

Competent communication must be appropriate *and* effective (Collier, 1988; Spitzberg & Cupach, 1984). The appropriateness criterion means that the competent communicator is capable of adjusting to the environment and requires knowledge of *what* is going on and *how* to deal with it (Spitzberg & Cupach, 1984). This "adjustment" may consist of a range of behaviors including changing the environment, exiting from the interaction, or applying communicative strategies to deal with problematic issues (Duran, 1983). But these behaviors will be selected based on culturally informed criteria or norms for appropriateness.

Effectiveness emphasizes communication behavior that accomplishes some desirable outcome (Hecht, 1978; Spitzberg & Cupach, 1984; Spitzberg & Hecht, 1984). Considering the potentials and consequences along with performance broadens the notion of competence and promotes more holistic approaches to communication.

Knowledge of ethnic culture is necessary to any consideration of appropriateness and effectiveness. Ethnic culture comprises a significant component of the environment, setting standards and norms, as well as guiding interpretations and evaluations. Symbols, meanings, and norms emerge out of cultural traditions, and ethnic cultures are constituted in codes, conversations, and communities. These communities use codes to determine the appropriate use of symbols. Such norms for appropriateness guide conversations and, when used effectively, lead to positive outcomes as defined by the community. Not only are effectiveness and appropriateness defined in terms of ethnocultural communities, but the very skills, motivations, and bases for knowledge that allow for the execution of communication are based upon cultural learning. What people consider to be the reasons for communicating effectively and what they consider to be the norms and behaviors leading to competence are all profoundly affected by the ethnic culture they share.

In Chapter 3 we described the communication patterns that *typify* African American culture. The commonalities shared by many African Americans express a culturally specific code for communication. In any analysis of ethnic patterns, however, we have to go beyond the observed behavior to understand the norms governing communication within a group. So both the observed patterns and the underlying rationale for behavior constitute the cultural code of an ethnic group, and evaluations of the code constitute competence.

Effective communication within an ethnic community requires that interactants have the requisite communication skills, be motivated to communicate, and have knowledge of self, other, situation, and topic (Spitzberg & Cupach, 1984; Spitzberg & Hecht, 1984). Ethnicity manifests itself in each of these areas and influences the ability of interactants to adjust to and accommodate one another (Giles et al., 1987; Giles & Coupland, 1991). This ability to adjust and accommodate becomes even more salient in interethnic contexts.

African American communication patterns differ from those evidenced by European Americans (Asante & Noor-Aldeen, 1984; Bachman & O'Malley, 1984; Duncan, 1978a, 1978b, 1978c; Hammer & Gudykunst, 1987a, 1987b; Hecht & Ribeau, 1984; Ickes, 1984; S. Jones, 1971; Kochman, 1981; LaFrance & Mayo, 1976). These differing patterns demonstrate the potential tension involved in interethnic interaction and the ways ethnic differences can inhibit effective communication. Also, members of different ethnic groups do not share a common set of communication norms (Collier et al., 1986) and are dissimilar in their willingness to shift their norms in order to adjust to the ethnicity of their dyadic partners (Collier, 1988). Though African Americans and European Americans may have differing styles, it is possible for them to communicate effectively if they are able to adapt their conversational patterns in order to adjust to or accommodate one another's styles.

Generally, interactants modify their messages to match or diverge from their conversational partners depending upon conditions. As reviewed in Chapter 2, ethnolinguistic identity theory has identified the general factors influencing divergence and convergence: individual focus, listener attributes, dependence on the group, group solidarity, power and dominance relationships, situational constraints, individual and group motivations, communicator repertoire, and expectations (Gallois et al., 1988). In some circumstances, modification in speech converges (moves toward each other's style) while in others such modification diverges (moves away from each other's style). Adjustments have been reported for variables such as pronunciation (Giles, 1973), vocal intensity (Natale, 1975), talk and silence sequences (Cappella & Planalp, 1981), pause and utterance length (Jaffe & Feldstein, 1970), and speech rates (Webb, 1972). These studies show that people linguistically converge toward each other's presentation when the costs are less than the rewards, there is a desire for communicative efficiency, and the social norms do not dictate alternative strategies (Beebe & Giles, 1984; Bourhis, 1985). However, divergence is likely to occur when the encounter is defined in intergroup terms and there is a strong desire for group identity or when there is the desire to disassociate self from other (Beebe & Giles, 1984; Bourhis, 1985).

Thus ethnic differences potentially can influence the adjustment process. Strong ethnic group identity can promote divergence as can peer group pressures. When dyadic partners do not share the same ethnic culture, it is more difficult to know how to adjust to each other and the adjustment process may require a communication style that is not a frequently used aspect of the cultural repertoire (e.g., when a faster speaking rate is required of southern African Americans).

In addition to differences in *how* to adjust, there are differences in the norms about *who* should do the adjusting. With the great power differential in United States society, members of the mainstream culture have often been able to assume that other groups will adjust to their style. In fact, earlier speech accommodation research has repeatedly examined and verified the presence of code switching in cross-cultural interactions (Giles et al., 1977); disempowered groups often shift to the mainstream style to accommodate cultural differences. However, rising controversies over issues such as bilingual and bicultural education suggest that social norms may be changing as emerging co-populations assert their own influence, and rightfully so. One survey respondent wrote us a note in which she claimed that "Black Folks are not concerning themselves with what White Folks are thinking. That was yesteryear when we looked for approval from Whites. TODAY we (Blacks) are seeking better educational opportunity and economic development. As we achieve this we will not need to concern ourselves with White acceptance and negative stereotyping." Therefore, dominant groups may no longer be able to depend upon other groups adapting to the dominant style.

These studies suggest problems inherent in African American/European American communication interactions, particularly as norms and power differentials shift. If interactants do not share common knowledge, motivation, and styles, then conversations may diverge. And if interactants do not agree on the direction or accountability for adjustment, effectiveness is problematic. Such problems can be viewed as "failure events." Failure events occur when interactions do not run smoothly; or when they violate norms, expectations, and preferences; or are somehow inappropriate (Cody & McLaughlin, 1985; McLaughlin, Cody, & O'Hair, 1983; Morris, 1985; Schonbach, 1980). In other words, communication has been unsuccessful.

If the interactants wish to improve the situation, they must "align" the interaction. Alignments are conversational improvement strategies for achieving accommodation once a failure event has been encountered, and the identification of alignment specifies those processes that tune the interaction to meet the interactants' preferences (Ball, Giles, & Hewstone, 1985; Morris, 1985). Alignment research emphasizes "cooperative efforts to guide the activity rather than efforts of 'offenders' to account for admittedly deviant behavior" (Morris, 1985, p. 70). Thus, alignment research is concerned with restorative processes in problematic situations.

Our analysis of the competence literature suggested to us that research could be most productive if it focused on communication norms, problematic events, and conversational improvement strategies. Norms reveal the "ought" aspect of the moral dimension and tell us what communicators have come to expect in interaction. Problematic events or communication issues tell us about the key events that constitute an agenda for effective communication. These issues are the criteria interactants use to evaluate success or failure, and if we identify the most salient problems or issues we can better understand what effective communicators do to achieve positive outcomes. Finally, we must learn what actors do to deal with conversations when they are less than optimal. How can conversations be improved? As a problematic event, communication requires adjustment and change during the conversational flow. Without a repertoire of improvement strategies, communication will stall when the first obstacle or nonscripted message is encountered.

We decided to examine the norms, issues, and improvement devices at the level of conversational choices or strategies. Much of the work on interethnic communication and failure events has been conducted at the "micro-level" of analysis. These studies focus on specific speech acts. While these studies are useful, it is important to complement this level of analysis with more macro-level studies. It has been suggested that communicators often make predictions about the direction and outcomes of their interactions and design strategies to actualize their preferences (G. Miller & Steinberg, 1975). While it seems clear that much communication occurs "mindlessly" or outside of awareness (C. Berger & Douglas, 1982; Folkes, 1985; Kitayama & Burnstein, 1988; Langer, 1978), when communicators are faced with atypical events outside of their scripted sequencing they become more aware and strategic (Douglas, 1983). Since difficult interactions should make being strategic ("strategicness") more salient, it is important to examine norms and issues in effective communication and communication improvement strategies.

Cultural Appropriateness

Our study of cultural appropriateness has focused on an understanding of the norms for intra- and interethnic communication. Appropriateness connotes normative conduct that is preferred and perceived as resulting in positive outcomes.[3] This conduct is contextually variant. Since we conceptualize communication as problematic, norms are implicitly and explicitly negotiated as individuals relate to each other. We assume that persons' conduct in conversation is both reactive and proactive as meanings are co-created and maintained. As a result, impressions of appropriateness are formed and reformed as persons converse. Appropriate behavior is consistent with situational demands, normative, and sanctioned by the response.

Relationships are one of the most salient contextual factors in defining norms. Within a culture the nature of the relationship between the interactants specifies appropriate and inappropriate conduct. Knowing someone is a friend rather than an acquaintance allows us to ask appropriate questions and bring up suitable topics. Research on African American norms examines these relational parameters, considering appropriate conduct and core symbols among acquaintances, friends, and unequal power relationships and in conflict situations.

Individuals may not be able to describe conversational norms. However, they are able to describe specific behaviors that were appropriate or inappropriate in specific situations (Collier, 1989), articulate an overall impression of self or other conduct (Spitzberg & Cupach, 1984), and make judgments about satisfaction with the conversation and relationship (Hecht, Ribeau, & Alberts, 1989). People do seem to have an easier time providing examples of inappropriate behavior than they do describing appropriate behavior. All but a few respondents in these studies were able to provide descriptions of inappropriate behaviors and most of these descriptions were quite detailed. The same was not equally true for appropriate behavior.

We have used interviews and open-ended questionnaires to study impressions of appropriateness. In most cases, respondents were asked to recall a recent conversation with a person from their own or other ethnic group. They described the topic, relationship with other(s), context, duration of conversation, and inappropriate or appropriate, effective or ineffective verbal and nonverbal communication. Respondents were then asked to explain their answers and describe the consequences for self-concept, ethnic identity, task accomplishment, relationship satisfaction, and so forth.

Respondents in these studies ranged in age from 18 to 55 years old. The majority lived in an urban setting and were employed full time while attending college part time. There were slightly more females than males in these studies.

These data were collected and coded by African American or interethnic research teams. Coders first copied individual responses on individual slips of paper. These responses were then categorized by individual coders based on thematic similarity. The coders then discussed their category systems, reached consensus, and named each category.

In the section below we summarize this work on African American cultural appropriateness. We consider first the norms for acquaintances, friends, and unequal power relationships. We conclude with a discussion of norms for conflict. Through this work we learn how African Americans handle the problematic elements of interaction and identify the core symbols that represent conversational norms. A summary of these norms appears in Table 4.1.

African American Norms for Acquaintances

Intra-ethnic communication with acquaintances is guided by four primary categories of norms: follow role prescriptions, be polite, adjust the content, and be expressive (Collier et al., 1986). These categories are shared, to some extent, with Mexican American and European American cultures. All groups place a great deal of emphasis on societal and individual politeness norms, including speaking "proper" English, being courteous, asking for feedback, actively listening, and taking time to help. However, these ethnic cultures differ in their emphases.

African Americans are in the middle of the three groups in their emphasis on role prescriptions, placing less stress on this rule category than Mexican Americans and more than European Americans. These groups agree that a person's position or place in the social

Table 4.1 African American Norms

Acquaintances

Follow Role Prescription
Be Polite
Adjust the Content
Be Expressive

Friends

Acknowledge or Respect the Individual
Develop Intimacy
Appreciate the Culture
Be Goal Oriented

Unequal Power Relationships

Allow Mutual Talk Time
Manage Time Appropriately (Do Not Rush)
Recognize and Respect Person With Less Power
Be Nonverbally Attentive
Greet Warmly
Avoid Overgeneralizing and Stereotyping
Avoid Negative Comments About Cultural Style
Be Friendly and Direct
Build Trust Slowly
Be Helpful With Task
Allow Input in Decisions
Be Direct
Check Out Information

Conflict

Adopt Problem Solution Orientation
Arguments Should Be Appropriate (Males)
Offer Information (Males)
Be Credible (Males)
Avoid Criticism (Females)

SOURCES: Collier, 1988, 1991, 1992; Collier et al., 1986.

system guides behavior. However, African Americans place the most emphasis on individual roles that express each person's personality or style and supersede positional or status roles. This finding is consistent with the core symbol of Uniqueness that was synthesized from the communication style literature in the previous chapter.

The content of the conversation and expressiveness play bigger roles in African American intra-ethnic conversations than for the other groups. They stress the need for these conversations to be supportive, relevant, and assertive. In this way the rule for expressiveness overlaps the core symbols of Sharing and Positivity discussed in the previous chapter.

Interethnic conversations with acquaintances have similar norms, but different emphases (Collier, 1988). Politeness is more individual than societal, and greater emphasis is placed on individual or idiosyncratic norms for politeness by African Americans than by Mexican Americans or European Americans. Role prescriptions are again important, but cultural identity prescriptions are the most important type. African Americans, however, continue to place more emphasis on professional roles than do the other two groups.

Collier (1988) also found that content norms are more important to African Americans than the other groups. Supportiveness is less important in inter- than intra-ethnic conversations for members of this ethnic culture. Expressiveness, however, is less important to African Americans in interethnic conversations than it is to the other groups, and this is a reversal of the findings for intra-ethnic communication.

African American Norms for Friends

Conversational norms with friends share an emphasis on the individual but also stress intimacy. We propose that appropriate behavior in these conversations can be represented in four core symbols:

(1) acknowledge or respect the individual,
(2) develop intimacy,
(3) appreciate the culture, and
(4) be goal oriented (Collier, 1992).

The high value African Americans place on individualism is stressed in the communication styles discussed in the previous chapter, norms for conversing with acquaintances discussed above, and now here in norms for conversing with friends. A strong individual identity is expressed through assertiveness and the value placed on individual accomplishment. These norms are consistent with the core symbols of Assertiveness and Uniqueness described in Chapter 3. Assertiveness and confrontation may be communicated through loud voices and argumentation style but are counterbalanced by the confirmation of the other. Thus, as we indicated in previous chapters, there is a dialectical tension between individualism (i.e., Uniqueness) and collectivism (i.e, Sharing) that requires a style that responds to both forces.

Friendship also requires a deep intimacy in the relationship and the conversation and this is consistent with the core symbol of Sharing discussed in Chapter 3. Talk among friends is about topics such as family and positive feelings are derived from receiving and giving advice. African Americans describe taking specific actions to establish trust as the most critical incident in conversations. Sensitivity, support, affirmation, honesty, and "sisterhood" are also used to describe conversations with friends. This intimacy base supports individuality and allows African Americans to criticize one another and assertively request actions without compromising friendship.

The third core symbol is an appreciation for the culture, another reflection of the core symbol, Sharing. It is appropriate for friends to discuss their culture. Similarities in beliefs and attitudes and common interests are stressed, and spirituality plays a role for some. Cultural background, itself, is a topic and expressions of "pride in our roots" are seen as appropriate to these conversations.

The final core symbol is goal orientation. Friends consider it appropriate to accomplish some task. Often this task may be the solution of some problem, particularly dealing with personal problems through advice. Sometimes the goal is mutual understanding. Goals may include expressing individuality, affirming the individual or the culture, or establishing trust and intimacy in relationships. Thus this rule category overlaps a number of the core symbols discussed in the previous chapter.

Unequal Power Relationships

Unequal power relationships between European American college advisors and African American students have been examined through a qualitative analysis of recalled conversations (Collier,

1988). African American students said that European American advisors should allow mutual talk time, manage time appropriately, show recognition and respect for the student as an individual, attend appropriately nonverbally, and greet warmly. In addition, advisors should avoid overgeneralizing, stereotyping, or criticizing the student's ability or preparation for college, should avoid negative comments about accents or language abilities, and should allow adequate time for interaction. To reinforce an appropriate relationship, advisors should be friendly, be direct, show respect for the individual student, and allow trust to build slowly. In approaching task discussions, advisors should provide adequate advice throughout the meeting, allow a mutual role in decision making, be direct, and check out information to avoid mistakes. Many African Americans expressed distance and anger at advisors who were insensitive, as one comment illustrates: "I feel just fine, it is the advisor who has the problem, not me." Clearly African American students preferred to be respected as individuals, and if they felt stereotyped were willing to end the relationship.

Conflict

Collier (1991) examined communication competence in conflict situations. The study described definitions of conflict and identified appropriate conflict behaviors. African American males and females were extremely consistent in their definitions of *conflict* as disagreement, contrary or differing views, and misunderstandings.

African American males and females were also asked to describe appropriate and inappropriate conflict management behaviors. Males and females were similar in their description of "problem solution" as appropriate behavior in conflict management. In this format, one interactant brings up a problem and the other helps by offering a solution or enabling a solution to emerge. One respondent gave the following advice: "I told him to stay in school and that I would help him study." Another said, "We decided together how to solve the problem and deal with our friend."

African American males emphasized that appropriate arguments should be given, information should be offered, and opinions should be credible. Examples include the following comments: "His case was full of holes." "He overgeneralized and tried to tell me

Black Americans and Africans are the same." "You shouldn't try to make a case when you are uninformed."

African American females pointed out that criticism is not appropriate. One said, "She told me I was selfish." Another reported: "I offended her because I said she was naive." Also, females viewed assertiveness as appropriate but only when the other's rights and views were considered. For example, one female said, "She pushed her own way and opinion and totally disregarded mine," and another reported, "He made no effort to understand my situation." A third example is illustrated in the following comment: "I went too far by telling my friend she should stop smoking if she cared at all about her health."

Friendship also plays a role. African American friends had mixed responses about the results of the conflict on their friendship. One said that the conflict "will never be resolved in my lifetime," while another commented that they "will need several more meetings." Overall, African Americans emphasized joint and responsible problem solution and sincere and informed support.

Cultural Effectiveness

Communication is said to be effective if it achieves positive outcomes. There are many different approaches to conceptualizing "positive outcomes." We believe that these outcomes are what members of the culture define them to be. Thus we reject Parks's (1985) notion that only communication that attains its "goals" is competent because we believe that not all cultures are as goal-oriented as U.S. mainstream culture, nor are all members of mainstream culture as focused on goals, and consequently other types of positive outcomes (e.g., those achieved through luck, goodwill, chance, spirituality) may more accurately capture a culture's view of effectiveness under certain circumstances. Recasting these other outcomes into goals honors or privileges the Eurocentric view.

Our approach to competence, then, is to articulate how members of the group say they cope with the problematic nature of communication. Most previous research treats communication as either competent or incompetent (Hammer, 1989; Martin, 1989;

Martin & Hammer, 1989; Pavitt & Haight, 1985; Ruben, 1977, 1989; Wiemann, 1977; Wiseman, Hammer, & Nishida, 1989) or satisfying/dissatisfying (Spitzberg & Hecht, 1984). Our approach assumes that communication is typically not either effective or ineffective but is better conceptualized as essentially problematic (Coupland, Wiemann, & Giles, 1991), requiring moment-to-moment strategies to correct or adjust to issues as they emerge. Two theoretical constructs form the basis for describing this process: communication issues and conversational improvement strategies.

Communication issues are the agenda for effective communication held in common by members of the group. When African Americans were asked to describe satisfying and dissatisfying conversations, certain criteria emerged that define the issues that must be dealt with for conversation to be effective. These issues are themes that run through these accounts and answer the question, "What does it take to be effective?" If all communication is problematic then these issues may be seen as the most salient problems. A summary of issues salient to interethnic effectiveness is presented in Table 4.2.

Conversational improvement strategies are techniques for dealing with problematic communication as it emerges. These strategies are enacted individually or jointly in order to improve conversations that are not meeting the implicit agenda established by the communication issues. We assume that most conversations do not flow smoothly from start to finish. Instead, they require adjustments to manage the issues, or the threat of emerging issues, as they arise. Achieving effectiveness thus becomes a continually developing and responsive process. A summary of these improvement strategies used in interethnic conversations appears in Table 4.3.

Effectiveness implies a communication outcome. While any number of criteria can be used to assess effectiveness, we propose *satisfaction* as a central feature and one particularly appropriate to this model. Communication satisfaction has been conceptualized as the emotional response to positive expectation fulfillment (Hecht, 1978). Satisfaction is an emotion that is experienced when expectations are met in a positive fashion (Hecht, 1978), such as when people establish effective relationships (Hecht, 1984; McLaughlin & Cody, 1982), function successfully in new environments (Vause & Wiemann, 1981), and, in general, lead healthy and successful lives

Table 4.2 African American Issues

Issue	Description
Negative Stereotyping	Use of rigid categories that distort individuality (direct and indirect).
Acceptance	The other confirms and respects one's opinions.
Expressiveness	Express thoughts and feelings.
Authenticity	Be genuine and open.
Understanding	Feeling that meanings are successfully conveyed.
Goal Attainment	Achieve goals or desired outcomes.
Powerlessness	Feeling controlled or manipulated.

SOURCES: Hecht & Ribeau, 1984, 1987; Hecht, Ribeau, & Alberts, 1989; Hecht et al., 1991.

(Maslow, 1954; Rogers, 1961; Thibaut & Kelley, 1959). Previous research has established satisfaction as an emotional response to effective interpersonal encounters (Bochner & Kelly, 1974; Hecht, 1978; Spitzberg & Hecht, 1984). Issues can be seen as a type of expectation; satisfaction will result if the issues are managed in a positive way (e.g., avoid stereotypes) and dissatisfaction will result from the obverse (e.g., use of negative stereotypes).

One of our primary research goals has been to articulate the issues and improvement strategies African Americans perceive in their satisfying and dissatisfying conversations with European Americans. This research has utilized a variety of techniques toward this end. Structured and unstructured interviews and open-ended questionnaires have been used to develop the lists of issues and improvement strategies, and scalar measures derived from respondents' descriptions of their interactions have been used to validate and compare across groups. We argue that all of these methods access the actors' interpretive frameworks, although the scalar items provide guideposts that orient respondents to issues that we wish to have addressed in a more specific way than interview questions. In the discussion that follows we will attempt to describe these issues and improvement strategies as they emerged from African American informants.

Table 4.3 African American Communication Improvement Strategies

Improvement Strategy	*Description*
Assert Point of View	More strongly argue your position and convince the other person.
Positive Self-Presentation	Impress the other person and/or contradict the stereotype.
Be Open and Friendly	Conversational partner should consider one's ideas or opinions rather than dismissing them without sufficient deliberation.
Avoidance	Avoid certain topics of conversation or simply avoid interaction with specific people.
Interaction Management	Regulate amount of talk, turn taking, and so forth.
Other Orientation	Involve the other person, find common ground, and create identification.
Inform/Educate	Clarify or give more information.
Express Genuineness	Express feelings and be honest.
Confront	Direct or indirect confrontation.
Internal Management	Control one's thoughts or feelings.
Treat as Individual/Equal	Leave race out of conversation.
Language Management	Avoid slang and articulate clearly.

SOURCES: Hecht & Ribeau, 1987; Hecht, Ribeau, & Alberts, 1989.

Interethnic Communication Issues

Our research describes seven primary issues African Americans perceive as salient to their communication satisfaction with European Americans (Hecht & Ribeau, 1987; Hecht, Ribeau, & Alberts, 1989; Hecht et al., 1991). These issues are Acceptance, Emotional Expressiveness, Authenticity, Negative Stereotyping, Understanding, Goal Attainment, and Powerlessness. Below are descriptions of the issues as they are described by African Americans who participated in our interviews and questionnaires.

Negative Stereotyping is the use of rigid racial categories that distort an African American's individuality. When stereotyping occurs, it runs counter to the core symbol of Uniqueness (see Chapter 3). These occurred in conversations in which the communication partner racially categorized and ascribed characteristics of the respondent's ethnic group rather than treating the person as an individual. African Americans told us that they believe that stereotyping is a fact of life in the United States. For example, an African American female reported dissatisfaction when her conversational partner "seemed to say to me that she (a third party) was Black and you know how they are."

In addition, several African Americans discussed a form of Negative Stereotyping that could be labeled "indirect stereotyping." This type of stereotyping occurred when the European American dyadic partner talked to the African American about what were believed to be "African American" topics (such as sports or music) and occurred during dissatisfying conversations. Our interview participants claimed that African Americans are very sensitive to indirect stereotyping and react with disdain and withdrawal. One African American male commented that the introduction of African American topics by European Americans is an attempt to find common interests, but he labels people who bring them up as "patronizing or unaware." For example, European Americans try to talk to him about basketball, but he does not play or have any real interest in that sport. He told us that he thinks about this type of stereotyping and "believes that many Blacks feel offended. More educated Blacks feel patronized." He also said that he feels that when most Blacks see disliked behavior or do not understand what a White person is saying, "they label the other person as racist."

Conversely, an African American female described a conversation as satisfying because she "didn't feel put on the spot to speak for the whole of the Black race." Another African American female was satisfied when her partner spoke to her "as another person and didn't let my color interfere with the conversation." A female added that language is important here. African Americans who speak nonstandard dialect are faced with more frequent stereotyping. She feels that many Whites are "predisposed to see the negatives in Blacks." Many of the respondents said they reacted with a great deal of emotion to stereotyping. Negative Stereotyping, when present, is a source of dissatisfaction and, perhaps because of the pervasiveness of prejudice, when absent acknowledges the core symbol of Uniqueness and is a source of satisfaction.

Acceptance is the feeling that another accepts, confirms, and respects one's opinions. This issue is tied to the core symbol of Sharing identified in Chapter 3. Most incidences of acceptance were recorded for descriptions of satisfying conversations. An African American female remarked that she was satisfied with one conversation because there was "mutual respect for each other's beliefs." A male commented that many African Americans overcompensate for "cultural deprivation" and "talk rather than listen in order to cover up." Most feel that their opinion is not respected and this leads them to get "more talkative and flippant." He referred to this as "not being taken seriously" by Whites.

A female remarked that acceptance may be a problem initially, but not after people get to know you. She said, "It depends on how you present yourself." She feels she has the upper hand if a White person does not accept her because she is comfortable with herself and lack of acceptance means the other person is fearful of her. She sees this as an advantage.

A second male pointed out that among African American males acceptance for each other is expressed nonverbally through actions such as similar dress and other signs of inclusion. Paradoxically, acceptance is also expressed while the person acts "cool" or removed.

Thus acceptance is an issue tied to a communication style of talkativeness, flippancy, and being cool. Two of the respondents also tied this back to stereotyping, noting that African Americans may try to preempt such behavior by controlling the conversation. One may use stylized interaction to avoid recognizing stereotyping when it occurs. These respondents commented on feelings of equality/inequality, mutual interest, liking, and communication barriers, with the expressed interpretation that the other person accepted him/her.

The third issue is *Emotional Expressiveness*, which refers to the communication of feelings and thoughts. This issue is tied to the core symbol of Positivity and emotionalism described in Chapter 3. Although a valued behavior in certain contexts, there are those who reported that withholding emotions and showing a tough exterior is important. In fact, it was suggested that some African Americans try to project a particularly "tough" or "cold" exterior in order to be seen as "cool." On the other hand, one respondent reported being dissatisfied because she did not express her own emotions; she reported, "I was dissatisfied that I maintained control and did not curse her out." So there are mixed opinions concerning the role of Emotional Expressiveness in conversations.

Emotional Expressiveness can refer to both one's own and one's partner's expression; lack of expressiveness for either is seen as dissatisfying. Expressiveness manifests itself verbally and nonverbally. While focusing on emotions, expressiveness also includes verbalizations of ideas and opinions. A number of African Americans remarked that expressiveness should not be limited to the emotional arena. To one male, expressiveness meant saying what you feel— "talking from the heart, not the head." Expressiveness is described as a valued behavior—"getting things off your chest." As presented in these opinions, expressiveness is a desirable attribute. In this sense expressiveness reflects the core symbol of Uniqueness.

There are some gender differences in discussions of this issue. According to an African American male, Whites often see Black males as removed from the conversation. He feels this is as a result of "feeling threatened and an attempt to hide a lack of a certain type of knowledge." This leads Black males to either withdraw or become even more talkative. Black females are more talkative, although often in a "flippant" manner. He felt that White expressiveness is less of an issue, although their lack of expressiveness would be interpreted as "racist or standoffish."

One female stated strongly that Black women do not encourage each other to be emotionally expressive. They have had to be so tough as the head of the household throughout history that now they tend to "talk tough and make fun of White women who are soft." This reflects Realism, a core symbol discussed in Chapter 3. She said that Black men criticize Black women for this and some give it as a reason for preferring White women. Both Black men and women stress "being cool"—not letting the other know what you are thinking or feeling. The remark of the second African American male under "Acceptance" supports this conclusion. Both agreed that there is a lot of anger underlying this.

A second female remarked that while expressiveness is important to her she feels this is not typical for African American females. "Talking tough" is a way of carrying oneself. She feels that White females see themselves as more petite and innocent than Black females, and she agrees with the other female that historically Black women have had to take charge and this has led to strength.

Thus there is disagreement among these group members as to the role of expressiveness, particularly Emotional Expressiveness. While the first group of responses suggests that expressiveness is associated with satisfying experiences, others argue that there are cultural forces that mitigate against expressiveness and result in highly stylized expression that demonstrates a tough exterior. Clearly verbal expressiveness, whether in the stylized talk or more genuine discussion, is valued when it occurs. The appropriateness of Emotional Expressiveness seems very situational, would require a considerable trust, and would only occur after the barriers had been brought down. The interpretation of expressiveness seems tied to the next issue, Authenticity.

Authenticity is the label applied to genuineness, with open disclosure being the positive instance and evasiveness the negative. One respondent derived satisfaction from a conversation because he "disclosed information about myself which I usually can't do with someone I don't know well." Another person was dissatisfied because she "was not direct about what I wanted to discuss with this person and did a lot of beating around the bush." Authenticity was inferred from discussions of private and personal information and from truthfulness. In addition, respondents who felt they could "be themselves" or who perceived the other as expressing opinions openly and freely attribute Authenticity to the conversation.

The concept of "realness" pervaded these discussions and questionnaire responses and is consistent with the core symbol of Realism identified in the previous chapter. Some commented on how unusual it was to have this genuine quality in interethnic communication. Their comments indicated that Authenticity might be valued in a White conversational partner, particularly by African American females.

All agreed that this was a factor in interethnic communication. One African American male commented that there are "so many phony conversations—White people try to impress Blacks with their liberalness." Blacks may or may not see through this, some buying into an illusion of equality. In the South the illusion is not as socialized as in the Southwest and, as a result, southern Blacks can see through "authentic" conversations. He commented on patronizing behavior again, noting that "even a sincere effort may come across this way."

Again, there may be gender differences in interpretation. Two of the females agreed that this issue is valued highly by African American women, and one commented that it is expressed in the phrase "being real." She continued, commenting that Black women "describe people in terms of their authenticity regardless of status level." If people are "unpretentious" and "down-to-earth" they are "real." Black women will say "be real" to someone who acts in a pretentious manner. The same individual cited African American literature that discusses this, including Tony C. Bambara's *Gorilla, My Love,* and Gloria Naylor's *The Women of Brewster Place.* The second woman commented that because this is so important she "doesn't accept people too readily." Instead, she "listens carefully to understand and assess authenticity."

Again, the highly stylized, African American male self-presentation was commented on. One male noted that among African American males "high talk and stylin' are valued. You dress as if you had money even if you don't." He noted that the symbol of the Cadillac is another example of this image. Not presenting the "real you" is accepted because the self has been demeaned by society for so long that it is acceptable to create another image.

Thus the stylized form of communication may serve a clear purpose in counterbalancing socioeconomic disadvantage of some African American males while, within the group, there is an understanding of what this image really means. This behavior may not compromise authenticity because it is understood as a message of strength.

Further evidence of the importance of Authenticity is the frequent admonition to "tell it like it is." This expression is recurrent for African American males and speaks of straightforward, to-the-point communication as opposed to avoidance of truth through double talking and fancy language. Despite the apparent contradiction of the high style image creation, Authenticity appears to be an important issue for males and females and may additionally reflect a preference in how the White communicator should behave. There may also be gender differences and the category may reflect a preference for how the White communicator should behave or emerge only after the other issues have been dealt with. This is consistent with the finding that lack of Authenticity is frequently associated with dissatisfaction.

Feelings of *Understanding* were also important to interactant satisfaction and may be related to the core symbol of Sharing presented in Chapter 3. Satisfaction for many respondents was keyed to the feeling that their meaning was successfully conveyed. For example, one respondent reported that "there was a genuine exchange of thinking, feeling, and caring." Responses suggesting that information was exchanged and learning took place fall into this theme as well. Cues that the other person did not believe the respondent were taken as signs of lack of Understanding. A greater proportion of these instances were represented in satisfying interethnic conversations.

Differing cultural backgrounds may underlie some of these misunderstandings. A female noted that differences in upbringing may cause problems. She told us that "if people don't share the same life experiences they can't be expected to truly understand each other. If Whites haven't been exposed to Blacks there will be a 'fear of the unknown.' "

Achieving objectives or obtaining desired ends from the communication effort constitute the issue of *Goal Attainment*. African American respondents seemed to desire a feeling of accomplishment, feeling satisfied when this was obtained and dissatisfied when it was not. One respondent noted dissatisfaction because "no information was exchanged in terms of what I was seeking." Goal Attainment referred to the respondent's ability to achieve a desired end, whether that be solving a problem, exchanging information, or finishing a project. Goal Attainment was observed more frequently in discussions of satisfying interactions than in dissatisfying interactions.

Some respondents suggested that, like Expressiveness and Authenticity, Understanding and Goal Attainment are interconnected issues. For example, an African American male noted that "Blacks and Whites may come away with different meanings from a conversation because concepts aren't defined in the same way. The members of the ethnic groups tend to think in a different manner.

Most times Blacks don't get a lot from conversations with Whites, so when it occurs it is highly valued—'like the gates opening.' " He noted that good conversations, ones that are open and honest, are rare. As a result, Blacks frequently come away from conversations with Whites feeling they have gained little. These discussions emphasized the difficulty of mutual understanding. Without understanding, goals cannot be attained. Thus both qualities are illusive, but valued.

The final issue was labeled *Powerlessness* and described feelings of being controlled, manipulated, and trapped. This can be seen as disconfirming all of the core symbols presented in Chapter 3. Conversely, satisfaction was manifested when interactants felt they had some control or influence over the conversation. One female explained her dissatisfaction by saying that the other interactant was "trying to persuade me using subtle tactics and assertiveness." An African American male described a dissatisfying conversation in which he did not get an adequate chance to express himself. He said that the other communicator "tried to carry on the conversation all by himself . . . he would keep talking and interrupted me whenever I tried to say something." Respondents felt powerless if they were interrupted and did not get a chance to complete their thoughts or felt that the other person controlled the topic. These conversations occurred among peers as well as in the presence of higher status others.

A female commented that success, in general, depends on the power relationship and communication skills. If you can articulate what you want and have the power to get it you will get something out of the conversation. She suggested that one of these factors may be missing for many Blacks in their conversations with Whites. Thus the expression of power is also important.

One male commented that in conversations among African Americans there is a lot that "Whites would consider antagonistic or brutal. Whites would be shocked to see this." He cited playing "the dozens," a put-down game described in Chapter 3, as an example. This type of assertiveness can be too powerful for White interactants. He said, "Whites wouldn't know how to take you if you acted really assertively. They would feel threatened." Similarly, a second male respondent commented that a better label for this issue would be "Mau Mauing"—a Black power strategy of extreme assertiveness and confrontation. He suggested that the label "powerlessness may be putting things in White terms."

Power and power dynamics play a major role in interethnic relations and provide a clear example of African American style or code switching (see Chapter 3). African Americans feel that if they practiced the same power strategies with Whites they use with each other their behavior would be badly misinterpreted. Power was an important undercurrent in many of the previous discussions and is reflected in the core symbol, Assertiveness, that is used to describe African American communication style in Chapter 3. Overall, however, this issue is most prevalent in dissatisfying conversations.

Validation of the Issues. The issues were initially obtained through content analysis of responses to open-ended questions in which African Americans described their effective and ineffective interactions with European Americans. Validation was obtained through interviews, additional open-ended questions, and a Likert-style survey. The interviews were conducted with representatives of the group in which the issues were described and commented upon (Hecht, Ribeau, & Alberts, 1989). These interviews supported external validity. Next, responses to open-ended questions asking for descriptions of effective and ineffective communication were coded using the issues (Hecht & Ribeau, 1987; Hecht, Ribeau, & Alberts, 1989). The coders were able reliably to recognize the issues in these descriptions of interethnic conversations. Finally, Likert-style items were written from the qualitative data to measure each of the issues. Confirmatory factor analysis supported the factorial validity of the issues (Hecht et al., 1991).

After identifying the issues we sought to ascertain their relationship to competent communication. This was accomplished in a series of studies in which satisfaction was used as the criterion of effectiveness.

In each of these studies the issues were found to be associated with communication satisfaction (Hecht et al., 1991; Hecht & Ribeau, 1987; Hecht, Ribeau, & Alberts, 1989). That is, the presence or absence of the issues or the successful or unsuccessful management of the issues was seen as salient to satisfaction with the interaction. In a quantitative study, the issues explained almost all of the variance in satisfaction $(R = .93)$ indicating that the issues provide a very effective model of interethnic communication satisfaction from an African American perspective. The relationship between the issues and satisfaction seems to be independent of personal characteristics such as gender, age, income level, and place of origin (Californian or Arizonan).[4] Further, these results show that while there is some variation from conversation to conversation and between methods of data collection, in general the presence of Negative Stereotyping and Powerlessness is dissatisfying, while interactions that involve Understanding, Acceptance, and Authenticity are satisfying.

Research also demonstrates some individual differences in perceptions of issues. Older respondents are more likely to see Authenticity as an issue than younger respondents, while younger respondents are more likely to report Goal Attainment as an issue (21%) than their older counterparts. In addition, women report that Expressiveness is an issue more frequently than do men. The issues appear to be independent of income level and there were no differences between California and Arizona respondents.

The communication issues are related to ethnic identity labels. African Americans who use different identity labels also seem to differ in the issues they see as salient to effective interethnic communication. People who label themselves Black American are most likely to feel negatively stereotyped, with those labeling themselves Black are next most likely, and those using the label African American the least likely to feel this way. Black Americans were also the most likely group to see Understanding as an issue. African Americans also occasionally perceive this as an issue.

Comparisons of the Issues in In-Group and Out-Group Conversations. In our view communication competence is a problematic event involving accommodation and adjustment. One of the circumstances that makes it problematic involves group membership. People who are considered members of one's own group, called in-group members, are treated differently from those who are perceived as being outside of the group (out-group members) (Giles & Coupland, 1991; Leung & Bond, 1984; Leung & Iwawaki, 1988; Tajfel, 1981). For example, research shows that speech patterns tend to converge when in-group solidarity is being expressed and diverge when out-group distinctions are being emphasized (Giles & Coupland, 1991).

So the in-group and out-group status of conversants is one of the ways in which communication is problematic and requires adjustment, accommodation, and negotiation. A communicator must decide whether the other is to be considered a member of the same (intragroup or interpersonal communication) or different (intergroup communication) group and this determination must be jointly negotiated with the other person. This reasoning leads us to examine the relationship between the issues and group status (Hecht et al., 1991).

We hypothesized that different issues would be salient in in-group and out-group conversations. In order to test this hypothesis we constructed a survey to measure the issues. We decided to add two issues that had emerged among Mexican Americans (Hecht et al., 1990) to test their salience to African Americans in the belief that sometimes issues may be salient that are not reflected in communicators' descriptions of conversations. These issues were shared worldview (having the same perspective on the world) and relational solidarity (close, intimate, personal bonding in relationships). Group membership status was operationalized by relationship intimacy; a scale was used with several items to determine if the relationship was closer, more like a friendship (in-group) or if the relationship was a more distant acquaintance (out-group). The surveys were administered to 129 African American students and community members in Phoenix, Arizona, who were asked to describe a recent conversation with a European American friend or acquaintance and rate their satisfaction with the interaction on a scale designed for this ethnic group (Hecht & Ribeau, 1984).

Analyses of these data show important differences in the issues salient to each type of relationship. In-group conversations place greater stress on Powerlessness and Relational Solidarity. Feelings of Powerlessness among friends seriously detracted from communication satisfaction, while attaining Relational Solidarity was a more important contributor to satisfaction in these conversations. We interpreted these findings to mean that in-group conversations stress control and relational bonding.

The analysis for out-group relationships manifested a different pattern. Stereotyping, Acceptance, Shared Worldview, and

Understanding were more salient concerns. We interpreted this to mean that satisfaction among out-group interactants depends more heavily on establishing a common ground (Acceptance, Shared Worldview, Stereotyping) and task concerns (Understanding).

These results demonstrate important differences between in-group and out-group communication. In order to maximize joint outcomes different issues must be attended to in each type of conversation. The skilled communicator will adjust both linguistically and strategically once a determination of relational status has been made.

Comparisons to European Americans. Once we felt confident that the issues were representative of the African American culture we sought to compare perceptions of these issues across ethnic groups. The group we chose for comparison was European Americans. The framework used here was an emically derived structure (J. Berry, 1980); that is, a framework derived "emically" from one cultural group (African American) and tested on a new group (European Americans) for the purposes of comparison.

We conducted a study to compare African American and European American communication satisfaction issues (Hecht et al., 1991). The African American issues were supplemented by the two additional issues that emerged from studies of Mexican American communication (described above), Shared Worldview and Relational Solidarity (Hecht et al., 1990). A survey was created to measure these issues and administered to 129 African American and 95 European American students and community members in the Phoenix, Arizona, area.

We were surprised to discover that the issues provided an excellent model of satisfaction for both groups. When satisfaction was regressed on the issues, the R^2 was .86 for African Americans and .93 for European Americans, indicating that the items explained almost all of the variance in satisfaction for each group. We reasoned that perhaps European Americans recognize the same issues once they are presented to them. It is also possible that there are differences in the ways the issues are enacted. Finally, the issues may be salient to different types of conversations for each group. This last alternative was examined in subsidiary data analyses.

Further analysis revealed that the issues are used differently by each group. The conversations were separated by ethnic group and group status (in-group/out-group). As described earlier, African Americans perceive Powerlessness (a control issue) as more salient to in-group conversations and Understanding (task issue), Stereotyping, Acceptance, and Shared Worldview (the latter three common-ground issues) more salient to out-group conversations. European Americans associated Goal Attainment (task issue), Relaxation, and Stereotyping (common ground issues) with in-group interaction and Authenticity, Relational Solidarity, and Acceptance (close bonding issues) with the out-group. The European American pattern mirrors that found in Illinois, Montana, and California U.S. samples (Hecht, 1984). A summary of these findings is presented in Table 4.4.

This study points out the differences in effective communication between European Americans and African Americans. While some of these themes have been discussed separately in the mainstream communicative competence literature (e.g., Bochner & Kelly, 1974; Spitzberg & Cupach, 1984; Spitzberg & Hecht, 1984; Wiemann, 1977) or in Eurocentric approaches to interethnic effectiveness (Abe & Wiseman, 1983; Hammer, Gudykunst, & Wiseman, 1978), the issues appear to have different meanings and uses in the various groups. The similarities, where they exist, may reflect the effects of acculturation or generalizable themes based on human social needs of acceptance, self-worth, and bonding. The results of the Hecht, Ribeau, and Alberts (1989) study indicate that where such overlap exists the categories are both experienced and expressed differently in each culture. Hecht et al. (1991) demonstrate that the issues are used differently by these groups and, therefore, also are functionally distinct for each group.

The categories of Powerlessness and Negative Stereotyping may be characteristic of many low-power groups. They also were found, for example, in Mexican Americans' conversational descriptions and rhetorical analyses of Chicano poetry (Hecht et al., 1990). Power is a pervasive issue in race relations in the United States, and power differentials have long existed between mainstream White culture and most other ethnic groups. Such groups are denied access to traditional sources of power, and this position frequently becomes

Table 4.4   A Comparison of African Americans and European
Americans on the Issues Salient to Interethnic
Communication Satisfaction

	African American	European American
Overall		
	Powerlessness	Identity
	Authenticity	Authenticity
	Understanding	Understanding
	Acceptance	Acceptance
	Relaxation	Goal
	Shared Worldview	Relational Solidarity
In-Group		
	<u>Control</u>	<u>Task</u>
	Powerlessness	Goal Attainment
		<u>Common Ground</u>
		Relaxation
		Stereotyping
Out-Group		
	<u>Task</u>	
	Understanding	
	<u>Common Ground</u>	<u>Close Bonding</u>
	Stereotyping	Authenticity
	Acceptance	Relation Solidarity
	Shared Worldview	Acceptance

SOURCE: Hecht et al., 1991.

institutionalized. At the same time, any "out-group" is stereotyped when its members are treated categorically rather than as
individuals. Separation of groups tends to deny the mainstream,
high-power group access to the out-groups except through limited
(and often biased) media contact. As a result, Powerlessness and
Stereotyping become salient issues for interethnic communication.

Recent studies suggest that racism in the United States now
tends to be expressed less directly (Pettigrew, 1981, 1985; Terkel,
1992; Zatz, 1987) or symbolically (Giles & Evans, 1986). For example, Zatz concludes that the effect of race on court sentencing is

moderated by variables such as bail status. While van Dijk (1987) finds direct expression of prejudice in topics of conversations when those conversations are held within the boundaries of an ethnic group (e.g., minorities as criminal, lazy, etc.), less direct expressions are found in argument forms (e.g., arguments about immigration, affirmative action, learning English).

It is interesting to note that these indirect forms may be used in a variety of cultures. In addition to van Dijk's (1987) comparative study, Wodak (1991) discusses indirect forms of anti-Semitism in Austria, and Stern (1991) notes such forms in Germany, labeling them Philosemitism.

Our studies support this interpretation. While traditional stereotyping was manifested, the less direct expression of stereotyping through the introduction of "African American topics" was also prevalent. Other forms of "overaccommodating" or "trying too hard" to adjust (Gallois et al., 1988) are similarly interpreted as indirect stereotyping. European American interactants' modification of their own behavior may appear so strained or extreme that it invokes a feeling of forced behavior or artificiality, "trying too hard." This interpretation is supported by the account of the European American respondent who was pleased that her African American conversational partner accepted her into her group. If such acceptance is overemphasized, overaccommodation is likely. Interviews with African Americans confirm this interpretation, providing numerous examples of this less direct form of stereotyping.

These interpretations may set up an "accommodative dilemma." A European American conversing with an African American may let certain topics or statements pass without commenting or acting on them for fear of being called racist or prejudiced. This may set up "attributional ambiguity" in the enactments of the European American and the interpretations of the African American.

The interpretation of "trying too hard" as stereotyping is certainly unlikely among European Americans and will be expressed and interpreted differently among other nonmainstream, ethnic co-populations in the United States. We have also seen that Powerlessness and Stereotyping function differently for each group, with African Americans finding Powerlessness most salient in the in-group setting and Stereotyping more salient to out-group interaction while European Americans manifest the reverse pattern.

The sense of Powerlessness among African Americans, however, may differ from that of other groups. Lessing, Clarke, and Gray-Shellberg (1981) argue that African Americans lack the in-group loyalty needed for a successful power struggle in the United States. Otto and Featherman (1975) note that early life cycle patterns influence feelings of Powerlessness. Martineau (1976) points out that African American neighborhood instability detracts from a sense of powerfulness and this pattern is different for White and African American populations. Thus, the meaning of Powerlessness may differ for African Americans as a result of both historical and sociological trends.

These studies have attempted to articulate an African American perspective on communication that emphasizes the problematic nature of communication. The issues may be seen as the most salient "problems" faced in intra- and interethnic encounters. But success is not an either/or event. Once acceptance has been established, the communicators cannot merely carry out the remainder of the conversation without encountering other problems or the need for further adjustment. These continuing concerns lead us to consider conversational improvement strategies.

Interethnic Conversational Improvement Strategies

Initial research identified 6 strategies that African Americans said could be used to improve interethnic communication (Hecht & Ribeau, 1987; Hecht, Ribeau, & Alberts, 1989; Martin, Larkey, & Hecht, 1991). Later research expanded this list to 12 strategies. These are conversational techniques that can be used by African Americans themselves, their European American counterparts, or by either interactant. The 12 strategies are described below with occasional reference to tests conducted on those strategies that were part of the original 6.

Original Strategies. Six strategies were identified in initial research (Hecht & Ribeau, 1987; Hecht, Ribeau, & Alberts, 1989; Martin et al., 1991). These include Asserting Point of View, Positive Self-Presentation, Be Open and Friendly, Avoidance, Interaction Management, and Other Orientation. *Asserting Point of View* was found exclusively as a response to a dissatisfying conversation as a strategy of persuasion and argumentation. Respondents felt that conversations could be improved by arguing their own position and convincing their conversational partner. Statements in the Asserting Point of View category imply active effort to change the other person's mind or obtain agreement rather than simply passively supplying more information for clarification (see "Inform/ Educate" below). Of course, suggestions to supply more information could be intended to persuade or pursue achievement of goals. Examples of this strategy are, "I continue to put across what I believe," "Just simply be more vocal in the conversation, this in itself will give you sense of control or power," and "Impress upon the other person the benefit of the action to them." One male said that a dissatisfying conversation could have been improved if he could "convince him [the conversational partner] to give the benefit of the doubt" to other people. Sometimes the strategy of assertion was indicated by descriptions of communication style. For example, "stress," "assert," or "emphasize my point" were phrases that were placed in this category. Thus assertiveness applies to both style and substance. Asserting Point of View was mentioned 43 times. Most of the responses in this category were elicited by either the description of the control/Powerlessness issue (44%) or the lack of accomplishing goals (25%).

The second category is *Positive Self-Presentation*. There were two main themes in this category. One theme was to mention or purposefully demonstrate positive attributes or accomplishments in order to impress the other. For example, "I try to make others see what I know, that is, when I'm being talked down to I try to show my intelligence." The other theme was to behave in a way that contradicts stereotype-based expectations—"I just make sure my actions and conversation don't fit the negative stereotype." Both strategies imply intentionally presenting self in a way that will produce the effect of impressing the other. Positive Self-Presentation was mentioned most often as a response to stereotyping.

The next theme, *Be Open and Friendly*, was recommended most frequently as a strategy for improving dissatisfying conversations. Respondents expressed a desire to have people consider their ideas or opinions, rather than dismiss them without giving them sufficient consideration. This category is similar to Positive Self-Presentation, but without the self-conscious attempt to impress.

Rather, it is usually phrased with simple admonitions to be tactful and polite, and to remain open and friendly, that is, "be considerate of the other person," "be polite and courteous," "make the person feel not intimidated." For example, a male wanted the other person to be "more open-minded," and a second male said the other person should "be more patient, not assume anything, find out first." This strategy was a desired change in the conversational partner.

One female asserted that open-mindedness is not highly valued. She felt that African Americans are more concerned with appearing strong rather than uncertain and saw openness as a White, middle-class female attribute. This is consistent with our data that show that open mindedness is seen as a strategy for the White interactant to invoke. The strategy appears to be used most frequently when Acceptance and Understanding are the issues.

The fourth theme was called *Avoidance* and was suggested as a strategy for dissatisfying conversations. Those who responded with this strategy felt the only recourse was to either avoid the topic or end the interaction. This strategy is usually simply described as "terminate the conversation," or "I remove myself from the conversation." Other variations include changing the subject, not getting involved with such conversations in the first place, or giving up trying to explain or accomplish anything (e.g., "I don't think it is beneficial to try to change the other person"). For example, one respondent said she could have improved the situation by "not bringing up the subject," while another female said the other person could have improved the situation "by leaving my house politely." These instances were very clear-cut and obvious. Respondents felt that certain conversations should not take place and that certain topics would just have to be avoided with specific people. Due to their conceptual similarity and additional responses indicating overlap, this category combined four of the original categories: Avoid, Give In, Nothing Self Can Do, Nothing Other Can Do. This issue is most frequently evoked when there are problems with Goal Attainment, Acceptance, Authenticity, and Understanding, while the "Giving In" subtheme is suggested by some when there is a feeling of powerlessness.

The fifth strategy, *Interaction Management*, may occur more frequently among descriptions of satisfying conversations. There are several strategies in this category, from managing the immediate interaction ("take turns," "work toward a compromise"), referring the problem to a later interaction or outside resources, ("request a time to talk it over," "contact personnel director"), or using alternative methods of communicating ("write a note"). Many respondents mentioned regulating the amount of talk and the rate. For example, one female wrote that a satisfying conversation could have been improved by "just talking a little more," and another female reported that her conversation could have been improved by "more time" together. Others discussed turn taking.

The conversation can be improved if either interactant adopts this strategy and suggestions of Interaction Management are fairly evenly distributed among the various issues. Overall, Interaction Management appears to be used when communication is *not* problematic to improve conversations that do not have any particularly salient issues or is used to divert and redirect the conversation when problems do occur.

Other Orientation occurred most frequently in descriptions of improving satisfying interethnic conversations and included attempts to involve the other person, find common ground, and create identification. Most of the comments in this category relate to listening to the other person's point of view, for example, "hear the person out," "learn by listening," "placing them in our shoes," "ask better questions," and "try to look at from both sides." Also, bringing up topics that both communicants share is suggested and described as a way to establish common ground—"think or talk about something that both can identify with," or "talk about something he could have related to." This strategy was used to improve all of the issues, with the highest response from the Acceptance, Authenticity, Goal Attainment, and Understanding issues. Responses suggest that either interactant can improve the conversation by being more other oriented.

Additional Strategies. More recent analyses have identified additional strategies. We have less information on these and, therefore, they require additional testing.

The theme of the "Inform/Educate" strategy is to clarify or give more information. The tone of this strategy is more passive than the argumentation and persuasion tactics described in the Asserting

Point of View category. For example, a female wanted to educate her partner about slavery in order to help him understand. Other examples include statements such as: "Tactfully educate by giving more information," "we must be ready to provide more information at all times," and "if the conversation is that important, try and explain whatever you feel is being misunderstood." A subgroup in this category felt that they should be more detailed, factual, and specific. For example, one female wrote that "if I had more facts I could have continued in my point of trying to make him realize these people need help."

This was mainly seen as a strategy for the respondent to employ, not the conversational partner. Most often, this suggestion is in response to the issue of Lack of Understanding. However, it is also often used as a strategy to overcome stereotyping. One of the frequently mentioned methods for clarification is to ask questions to assure understanding such as simply, "ask them for more information" or "ask what it is they don't understand." This was by far the most frequently mentioned strategy and is used more often in response to the Lack of Understanding issue.

"Expressing Genuineness," that is, expressing feelings and being honest or genuine—"be yourself"—is a strategy often mentioned, particularly in response to the issues of feelings *not* being expressed or a lack of genuineness. This strategy is sometimes presented as a method to lead or model the behavior in hopes that the other will follow. Also, this strategy is used as a response to an unfavorable conversation—"share your feelings of a lack of accomplishment," "ask the person to be for real," or "describe feeling you have about the situation and tell the person 'it makes me feel bad when you . . .' " Such statements might be considered a form of confrontation, but the focus seems to be more on changing the other's behavior by being completely honest rather than on confronting the other person. This was a popular strategy and is used most frequently in reaction to the expressing feelings issue and genuineness.

"Confront" is described as either a direct confrontation of the issue or using questions to place the burden back on the other person. Direct confrontation statements include, "State that you feel that the other party feels hesitant about being authentic with you," "correct misconceptions in a shrewd, effective manner," or "I believe you must always confront stereotyping by saying, 'It sounds as if you are making generalizations that may not be applicable to me.' "

Examples of questions include: "Just say, 'but how do *you* feel about it?' If they don't answer, it's obvious that it at least makes them feel uncomfortable" or "ask why and how they got that stereotyping." These questions are not asking for information as much as they are apparently intended to put the problem back on the shoulders of the other. This strategy is used most frequently when the other person is stereotyping but is also used when genuineness is an issue.

"Internal Management" is the next category. Many of the comments did not recommend actual behaviors or scripts that one could use in response to the issues. Rather, there were suggestions for how to handle one's internal response—how to think or feel about the situation. Usually these suggestions prescribed acceptance, objectivity, and nondefensiveness as internal attitudes, rather than behaviors. Examples include, "I do my best to control my thoughts," "think first of who you are, how you feel about yourself," and "put situation in proper perspective, that is, lose a battle to win the war." Internal management is frequently commented on, often in response to the acceptance issue but also used for the other issues as well.

The "Treat as Individual/Equal" category makes direct suggestions to leave race, color, or stereotypical assumptions out of the conversation, such as, "Talk to each other without having the sense of color in the conversation." Additionally, it includes direct suggestions to treat others as individuals such as, "decisions should be made based on each individual" or "get to know me then judge me." Treating people with respect also falls in this category since it might be seen as a way to demonstrate that one is dealing with others on equal footing. Other examples included a female who wanted the other person to "not take a self-righteous position" and a second female who would have been more satisfied if her partner "had been less inclined to a superior attitude." This strategy is suggested most frequently in response to stereotyping and, for the most part, the expectation was that the other person would adopt this strategy (e.g., "have them evaluate me on my own merit").

"Language Management" only had a few items. However, these seemed to be sufficiently different from the other categories to warrant separate treatment. The suggestions were mostly related to avoiding slang and jargon or by articulating clearly in order to be understood. "Refrain from using unfamiliar jargon" and "talk the same language" are typical examples. Language management was not frequently mentioned and is suggested as a way of responding to the Understanding issue.

Validation of the Conversational Improvement Strategies. Studies show that use of the original set of improvement strategies is related to satisfaction (Hecht & Ribeau, 1987; Hecht, Ribeau, & Alberts, 1989; Martin et al., 1991). Research has not, as yet, addressed the additional strategies. Dissatisfying conversations can be improved by either being more open-minded or by avoiding the topic or the entire conversation, and this is true regardless of age, gender, income, or geography. However, even though the improvement strategies influence satisfaction notwithstanding these personal characteristics, research does show that people with family incomes below $25,000 are more likely to suggest Interaction Management to improve conversations while those with incomes above this mark were more likely to suggest increased Other Orientation.

Research has also shown that the identity label a person adopts is associated with the strategies she or he is likely to use to improve interethnic conversations. Those using the label Black American or African American are more likely to suggest Assertiveness to improve conversations than are those who label themselves as Black. Conversely, those using Black and Black American are more likely than those using African American to report that communication can be improved by exhibiting more Other Orientation.

The African Americans we interviewed and surveyed felt that the improvement strategies might work under certain circumstances. However, where stereotyping and acceptance are issues, they did not hold out much hope. One male did not see much hope for improving dissatisfying conversations. Describing it as "bouncing off a brick wall," he said that most Blacks look for keys in the beginning. If they "see signs of racism, patronizing behavior, or other put downs, they turn off quickly." The importance of stereotyping and acceptance is stressed here. He also noted that after "the first few minutes of a bad conversation it is almost a lost cause." Others held out some hope when the other issues were salient, feeling that some of the strategies might work but cautioning against placing too much faith in any attempt by African Americans where power is unequal. This is consistent with our findings that indicate that Avoidance by the self and open-mindedness by Whites are the two most salient strategies.

The original strategies provide an effective set of remediation tactics for Powerlessness, Acceptance, Understanding, and Goal Attainment, and a moderately effective set of strategies for Stereotyping and Authenticity. Additional strategies are needed for Expressiveness and these may be present in the extended list provided above, but this later list has not yet been tested for its relationship to the issues. Overall, Avoidance and Other Orientation seem to be the most useful strategies across the issues.

Interethnic Conversational Improvement Strategies in In-Group and Out-Group Conversations. Our discussion of the communication issues explained the importance of distinguishing between in-group and out-group relationships. We applied the same concept to conversational improvement strategies in an effort to see if different strategies are used with different conversations.

A survey measure of the improvement strategies was constructed and administered to the same sample of 129 African Americans described previously. After recalling a conversation, respondents were asked to indicate how the conversation could have been improved. Regression analyses were then computed separately for in-group (with friends) and out-group (with acquaintances) conversations to see if the choice of improvement strategy was related to the type of issue.

Similar improvement strategies are used with the three issues identified with satisfying communication, Goal Attainment, Understanding, and Acceptance. Avoidance seems to be the sole strategy used in in-group conversations for these issues, while in out-group conversations Other Orientation is used as well. The issue of Understanding is an exception. For this issue *both* Avoidance and Other Orientation are associated with *both* in-group and out-group conversations.

When Powerlessness is problematic in in-group conversations, Interaction Management is used. In out-group conversations, Nothing Other Can Do and Giving In are strategies used. The issue of

Stereotyping in out-group conversations is associated with Nothing Other Can Do.

The relationship between Stereotyping and strategies is interesting and not easy to interpret. No strategies were associated with Stereotyping for in-group conversations for African Americans, and Nothing Other Can Do about it for out-group. This is a difficult issue that people have not learned to deal with. Cultural representatives in the Hecht, Ribeau, and Alberts (1989) study said they just "turned off" people they perceived to be racist. The data in this study also indicate that African Americans seem resigned to the lack of control over racism and feel that little can be done to improve these situations in distant relationships. Future research is needed to suggest ways of coping with this issue.

To summarize, different strategies are used in in-group and out-group conversations on all issues except for Understanding. For the three issues identified in satisfying conversations, the strategy most strongly associated with in-group conversations (Avoidance) is described as the joint responsibility of both self and other. Interaction Management, associated with in-group conversations when Powerlessness is an issue, also requires joint action.

However, additional strategies are identified with out-group conversations—Other Orientation and Giving In—and shift the responsibility to the other interactant. The exception to this is the fact that African Americans feel there is Nothing Other Can Do when Powerlessness and Stereotyping occur in out-group conversations.

Overall, out-group conversations are associated with strategies that put more of the responsibility on the other person. Here, Other Orientation and Giving In are used when the conversation is extremely and negatively problematic, implying that it is the other person's responsibility to deal with the issues (i.e., should agree with self, not offend me and ask me what I wanted, should be more oriented to me, should practice more Other Orientation).

This focus on the other's responsibilities is somewhat tempered for African Americans' in-group conversations. Avoidance is associated with in-group conversations—implying that when there are problems in Authenticity, Goal Attainment, Acceptance, and Understanding, both interactants should avoid topics that are problematic.

A Comparison of African American and European American Conversational Improvement Strategies. Again, paralleling the analyses of the issues, a comparison was conducted between African American and European American communicators utilizing the same sample and survey (Martin et al., 1991). These analyses indicated that European Americans did not generally report using the improvement strategies in response to the issues. When significant relationships were observed, they were moderate to weak and always of lesser magnitude than those observed for African Americans. These findings tell us that the improvement strategies are more characteristic of African Americans than European Americans. There were, however, certain similarities and other more specific differences in the findings.

The major similarity between European Americans and African Americans is that, for both groups, Avoidance and Other Orientation are the most frequently used strategies to improve problematic conversations. It is interesting that the strategies mentioned most frequently are those that require either joint action or the responsibility of the other person. There are few "self" strategies (e.g., Assertiveness) associated with these issues.

In addition, it seems that the more distant the relationships (out-group conversations), the more the strategies focus on the other interactant's responsibility. In contrast, the closer the relationship (in-group conversations), the more joint strategies are used. However, while this general relationship between degree of intimacy in conversation and locus of responsibility seems to hold for both groups, there is a difference in the types of strategies used.

The major differences revolved around the number of strategies associated with each issue. African Americans seemed to report differential patterns of strategy use for Powerlessness and Stereotyping (issues generated from dissatisfying communication) and those issues associated with satisfying conversations (Acceptance, Understanding, Goal Attainment). This differential pattern did not emerge in the European American data. This is understandable given that the framework (issues and strategies) was developed from African American samples and in this study was extended to European Americans.

The findings for the in-group/out-group distinction also demonstrate similarities and differences. As noted, African Americans tend to place responsibility on the other for conversational improvement, although less so among members of the in-group. Reliance on the other is even stronger among European Americans and this extends to in-group conversations where Other Orientation, a strategy that the conversational partner is expected to use, is most frequently used.

If both groups place more responsibility on the other person for improving problematic interaction, particularly in out-group conversations, it may explain some of the difficulty reported in interethnic communication identified in previous research. Each interactant may feel the other is responsible for improving the conversation, and this is particularly true when relationships are not intimate.

The differences between the two groups in expectations for in-group and out-group conversations further explains the difficulty. If African American interactants hold expectations that problematic in-group conversations should be improved by some joint conversational strategies and European Americans expect that it is the responsibility of the other person, it is easy to see how misunderstandings and negative outcomes might occur. This particular mix of approaches to in-group relationships may impose more of the responsibility for improving these conversations on the shoulders of the African Americans.

Intra-Ethnic Communication Effectiveness

Finally, we have also addressed intra-ethnic communication satisfaction, although in a more limited way (Hecht & Ribeau, 1984). Like the interethnic research, these studies attempted to identify the African American perspective on these conversations. Responses to open-ended questions in which respondents described satisfying and dissatisfying conversations were used to construct scalar items in surveys that elaborated the findings.

In this research we focused on intra-ethnic communication among friends in three ethnic groups (Hecht & Ribeau, 1984). The study, however, was conducted before the issues had crystallized into their present forms although the findings parallel the later issues. This work showed that the largest differences were between Mexican Americans and European Americans, with African Americans closer to European Americans. Mexican Americans seem to place greater emphasis on a closely bonded relationship (relational solidarity) with rewards derived from within the relationship. The dyadic unit is seen as joined together, with self-interest subsumed in relational interest. The bonding is implicit. This viewpoint would be typified by the statement, "We are doing something together that we are both getting something out of." In addition, satisfying communication for this group also revolves around nonverbal communication and acceptance of self. More on the Mexican American perspective is presented in Hecht et al. (1990).

European Americans, and to a lesser extent African Americans, are more self-oriented and their rewards tend to be external. From this cultural perspective, the other person is viewed as an external source of rewards for one's self. This perspective might be typified by the statement, "I'm doing something with you and will get my needs met (and you might, as well)." In addition, European American and African American groups seem to place greater emphasis on the future of the relationship (this seems to be assumed among Mexican Americans) and explicit confirmation that the message and the relationship are being accepted.

While the differences between African Americans and European Americans were not as pronounced, they were present nonetheless. African Americans seems to require deeper, more intimate involvement in the topic. Intimacy for this group is intrinsic to the relationship and therapeutic and is built on trust. Greater Other Orientation is also presented, leading us to conclude that satisfaction for African Americans may revolve around having conversational goals met through the actions of others. Consistent with their position between the other two groups, bonding seems to be conditional depending on goal attainment and reciprocity.

In contrast to African Americans, European Americans place greater emphasis on emotional aspects of conversation and appear to be more future oriented. This is consistent with previous findings for this group that revealed communication satisfaction among friends to be more strongly influenced by signs of intimacy that confirm the future of the relationship and a relaxed atmosphere that sets the emotional tone of the conversation (Hecht, 1984).

These studies show that the issues of Expressiveness, Authenticity, Understanding, and Goal Attainment and the conversational improvement strategy of Other Orientation are also salient to African Americans in the intra-ethnic setting. Expressiveness is reflected in an African American emphasis on a deeply intimate involvement in the topic of intra-ethnic interaction. The passion associated with such involvement is communicated through expressive style. Authenticity is also important in intra-ethnic communication. African Americans stress a genuine involvement with the topic and the importance of an intimacy that is intrinsic to the relationship. Combined, Expressiveness and Authenticity speak to a kind of intimacy that is stressed in in-group conversations. African Americans seem to place particularly high value on trust and helping one another.

Understanding and Goal Attainment also appear to be salient African American issues in intra-ethnic communication. African Americans seem to require explicit confirmation that both parties are going in the same direction or are on the "same wave length." Relatively unambiguous cues are needed to express understanding when members of this group communicate with each other. As with Understanding, in intra-ethnic conversations African Americans seem to desire confirmation that the interactants share the same goals and they are being met. Beyond the issues of Understanding and Goal Attainment is the need for expressions of these outcomes. Here, Expressiveness, Understanding, and Goal Attainment seem to merge into an emphasis on explicit confirmation of mutual agreement about where the conversation is going.

Finally, research shows that African Americans place more emphasis than European Americans on Other Orientation in intra-ethnic interaction. Thus it appears that in intra-ethnic settings Other Orientation may be an issue as well as a means for improving conversation.

Conclusion

In this chapter we have attempted to articulate an African American perspective on communication competence. These studies are based on the assumptions articulated in the opening chapter. We examine how ethnic culture emerges in social interaction and explicate African American perceptions of patterned conduct.

A number of sensitizing constructs are used in these analyses. The chapter seeks to describe African American prescriptions for appropriate and effective communication. We approach these prescriptions by conceptualizing communication as a problematic event and eliciting the patterns, interpretations, and taken-for-granted elements of conversation. As a result we identify conversational issues and improvement strategies. In addition, we use core symbols to represent norms.

This work is in its infancy. While we can point to specific findings, much more research is needed before we can be said to truly understand the African American code of competence and the conversational style in which it is enacted. To date we have information about certain issues that appear highly salient to the group and a set of strategies that can be used to improve conversations. Other questions are equally salient. What of the issues in communication between African Americans and other groups (e.g., Mexican Americans, Asian Americans, types of European Americans)? What are the patterns to these issues and how are they related to the culture itself? Ethnic identities? Communication style? Other methods (e.g., videotaped conversations, ethnographies, experiments) also can be utilized to identify additional issues, learn how the issues emerge, see what other variables influence the issues, and develop a system for classifying and understanding these problematic elements. Do these issues reappear in relationships over time? Are some more characteristic of earlier stages of relationships? How do power dynamics (e.g., in organizations) influence the issues?

Our understanding of communication improvement strategies is just in its infancy and relies too heavily on self-report data. We need to videotape conversations involving African Americans and observe how the issues are dealt with through specific conversational acts. We also need longitudinal studies of relationships to learn how friends, co-workers, and married couples manage these issues through relational strategies. As throughout this book, we hope our work can be a springboard to answering questions such as these.

Notes

1. A number of authors have dealt with this topic, including Hammer, Gudykunst, and Wiseman (1978), Imahori and Lanigan (1989), Kealey (1989), Martin and Hammer (1989), Olebe and Koester (1989), Ruben (1989), Spitzberg (1989), and Wiseman, Hammer, and Nishida (1989).

2. For other examples, see Abe and Wiseman (1983), Collier (1988), Gudykunst & Hammer (1988), and Hecht & Ribeau (1984, 1987).

3. In this book *rules* and *norms* are used synonymously. Others (e.g., Shimanoff, 1980) distinguish between the two terms. For purposes of convenience we will use the term *norm*.

4. Here we are testing to see if these characteristics mediate the relationship between the issues and satisfaction. Below we examine how the characteristics are related to the issues alone. These findings show that regardless of personal characteristics the issues influence satisfaction. However, these same findings suggest that future research test a model that predicts:

personal characteristics→issues→communication satisfaction

CHAPTER FIVE

Conclusions

This book discusses African American communication and culture. We have examined research and talked to and surveyed African Americans in an attempt to explain the social, political, economic, and historical context of African American communication, understand their ethnic identity, and describe their communication styles and competencies. These efforts have lead us to a number of conclusions and to begin the development of a new theory of identity that encompasses these diverse factors. In this chapter we will briefly highlight some of these conclusions and articulate and apply the theory. Finally, we will consider methodological issues that transcend any individual area of research and suggest applications of the findings.

Status of African Americans in the United States

It is clear that conditions in the United States have not been conducive to positive African American self-images and interethnic relationships. From their first experiences in the geographic area now known as the United States, African Americans have experienced repression and discrimination and, in general, have been disadvantaged. While there are some signs that prejudice might be decreasing (L. Gordon, 1986) and economic conditions improving, the overall trends are still not positive. Further, work in life-span development (MacLaury & Hecht, in press) suggests that improvements in interethnic social relationships are highly dependent upon the events that shape an age cohort and the quality of interactions, and thus it may be difficult to alter the dynamics within an age cohort. More intra- and interethnic research across the life span is needed to clarify the conclusion.

The complex issues creating African American social reality are multifaceted. Race, class, and gender discrimination interact in a manner that challenges the institutions that usually provide group stability and hope for a better tomorrow. In addition, a decline in the domestic economy for all U.S. residents seems to ensure that the poor will remain separated from the "American Dream."

Due in part to the disadvantaged status of African Americans in the United States, most of the research dealing with this group is conducted from a Eurocentric perspective. We acknowledge that our own work is strongly influenced by these traditions. However, we represent as accurately as we can the African American perspective as expressed to us by the bearers of this cultural tradition. We believe this work is part of a larger movement away from putting European Americans at the center of the research experience (the assumed norm) and toward understanding various groups within their own ethnocultural framework. This move is reflected in the phrase *cultural diversity,* which is being used by some instead of *assimilation* as a metaphor for dealing with ethnic differences. The cultural roots of the African American experience, which extend beyond the shores of the United States, and the persistence of racism in spite of organized political resistance have accentuated the uniqueness of African American life and culture.

A Communication Theory of Ethnic Identity

In Chapter 2 we discussed theory and research on self, identity, and ethnic identity. No single paradigm has emerged that synthesizes the diverse approaches nor has any approach fully integrated communication. We predicate our work on the assumptions that ethnic culture is socially and historically emergent, is co-created and maintained as a function of identity, and is constituted as a system of interdependent patterns of conduct and interpretation. Thus identity is central to our study of ethnic culture and communication central to both identity and ethnic culture.

For this reason we decided to apply a communication perspective to the study of African American ethnic identity. This means that we use what we know about communication to construct a theory of ethnic identity. We hope that in deriving this new theory we can explain aspects of ethnic identity that can only be revealed through a communication orientation. The theory is grounded in our descriptive and explanatory research and offered here in preliminary and tentative form in order to encourage testing by the research community.

Our primary concern in Chapter 2 was to understand the communicative processes involved in the development, maintenance, and revision of identity. In this pursuit we encountered sociological, psychological, and anthropological approaches. These approaches stress individual and social conceptualizations of identity. The individual conceptualization is associated with social psychology and views identity as a characteristic of the person and personality. From this perspective, identity is a person's way of perceiving self. The social conceptualizations are derived from sociology and anthropology and view the self as centered in social roles and societal practices.

Our emphasis on the communicative aspects of identity changes these foci. In attempting to articulate a communication approach to identity we seek to integrate these divergent perspectives and add a communication emphasis. The basic premise of this new theoretical stance is that identity is inherently a communication process and must be understood as a transaction in which messages are exchanged. These messages are symbolic linkages between and among people that, at least in part, are enactments of identity. The new theory extends identity beyond individual and societal constructions to the interaction and complements the view of social identity located in roles and role theory with identity as relational.

Basic Concepts of the Theory

The book has already presented a number of sensitizing concepts to describe communication and culture. These include core symbols, prescriptions, code, conversation, and community. We also see identity as a problematic event. These concepts become the bases for our communication theory of identity.

Identity, itself, may be seen as a core symbol. As we have seen, societies orient themselves around their concept of identity and researchers have bifurcated these orientations into individualist and collectivist camps. Identity becomes a way of understanding constellations of behaviors that can be interpreted as creating, expressing, protecting, and changing identity. Within this larger, ethnocultural concept of identity there exist smaller systems of meanings and behaviors that can also be considered the core symbols of a particular type of identity. For example, researchers have argued that "power" is a core symbol around which gender roles historically have been organized in the United States (Henley, 1977).

Identities also prescribe modes of conduct. Defining who you are tells you what you should be doing. One can view competence on an individual level as the successful enactment of identity. Relationally, one can say that competent conversation confirms the identities of all interactants. Communal identities become the means for public communication.

Code, conversation, and community also provide ways of understanding identity. Identity is a code for being. It provides the means for understanding self, interaction, relationships, and society by defining the nature of self and social life.

There are at least two ways in which identity is a conversation. First, identity may be viewed as a narrative told to oneself or existing within a culture. Second, identity is enacted as a way of doing conversation.

The notion of community is fundamental to identity. Identities are located in communal memberships. Philipsen (1987) argues that the function of cultural communication is to provide shared and individual identities. This is accomplished through the creation, affirmation, and enactment of identities. Philipsen (1987) identifies three prominent forms of cultural communication by which this is accomplished: *ritual, myth,* and *social drama.* These forms achieve the functions of uniting groups, coordinating action, and defining boundaries.

Ritual is defined as "a communication form in which there is a structured sequence of symbolic acts, the correct performance of which constitutes homage to a sacred object" (Philipsen, 1987, p. 250). Philipsen provides the example of the "call-response" ritual sequence in African American churches. As described by Daniel and Smitherman (1976), the sequence consisting of a call by a minister and a response by the congregation promotes unity.

A *myth* is a symbolic narrative whose function is to bind together the thoughts of a group and promote coordinated social action (Philipsen, 1987). Philipsen cites as an example Hannerz's (1969) study of "street corner mythmaking" in which African American males gather to tell stories about successful confrontations with European American society. These myths help create and crystallize community standards and criteria that allow smoother coordination of interaction.

Finally, Philipsen (1987) describes *social dramas* in which group standards are breached and resolved. Through these dramas transgressors can be reintegrated into the community and the boundaries defined and enforced.

In addition to these cultural forms we believe that identity is also enacted in a form called *everyday interaction* or *everyday talk* (Duck, 1990). In many ways, the mundane workings of everyday existence provide a powerful statement of identity by building the roots of those identities into the most frequent human actions. Further, these interactions and the elements of identity they enact exist on both *content* and *relationship levels* (Watzlawick et al., 1967). Thus they comment on the topic or substance of interaction as well as the relationship between the people. For example, the phrase "I don't do windows" not only sets limits on behaviors, but also achieves a humorous statement of relationship and provides important information regarding self-perception.

It is through these forms and functions that individuals and communities define and communicate a shared sense of identity and that the emergent quality of identity manifests itself. We agree with Hoelter (1985) that social networks, interactive groupings of people, are central to identity. However, identity also can be maintained symbolically (Gans, 1979). *Symbolic identities* require the individual to enact rituals and performances but may be maintained without actual interaction with reference groups/networks.

Conversely, since reality is socially constructed (P. Berger & Luckmann, 1966), we believe that it is not only participation in the network and group roles per se that matter, but also the *meanings* assigned to such actions. It is not enough to know that a person interacts with a certain group or maintains symbolic representations of group membership. We must also ascertain what that interaction or symbol means to the person and communicates to others. The semantic properties of these interpretations are represented by labels and core symbols.

Finally, identity is understood as *problematic*. Identity is a message that exists on competing levels (e.g., individual/social) and is influenced by diverse social (e.g., individualism/collectivism) and individual forces. Counter- and co-identities push and pull us. People, groups, and places change in a continual transactional process that alters the codes and prescriptions we live under. In this nebulous nexus of mediating and moderating variables, identities are created, negotiated, defended, and modified.

These basic concepts provide a structure and language to discuss the Communication Theory of Identity. As an interpretive process, these structures require a frame of reference. How are we to locate core symbols? prescriptions? codes? conversations? communities?

Frames of Reference

Our communicative analysis of identity has lead us to a theory that explicates four frames of identify: *personal, enacted, relational,* and *communal*. The theory builds off of the integrative work of De Vos and Roosens. De Vos (1982) argues that ethnic identity exists on four levels: social structure, social interaction, subjective experience, and fixed patterns of behavior and emotional expression. Similarly, Roosens (1989) maintains that ethnic identity consists of overlapping cultural, social, and psychological dimensions. The current approach does not accept De Vos's structuralist perspective nor Roosens's dimensional approach but substitutes the interpretive perspective and the dialectical approach articulated in Chapter 1. Further, the theory adds a relational dimension and a communication emphasis.

The four frames define for us the "location" of identity. Identity is "stored" within individuals, relationships, and groups and is communicated within and between relational partners and group members. Even when identity is symbolic and face-to-face interaction with other members is cut off, communication rituals use symbols to bind groups together. These four levels or frames permeate all understandings of identity and may be considered individually, in pairs, or in groups.

Frames are means of interpreting reality that provide a perspective for understanding the social world (Hecht, 1984). Frames exist on two levels. In their most abstract usage, there are researcher-adopted frames of reference that are analogous to other ontological and epistemological positions that orient the researcher's "viewing lens." These frames tell us what to look for and where to look. For example, the communal frame might focus a researcher on the rituals or norms handed down to new members. At this level of analysis the frames are sensitizing constructs for social research.

These frames are not only research or analytical perspectives but are also ways people have of conceptualizing their own identity. People who see themselves as invested in what they do (e.g., "I am an artist") are emphasizing the enacted level while those whose self-concept is tied to their image as a relational partner (e.g., "I am a father") are more concerned with the relationship level. Here the frames act as organizing principles for social life. Similarly, gang membership, religious affiliation, and corporate memberships all emphasize the communal level. So the frames are useful to researchers and also are part of the lived experience of social actors.

The Interpenetration of Frames. These levels or frames of identity do not exist isolated from each other. Instead, they may operate jointly as when the personal and communal frames match or there may be a dialectical tension between and among the levels. For example, Montgomery (1992) discusses the tension between what we would call personal and relational enactments as couples seek to define self and relationship through communication. Montgomery also discusses the tensions between what we call Relational Identity and Communal Identity as the couple seeks to negotiate its relational definition with that provided by the cultural group. Thus a communication analysis of identity will consider how individuals frame and enact their personal identity and how these identities are relationally and communally expressed, negotiated, and defined.

Personal meanings are not only expressed in enactment but created through enactment. In fact, one can only come to know a personal identity through its enactment and, conversely, enactments must be of a personal, relationship, and/or communal frame. These interpenetrations have become the substance of our emerging research agenda.

Our notion of interpenetrating frames provides the basic structure for our Communication Theory of Identity. In the next section we will attempt to articulate the basic assumptions of the theory, starting first with overall assumptions and then articulating the assumptions associated with each of the frames.

Basic Assumptions of the Theory

Our assumptions are derived from the discussion of the nature of identity in Chapter 2 and applied to each of the frames as well as their interpenetrations with each other. It is our belief that these assumptions are observable/testable, but some may view them as more axiomatic in nature. The first five assumptions involve dialectics. The eight overall assumptions are:

(1) Identities have individual, enacted, relational, and communal properties;
(2) Identities are both enduring and changing;
(3) Identities are affective, cognitive, behavioral, and spiritual;
(4) Identities have both content and relationship levels of interpretation;
(5) Identities involve both subjective and ascribed meanings;
(6) Identities are codes that are expressed in conversations and define membership in communities;
(7) Identities have semantic properties that are expressed in core symbols, meanings, and labels;
(8) Identities prescribe modes of appropriate and effective communication.

Identity as a Personal Frame. Identity is a personal frame of reference for the individual, stored as self-cognitions, feelings about self, and/or a spiritual sense of self-being. As a characteristic of the individual, identity has been known as self-concept or self-image and provides an understanding of how individuals define themselves in general as well as in particular situations. The following are the assumptions of Identity as Personal Frame:

(9) Identities are hierarchically ordered meanings attributed to the self as an object in a social situation;
(10) Identities are meanings ascribed to the self by others in the social world;
(11) Identities are a source of expectations and motivations.

Identity as an Enactment Frame. Identities are enacted in social interaction through communication. This frame focuses on the messages that express identity. Not all messages are about identity, but identity is part of all messages. Thus, identity may be expressed as part of a message or may be the central feature of the message, and messages may express more than identity (i.e., they tell us about the task, relationship, etc.). Within a single speaking turn, one may provide an identity-rich message along with those that are less expressive of identity and more expressive of some other communicative function. The characteristics of Identity as Enactment are:

(12) Identities are emergent;
(13) Identities are enacted in social behaviors, social roles, and symbols.

Identity as a Relationship Frame. Since communication has both content and relationship dimensions (Watzlawick et al., 1967), it is impossible to consider Identity as Enactment without also considering Identity as Relationship. Identity is mutually constructed in social interaction. One party's social behavior merges with another's in a relational perspective that defines identity as a mutual property; mutual because it is jointly negotiated and mutual in that it becomes a property of the relationship.

Thus the relationship frame has three levels. First, identity is relational because people define themselves in terms of others and shape their enactments to their interactional partners. The person I am with you is not the person I am with someone else. Second, identity is relational because people define themselves in terms of their relationships. People gain identity through relationships with others such as marital partners, occupations, and friendships. Third, identity is relational because relationships, themselves, take on identities and the dyad becomes an entity. A dating couple establishes an identity as a couple that aligns it within the larger group.

Identity is jointly constructed for participants, emerges out of social interaction, *and* is a property of the relationship (i.e., relational identity). This latter property seems consistent with the notion of relationships as cultures (Montgomery, 1992; Wood, 1982). Identity as Relationship shares the assumptions of Identity as Enactment, although this time the focus is on the mutual or relational aspects.

    (14) Identities emerge in relationship to other people;
    (15) Identities are enacted in relationships;
    (16) Relationships develop identities as social entities.

Identity as a Communal Frame. Identity may also be seen as a communal frame (Middleton & Edwards, 1990; Philipsen, 1987). Identity is something held in the collective memory of a group of people that, in turn, bonds this group together. Thus the group is the locus of identity (i.e., the group has the identity), not the individual, the conversation, or the relationship. Communities define a repertoire of identities that are jointly held/remembered and taught to new members.

The characteristics of Identity as Personal Frame may be transposed to Identity as Communal Frame. For example, the community will have a hierarchy of identities, with some identities more central to its notion of membership than others. In addition, the following proposition is offered:

    (17) Identities emerge out of groups and networks.

An Application of the Theory

When we first began to examine African American ethnic identity, we were primarily interested in the labels people chose to describe their ethnicity, the meanings assigned to those labels, and the communication that expressed the identity. Labels and meanings had initially been conceptualized as the personal frame of identity, while the communication was seen as the enactment of identity. But our respondents' answers did not conform to our preconceived categories. They discussed the *communal* aspects of identity when they told us about the ancestral roots reflected in their label usage and the assimilationist pressures of mainstream society. They also told us about the *relationship* frame when telling us about social approval and relationships with in-group and out-group members.

Our exploration of communication competence has begun to identify the problematic elements of interethnic communication between African Americans and European Americans. Our theory of identity helps us to reinterpret recent research findings (Hecht et al., 1991). In that study we tested a model of interethnic communication presented in Figure 5.1 (see Model No. 1). This model was not supported by structural equations modeling, although the regression of satisfaction on issues and identity produced a very strong effect. Initially we were somewhat disappointed by these findings. However, by reconceptualizing the elements of the model we now understand that the issues are, at least in part, an enactment of identity. The revised model that is presented as Model No. 2 in Figure 5.1 more accurately reflects this new theoretical position. Conceptually ethnic labels, identity salience, and communication issues cannot be causally separated as in Model No. 1 because they are all part of identity (personal and enacted respectively). A more complete model would add relational and communal frames. In fact, differences emerged when analyses were conducted separately for friends and acquaintances, and for the African American and European American ethnic communities.

Future Directions

In developing this theory our work has evolved from an emphasis on ethnic labels, their meanings, and their enactments to an exploration of the personal, enacted, relational, and communal frames of ethnic identity. Since the theoretical perspective emerged out of our work, much still needs to be done to apply the new theory fully.

The communal and relational aspects in particular were derived from our interpretations of interviews and questionnaires.

Model #1:   Original Model

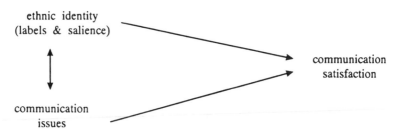

Model #2:   Revised Model

Figure 5.1. Models of Interethnic Communication

Respondents described their identity in terms of their relationships with other people (e.g., equality, power) and membership in a group (e.g., who "we" are). The communal identities are implied by the patterns that emerged in the personal identities but must be explored on a group level. Suggestions for developing this line of research can be considered across all four frames, for each individual frame, and for the interpenetration of frames.

Across all four frames we must develop a better understanding of how these identities develop and change. Are there key events that mark "turning points"? Are there stages that characterize initial development? How are changes in one frame (e.g., personal identity) played out in the other frames? How are these changes linked to historical trends and life-span development? Clearly the use of the label "Black" increased during the 1960s under the influence of the Black Power social movement. We may be observing a 1990s trend toward the label "African American" with the pronouncements of leaders such as Jesse Jackson, and this trend may reflect an increasing emphasis on ethnicity rather than race.

Numerous questions also remain about the enacted frame. Are all behaviors to be considered enactments of identity? At the very least certain behaviors are more salient to the enactment of identity than others. How does this come to be? Do people become aware of behaviors that, when performed, are enactments of identity? How are these behaviors interpreted? Work on impression formation may inform this inquiry (e.g., Fiske & Neuberg, 1990), but more direct links to identity are needed. When do people consciously and strategically perform these behaviors to enact an identity? Do others perceive this as strategic? Goffman's (1959) studies of facework and Ting-Toomey's (1988) recent extensions provide a beginning to this process.

These studies of enactment might also profitably apply Philipsen's (1987) notions of ritual, myth, and social drama. How do we enact personal identities through individual rituals (e.g., ironing socks, eating vegetables only, making up our beds each morning), relational identities through dyadic rituals (e.g., nicknames, secret signals, common dress style), and communal identities through group rituals (e.g., spectator sports, bridal showers, mass education)? What myths and social dramas mark each of these?

The relational level of identity is one that has received scant attention. We must consider more directly how people in pairs (e.g., friends, romantic partners) and groups (e.g., families, clubs, cliques) establish a relational identity and consider the ethnic aspects of these. African American fraternities and sororities would be excellent groups to study because they combine rich ethnic traditions with the dynamics of collective behavior. Further, we must understand how intra- and interethnic relationships come to establish these identities. Questions of interethnic marriages and friendships are particularly salient because of their prevalence in contemporary society and potential to explain the intricacies of ethnic social worlds. The role of social networks in ethnic identity is also an important area of study. How are our social relations associated with our personal and enacted identities? Are there particular social support systems for ethnic identities and what roles do these play?

Recent emphases on social cognition across the social sciences suggest an approach to the communal frame that may be profitable. In particular the construct "cognitive prototype" may be useful in exploring communal conceptions of African American communication and communicators. Prototypes are models or exemplars. For example, students have a prototype of *teacher* that tells them what an ideal teacher or a certain type of teacher (e.g., student-oriented, easy) is like. Pavitt and Haight (1985) recently have begun to articulate the structures of European American prototypes. Their work suggests that prototypes also should have a content domain. We might ask, then, what prototypes are held within the African American community? While social cognition scholars typically proceed at the individual level of analysis—and this may be a useful place to start—we might also ask how identities are reflected in cultural forms such as African American art, literature, music, and narratives.

More work is also needed to examine these frames and their interpenetrations. As we struggle with trying to fit new theoretical frames into existing methodological competencies, we are still utilizing tools such as correlations, surveys, and so forth, in a rough operationalization of this approach. We began by looking at trends or similarities among persons using a common personal identity as means to get at communal identity. It is now clear that a primary focus on the communal frame and an understanding of how the communal is interpenetrated with the other frames is going to require rhetorical/critical analyses (e.g., Hecht et al., 1990) and ethnographies (e.g., Carbaugh, 1989). What aspects of African American communication style are characteristic of which personal and communal identities? What happens when an individual's personal identity does not match the communal identities of the peer group? What happens when they match very closely?

Similarly, enactment and relationship foci will require direct observations in addition to self-reports. A method of stimulated recall in which interactants view and provide interpretations of videotapes of recently completed interactions can complement observer analyses. Through combining these methods we obtain descriptions of interaction from the perspectives of people who are removed from the interaction and can match those with the self-perceptions of the actors. By interviewing the dyad together about their relationship and having nonparticipants code the relational properties of their talk, we can also better understand the relationship frame.

If identities are negotiated in everyday conversations and if identity negotiation is a process, then we need much more information about the negotiation process itself. What happens when an avowed or self-selected identity (African American) is different from an ascribed or imposed identity (friend)? Are there discursive cues in conversational text that indicate avowed and ascribed identity (Collier & Thomas, 1988)? Can such cues be pinpointed through content analysis of texts?

Also we need to identify the scope conditions, salience, and intensity with which particular identities are adopted. Are there particular conditions that covary with strong and intense advocacy of African American identity? It may be that when individuals are the single representative of their ethnic group, they are much more likely to think of their ethnic identity in certain ways (Saenz & Lord, 1989). It may also be that in conflict with members of an out-group, the intensity of identity avowal may be stronger.

It should be clear that this theory is in the early stages of development. Its promise is to open new doors to understanding ethnic identity. Its challenge is to work through the complexity it suggests and live with the vagaries and indeterminancies that it incorporates. In the next section we use the theory to reinterpret our work on ethnic labels and communication competence in order to provide a more specific example of its use and scope.

Research Methodology

Our research and theory development provide a framework for understanding ethnic identity and intra- and interethnic communication. This work also suggests methodological directions for future research. In this section we consider some of these directions.

In our discussion to this point there are numerous calls for methodological diversity. We are firmly committed to a research strategy of triangulation—approaching research questions from different methodological stances (Denzin, 1978). Each stance (interview, ethnography, survey, experiment, etc.) has its own advantages and disadvantages. We believe that by juxtaposing these methods we can overcome their individual biases.

Our respective research programs have included various research methodologies that can be compared and contrasted in order to "triangulate" or validate findings. We have used open- and closed-ended surveys and interviews to obtain respondents' descriptions of recalled conversations, their impressions and their interpretations of others' conduct, and their evaluations of the extent to which conduct was appropriate/inappropriate and effective/ineffective. These methods also have been used to validate and extend the findings (e.g., Hecht, Ribeau, & Alberts, 1989).

Data have been collected at a variety of locations throughout the United States including the East, Midwest, West, and Southwest, although the latter two locations predominate in our work. The research teams have been multiethnic in their composition and have included both male and female researchers and coders.

Our work also has informed us about methodological issues particularly salient to African Americans. We start this discussion by describing the issues that have been raised in our research. We will then review some of the issues that other researchers have pointed to in their discussions of studies involving African Americans.

In the beginning of our work, we sought to avoid placing European Americans at the norm or the center of our work by working with African American participants only. However, some of the African American participants felt that investigating only members of their group was racist in itself. These people felt that we were placing too much of a burden on them to account for interethnic relationships. This was particularly true when we asked about communication improvement strategies. In this concern they were joined by journal reviewers who felt that despite asking what *either* party could do to improve the conversation, asking only African American respondents implied it was their exclusive responsibility.

A second complaint from our research participants was directed at the entire area of study. These people interpreted our questions as assuming that African Americans are particularly concerned (perhaps overly concerned) about their conversations with European Americans. Here we see a possible reaction to "minority" status and powerlessness. The respondents reacted to the perceived ethnic aspect of the question, ignoring the responsibility of successful communicators to be aware of what others think. This interpretation led them to argue that African Americans were no longer concerned or should no longer be concerned with how European Americans perceived them. Thus they were upset by our questions.

This stance is reflected in Collier's (1988) study that demonstrated that inappropriate European American advisor behaviors had less impact on the self-concept of African American college students than other ethnic groups. In fact, the African American students recommended that the student should just leave the office and end the advising relationship if an advisor was rude or stereotyping. Respondents said that their self-concepts were not and should never be determined by European Americans.

A third area of concern about our approach to ethnic labeling was raised primarily by scholars. We used the labels (e.g., Black, Black American, African American) to reflect the differences within the community, arguing that the use of a single label implied a mistaken homogeneity. Michaels (1982), for example, argues that the label Black mistakenly obscures religious, linguistic, regional, and class differences within the group. Other scholars opposed our use of labels to reflect different types of ethnic identities, arguing that by subdividing the group we were diffusing its power.

Some respondents also approached us and argued that because we were pinpointing differences between African Americans and other ethnic cultures, we were actually reinforcing stereotypes and prejudices. Their point was that describing African Americans as a group would simply teach the readers of the research that African Americans were all similar to one another and different from everyone else. The respondents were quite uncomfortable with the attention being placed on differences across groups and the lack of attention being placed on the differences within the ethnic group. This attention to differences reflects the core symbol of Respect for the Individual described in Chapter 3.

Two objections were voiced about our use of African American research assistants in some studies. The first of these was raised by potential African American participants being recruited into the study by our research assistants and the second was raised by our research assistants themselves. Some community members were concerned that European American researchers were using African American assistants as "fronts." While less polite terms were also used, the perception and the objection was that African Americans were being exploited for the purposes of the European American researchers. This is not a new concern, but it recurs because of the perception that studying African American people over the years has not significantly influenced the patterns of racism and discrimination.

Related research supports the notion that the race of the interviewer influences responses of both European American and African American respondents (Athey, Coleman, Reitman, & Tang, 1960; Hatchett & Schuman, 1975; J. Williams, 1964). These effects are found when the topics are militant, sensitive, or express hostility toward a group, when the social distance between the interviewer and interviewee is high (particularly when the interviewee is an African American with less education and lower socioeconomic status), and when dealing with racial opinions rather than facts. More militant male interviewees are likely to manifest this pattern, which seems to hold across geographic regions in the United States. Further, there is support for the notion that African American respondents provide more extreme opinions to African American interviewers and less extreme information to European Americans. Thus there are patterns of less frankness and decreased accommodation that influence responses.

A different issue was raised by the African American students who helped us develop and apply the category systems. These assistants were particularly sensitive about being asked to *speak for* the group. They felt there were times when they were expected to tell us how all African Americans communicated with European Americans.

All of these issues have validity. In a sense we practiced a form of separatism by examining only African Americans and did privilege their conversations with European Americans by focusing their attention on these particular interactions. Dividing the group by labels does create smaller, less powerful groups, and, potentially, highlighting differences within the community can create rifts. And, on some level, we were "using" the research assistants by asking them to recruit other African Americans and/or to tell us about their community.

These issues will probably always be present in the perceptions of African Americans asked to participate in research projects. The history of the group in the United States may sensitize them to being "studied" as a form of exploitation. We apologize for contributing to this perception. Our primary suggestion to other researchers is more effective communication. Participants, research assistants, and coders need to be told enough to understand the purpose of the study. When faced with these objections it is clear that sometimes we did not do an effective job communicating our goals.

What can be done? Overall, it is important to keep in mind the history of race relations. If the researchers are European American they must go beyond the normal means to eliminate suspicions. Even if the researchers are African American they must be sensitive to these issues. We recommend three specific strategies. First, the researcher should probably accompany the assistant on at least preliminary recruitment contacts (e.g., with representatives of the group). Second, questionnaires should be pilot tested for language and interpretation. Third, research assistants should read previous articles and research papers to understand the line of research, and their role as a coder should be limited to that of a cultural representative. That is, they can tell us their experience and their understanding of the experiences of others they know, but they can never speak for the group nor should they be asked to "inform on" (or squeal on) their ethnic group.

One technique for operationalizing these suggestions can be seen in several of our studies that asked respondents to describe the behavior of specific people or to describe specific conversations. Respondents are asked about the conduct of others with whom they are familiar. Then, coders are asked to identify patterns in the particular data set. In this way, neither respondents nor coders are asked to speak for all African Americans.

A number of other research issues have emerged in our work as well as that done by others. We have found that terminology is extremely important. In one study of ethnic labels we pilot tested a survey listing these terms: Black, Black American, African American,

Negro, and Colored. The terms *Negro* and *Colored* were perceived as, at best, outdated, and, at worst, racist. Perhaps if more of our sample were older adults (aged 50 and older), this perception would not have arisen. But others, too, have cautioned about these issues. Byrnes and Kiger (1988) reported that dated stories about sharing an elevator and shopping in the same store were perceived as racist in a contemporary context. Whereas these situations may be seen as problematic and a valid indicant of racial attitudes sometime in the past, their use in current research may offend. Michaels (1982) argues that the use of racial categories as measures is not only unreliable, but invalid. Pointing to census data, he argues that responses to racial checklists do not correlate well with related questions of ancestry and language and may reflect ideology.

Based on this concern with language, Byrnes and Kiger (1988) suggest more sensitive and *in*direct tests of racial attitudes. Since racism is less direct in many strata of U.S. society, attitude scales may need to be more subtle to measure underlying racism. For example, European Americans are less comfortable with intimate contact with African Americans and more likely to express negative attitudes about these than about less intimate relationships. Similarly, European Americans are more likely to object to job or housing discrimination than to negative remarks about African Americans in general (Byrnes & Kiger, 1988).

Other issues also are relevant to the use of questionnaires with African Americans. It has often been argued that questionnaires should not be used in cultures other than those for which they were created without appropriate checks (e.g., Cronbach, 1984; Eysenck, 1983). However, one may extend this argument to members of various ethnic cultures as well. In one of our studies we developed separate scales for measuring the communication satisfaction of African Americans, Mexican Americans, and European Americans from each group's descriptions of specific conversations (Hecht & Ribeau, 1984). Others have noted ethnic differences in responses to questionnaires. Bachman and O'Malley (1984) found that African Americans tended to be more extreme in their response style.

Finally, we would like to comment on the use of coders in our research. In several of the studies coders first individually categorized descriptions of appropriate or inappropriate behavior and then discussed the episodes on which they disagreed. In this manner categories emerged as a consensually negotiated and interpreted system of meanings. Next, the categories were used to code the data. Again, disagreements over the placement of acts in categories were negotiated. The final codings, too, were jointly negotiated and interpreted.

We believe that these methods produce analyses that reflect an intersubjective interpretation of respondents' descriptions. But there is a "value added" element to the procedures. The three authors of the book collaborated in their first experience of coding by means of discussion and consensus in 1986. Since then we have witnessed the richness of the negotiations as a source of data in its own right. These discussions enhanced the coding systems and improved our understanding of the data. We now propose an additional step in the analysis. A textual analysis of coding discussions and differences in interpretations would be a substantial addition to the literature on cultural and intercultural communication, particularly when ethnically and culturally diverse coding teams are used.

Practical Applications

Finally, we feel our work has application to the lives of African Americans and the people they interact with in U.S. culture. Unfortunately, these applications are just now filtering into our work. We believe that theory and research can be tested through such application—effective social theory should be applicable to the lives of group members.

Several practical applications may be derived from the results of our research. Some of these have been suggested in this chapter and throughout the book. At the broadest level these findings inform us about the issues salient to African Americans and suggest a repertoire of strategies for improving conversations.

These findings also have important implications in the counseling arena. Collier (1988) found frequent rule violations by European American advisors that are very damaging to their relationships with African American students. The counseling literature abounds with criticisms of the cultural bias inherent in the dominant training model and counseling style being taught (Atkinson, Morten, & Sue, 1979). Clients are expected to self-disclose readily, to talk openly about feelings, and to adapt to the dominant culture's perception of psychological well-being. It is clear that these criticisms apply to academic advising as well. Academic advising can be improved through greater attention to the identities described in Chapter 2, the styles and core symbols articulated in Chapter 3, and the communication issues and improvement strategies explained in Chapter 4.

Education is still another area in which we hope our research can be applied. Universities such as Stanford, University of California at Berkeley, and Arizona State University have instituted requirements for courses in "American culture" and/or cultural diversity. The information in this book may prove useful as text material in these courses. In addition, educators who are teaching African American students or teaching teachers of African American students may use this book to become more familiar with African American ethnic identity and communication style. Understanding these identities and styles and the problematic nature of interethnic interaction may enable student-instructor relationships to be more positive and productive. Similarly, the information may prove useful to those in the service professions (e.g., health care professionals, government workers, community outreach personnel).

Conclusion

This book examines African Americans and their perceptions of identity and communication. In this concluding chapter we provide directions for future studies. But descriptions of African American communication must continually evolve as the social and historical context changes and the identities and communication styles unfold. As we said in the first chapter, this book is meant as a beginning, tracing one approach to the study of the communication of African Americans and other ethnic groups.

References

A rap on Arizona. (1992, January 9). *The Arizona Republic,* p. A12.

Abe, H., & Wiseman, R. (1983). A cross-cultural confirmation of the dimensions of intercultural effectiveness. *International Journal of Intercultural Relations, 7,* 53-67.

Abrahams, R. D. (1963). *Deep down in the jungle.* Chicago: Aldine Press.

Abrahams, R. D. (1976). *Talking black.* Rowley, MA: Newbury House.

Aiello, J., & Jones, S. (1971). Field study of the proxemic behavior of young school children in three subcultural groups. *Journal of Personality and Social Psychology, 19,* 351-356.

Aiello, J., & Thompson, D. (1980). Personal space, crowding, and spatial behavior in a cultural context. In I. Altman, A. Rapaport, & J. Wohlwill (Eds.), *Human behavior and environment: Advances in theory and research: Vol 4. Environment and change* (pp. 107-178). New York: Plenum.

Akinnaso, F., & Ajirotutu, C. S. (1982). Performance and ethnic style in job interviews. In J. J. Gumperz (Ed.), *Language and social identity* (pp. 119-144). New York: Cambridge University Press.

Alba, R. (1985). The twilight of ethnicity among Americans of European ancestry: The case of Italians. *Ethnic and Racial Studies, 8,* 134-158.

Aleshire, P., & Thomason, A. (1992, January 9). Video branding Arizona as racist is rapped back. *The Arizona Republic,* pp. B1, B6, B7.

Allard, R., & Landry, R. (in press). Subjective ethnolinguistic vitality: A comparison of two measures. In R. Landry & R. Allard (Eds.), *Ethnolinguistic vitality* (Special issue of the *International Journal of the Sociology of Language).*

Altman, I., & Taylor, D. A. (1973). *Social penetration: The development of interpersonal relationships.* New York: Holt, Rinehart & Winston.

Altman, I., Vinsel, A., & Brown, B. B. (1981). Dialectic conceptions in social psychology: An application to social penetration and privacy regulation. *Advances in Experimental Social Psychology, 14,* 107-160.

Altman, K. E., & Nakayama, T. K. (1991). Making a critical difference: A difficult dialogue. *Journal of Communication, 41,* 116-128.

Aries, E., & Moorehead, K. (1989). The importance of ethnicity in the development of identity of black adolescents. *Psychological Reports, 65,* 75-82.

Asante, M. K. (1978). Systematic nationalism: A legitimate strategy for national selfhood. *Journal of Black Studies, 9,* 115-128.

181

Asante, M. K. (1980). *Afrocentricity: The theory of social change.* Buffalo, NY: Amulefi.

Asante, M. K. (1987). *The Afrocentric idea.* Philadelphia: Temple University Press.

Asante, M. K., & Noor-Aldeen, H. S. (1984). Social interaction of black and white college students. *Journal of Black Studies, 14,* 507-516.

Athey, K. R., Coleman, J. E., Reitman, A. P., & Tang, J. (1960). Two experiments showing the effect of the interviewer's racial background on responses to questions concerning racial issues. *Journal of Applied Psychology, 44,* 244-246.

Atkinson, D. R., Morten, G., & Sue, D. W. (1979). *Counseling American minorities: A cross-cultural perspective.* Dubuque, IA: William C. Brown.

Babad, E. Y., Birnbaum, M., & Benne, K. D. (1983). *The social self.* Beverly Hills, CA: Sage.

Bachman, J. G., & O'Malley, P. M. (1984). Yea-saying, nay-saying, and going to extremes: Black-white differences in response styles. *Public Opinion Quarterly, 48,* 491-509.

Ball, P., Giles, H., & Hewstone, M. (1985). Interpersonal accommodation and situational constraints: An integrative formula. In H. Giles & R. St. Clair (Eds.), *Recent advances in language, communication and social psychology* (pp. 263-286). London: Lawrence Erlbaum.

Bambara, T. C. (1981). *Gorilla, my love.* New York: Random House.

Banks, J. A. (1981). *Multi-ethnic education: Theory and practice.* Boston: Allyn & Bacon.

Banks, J. A. (1984). *Teaching strategies for ethnic studies* (3rd ed.). Boston: Allyn & Bacon.

Banks, S. P. (1987). Achieving "unmarkedness" in organizational discourse: A praxis perspective on ethnolinguistic identity. *Journal of Language and Social Psychology, 6,* 171-189.

Baraka, I. A. (1963). *Blues people: Negro music in white America.* New York: Morrow.

Barresi, C. M. (1990). Ethnogerontology: Social aging in national, racial and cultural groups. In K. F. Ferrero (Ed.), *Gerontology: Perspectives and issues* (pp. 248-265). New York: Springer.

Barth, F. (Ed.). (1969). *Ethnic groups and boundaries.* Boston: Little, Brown.

Bateson, G. (1972). *Steps to an ecology of mind.* New York: Chandler.

Baugh, J. (1983). *Black street speech: Its history, structure and survival.* Austin: University of Texas Press.

Baxter, L. A. (1988). A dialectic perspective on communication strategies in relationship development. In S. W. Duck (Ed.), *A handbook of personal relationships* (pp. 257-274). New York: John Wiley.

Beebe, L. M., & Giles, H. (1984). Speech accommodation theories: A discussion in terms of second language acquisition. *International Journal of the Sociology of Language, 46,* 5-32.

Bellah, R., Madsen, R., Sullivan, W., Swidler, A., & Tipson, S. (1985). *Habits of the heart: Individualism and commitment in American life.* Berkeley: University of California Press.

Berger, C. R., & Calabrese, R. J. (1975). Some explorations in initial interaction and beyond: Toward a developmental theory of interpersonal communication. *Human Communication Research, 1,* 99-112.

Berger, C. R., & Douglas, W. (1981). Studies in interpersonal epistemology III: Anticipated interaction, self-monitoring, and observational context selection. *Communication Monographs, 48,* 183-196.

Berger, C. R., & Douglas, W. (1982). Thought and talk: "Excuse me but have I been talking to myself?" In F. Dance (Ed.), *Human communication theory* (pp. 42-60). New York: Harper & Row.

Berger, P. (1966). Identity as a problem in the sociology of knowledge. *European Journal of Sociology, 7,* 105-115.

Berger, P., & Luckmann, T. (1966). *The social construction of reality.* Harmondsworth, UK: Penguin Books.

Bergman, P. M. (1969). *The chronological history of the Negro in America.* New York: New American Library.

Bernal, M. E., Saenz, D. S., & Knight, G. P. (1991). Ethnic identity and adaptation of Mexican American youths in school settings. *Hispanic Journal of Behavioral Science, 13,* 135-154.

Berry, J. (1980). Introduction to methodology. In H. Triandis & J. Berry (Eds.), *Handbook of cross-cultural psychology* (Vol. 2, pp. 1-28). Boston: Allyn & Bacon.

Berry, M. F., & Blassingame, J. W. (1982). *Long memory.* New York: Oxford University Press.

Blau, P. (1977). A macrosocial theory of social structure. *American Journal of Sociology, 83,* 26-53.

Block, C. B. (1980). Black Americans and the cross-cultural counseling and psychotherapy experience. In A. J. Marsella & P. B. Pedersen (Eds.), *Cross-cultural counseling and psychotherapy* (pp. 148-164). Elmsford, NY: Pergamon.

Blubaugh, J., & Pennington, D. (1976). *Crossing differences: Interracial communication.* Columbus, OH: Merrill.

Blumer, H. (1969). *Symbolic interactionism: Perspective and method.* Englewood Cliffs, NJ: Prentice-Hall.

Bochner, A. P., & Kelly, C. W. (1974). Interpersonal competence: Rationale, philosophy, and implementation of a conceptual framework. *Speech Teacher, 23,* 279-301.

Bogel, D. (1973). *Toms, coons, mulattoes, mammies and bucks.* New York: Viking.

Bolling, J. L. (1974). The changing self-concept of black children—The black identity test. *Journal of the National Medical Association, 66,* 28-31.

Bond, M. H., & Hewstone, M. (1986). *Social identity theory and the perception of intergroup relations in Hong Kong.* Unpublished manuscript.

Bosmajian, H. A. (1978). Freedom of speech and the language of oppression. *Speech Teacher, 21,* 209-221.

Bourhis, R. Y. (1985). The sequential nature of language choice in cross-cultural communication. In R. L. Street, Jr., & J. N. Cappella (Eds.), *Sequence and pattern in communicative behaviour* (pp. 120-141). London: Edward Arnold.

Bourhis, R. Y., & Giles, H. (1977). The language of intergroup distinctiveness. In H. Giles & R. St. Clair (Eds.), *Language, ethnicity, and intergroup relations* (pp. 119-135). London: Academic Press.

Bourhis, R. Y., Giles, H., & Rosenthal, D. (1981). Notes on the construction of a "subjective vitality" questionnaire for ethnolinguistic groups. *Journal of Multicultural and Multilingual Development, 2,* 145-155.

Brewer, M. (1979). In-group bias in the minimal group situation. *Psychological Bulletin, 56*, 307-324.

Brittan, A. (1973). *Meanings and situations.* London: Routledge & Kegan Paul.

Broom, L., & Selznick, P. (1977). *Sociology.* New York: Harper & Row.

Brown, P., & Levinson, S. (1978). Universals in language usage: Politeness phenomena. In E. Goody (Ed.), *Questions and politeness* (pp. 56-289). London: Cambridge University Press.

Bugenthal, J. F. T., & Zelen, S. L. (1950). Investigations into the self-concept. *Journal of Personality, 18*, 483-498.

Bumpass, L. (1984). Children and marital disruption: A replication and update. *Demography, 21*, 71-81.

Burke, K. (1954). *Permanence and change* (2nd ed.). Berkeley: University of California Press.

Burke, K. (1959). *Attitudes towards history* (3rd ed.). Berkeley: University of California Press.

Burke, P. J. (1980). The self: Requirements from an interactionist perspective. *Social Psychology Quarterly, 43*, 18-29.

Burke, P. J., & Franzoi, S. L. (1988). Studying situations and identities using experiential sampling methodology. *American Sociological Review, 53*, 559-568.

Burke, P. J., & Reitzes, D. C. (1981). The link between identity and role performance. *Social Psychology Quarterly, 44*, 83-92.

Burke, P. J., & Tully, J. (1977). The measurement of role/identity. *Social Forces, 55*, 881-897.

Burleson, B. R., Wilson, S. R., Waltman, M. S., Goering, E. M., Ely, T. K., & Whaley, B. B. (1988). Item desirability effects in compliance-gaining research: Seven studies documenting artifacts in the strategy selection procedure. *Human Communication Research, 14*, 429-486.

Byrnes, D. A., & Kiger, G. (1988). Contemporary measures of attitudes toward blacks. *Educational & Psychological Measurement, 48*, 107-119.

Campbell, D. T. (1967). Stereotypes and the perception of group differences. *American Psychologist, 22*, 817-829.

Cappella, J. N., & Planalp, S. (1981). Talk and silence sequences in informal conversations III: Interspeaker influences. *Human Communication Research, 7*, 117-132.

Carbaugh, D. (1987). Communication rules in Donahue discourse. *Research on Language and Social Interaction, 21*, 31-61.

Carbaugh, D. (1988). Comments on "culture" in communication inquiry. *Communication Reports, 1*, 38-41.

Carbaugh, D. (1989). *Talking American: Cultural discourses on Donahue.* Norwood, NJ: Ablex.

Carmichael, S., & Hamilton, C. V. (1967). *Black power: The politics of liberation in America.* New York: Vintage.

Cazenave, N. A. (1983). Black male-black female relationships: The perceptions of 155 middle-class black men. *Family Relations, 32*, 341-350.

Cheek, J. M. (1976). *Assertive black . . . puzzled white.* San Luis Obispo, CA: Impact Publications.

Cheek, J. M., & Briggs, S. R. (1982). Self-consciousness and aspects of identity. *Journal of Research in Personality, 16*, 401-408.

Cheek, J. M., & Hogan, R. (1983). Self-concepts, self-presentations, and moral judgments. In J. Suls & A. G. Greenwald (Eds.), *Psychological perspectives on the self* (Vol. 2, pp. 249-273). Hillsdale, NJ: Lawrence Erlbaum.

Clark, M. L. (1985). Social stereotypes and self-concept in black and white college students. *Journal of Social Psychology, 125,* 753-760.

Clark, R. A. (1979). The impact of self interest and desire for liking on selection of persuasive strategies. *Communication Monographs, 46,* 257-273.

Cody, M. J., & McLaughlin, M. L. (1985). Models for the sequential construction of accounting episodes: Situational and interactional constraints on message selection and evaluation. In R. L. Street, Jr., & J. N. Cappella (Eds.), *Sequence and pattern in communicative behaviour* (pp. 60-69). London: Edward Arnold.

Cogdell, R., & Wilson, S. (1980). *Black communication in white society.* Saratoga, CA: Century-Twenty-One Publishers.

Collier, M. J. (1988). A comparison of intracultural and intercultural communication among acquaintances: How intra- and intercultural competencies vary. *Communication Quarterly, 36,* 122-144.

Collier, M. J. (1989). Cultural and intercultural communication competence: Current approaches and directions for future research. *International Journal of Intercultural Relations, 13,* 287-302.

Collier, M. J. (1991). Conflict competence within African, Mexican and Anglo American friendships. In S. Ting-Toomey & F. Korzenny (Eds.), *Cross-cultural interpersonal communication* (pp. 132-154). Newbury Park, CA: Sage.

Collier, M. J. (1992). *Ethnic friendships: Enacted identities and competencies.* Manuscript submitted for publication.

Collier, M. J., Ribeau, S., & Hecht, M. L. (1986). Intercultural communication rules and outcomes within three domestic cultural groups. *International Journal of Intercultural Relations, 10,* 439-457.

Collier, M. J., & Thomas, M. (1988). Cultural identity: An interpretive perspective. In Y. Y. Kim & W. B. Gudykunst (Eds.), *Theories in intercultural communication* (pp. 99-120). Newbury Park, CA: Sage.

Collier, M. J., & Thomas, M. (1989). Cultural identity in inter-cultural communication: An interpretive perspective. In W. B. Gudykunst & Y. Y. Kim (Eds.), *Theorizing intercultural communication: International and intercultural communication annual, 12* (pp. 94-120). Newbury Park, CA: Sage.

Collins, P. H. (1990). The social construction of black feminist thought. In M. Malson, E. Mudimbe-Boyi, J. O'Barr, & M. Wyer (Eds.), *Black women in America* (pp. 297-326). Chicago: University of Chicago Press.

Color bias is ruled possible within race. (1989, May 14). *The Arizona Republic,* p. B2.

Comer, J. P. (1980). White racism: Its root, form, and function. In R. L. Jones (Ed.), *Black psychology* (2nd ed.) (pp. 361-366). New York: Harper & Row.

Conquergood, D. (1991). Rethinking ethnography: Towards a critical cultural politics. *Communication Monographs, 58,* 179-194.

Cooke, B. G. (1972). Nonverbal communication among Afro-Americans: An initial clarification. In T. Kochman (Ed.), *Rappin' and stylin' out: Communication in urban Black America* (pp. 32-64). Urbana: University of Illinois.

Cooke, B. G. (1980). Nonverbal communication among Afro-Americans: An initial clarification. In R. L. Jones (Ed.), *Black psychology* (2nd ed.) (pp. 139-160). New York: Harper & Row.

Coppola, C. (1992, January 15). Black groups back Public Enemy. *Tempe Daily News Tribune*, p. B1.

Coupland, N., Coupland, J., & Giles, H. (1991). *Language, society and the elderly.* Cambridge: Basil Blackwell.

Coupland, N., Wiemann, J. M., & Giles, H. (1991). Talk as "problem" and communication as "miscommunication": An integrative analysis. In N. Coupland, H. Giles, & J. M. Wiemann (Eds.), *Miscommunication and problematic talk* (pp. 1-17). Newbury Park, CA: Sage.

Covin, D. (1990). Afrocentricity in O Movimento Negro Unificado. *Journal of Black Studies, 21,* 126-146.

Cromwell, V. L., & Cromwell, R. E. (1978). Perceived dominance in decision-making and conflict resolution among anglo, black and chicano couples. *Journal of Marriage and the Family, 40,* 749-759.

Cronbach, L. J. (1984). *The essentials of psychological testing* (4th ed.). New York: Harper & Row.

Cross, W. E., Jr. (1971). The Negro to Black conversion experience: Towards the psychology of black liberation. *Black World, 20,* 13-27.

Cross, W. E., Jr. (1978). Models of psychological nigrescence: A literature review. *Journal of Black Psychology, 5,* 13-31.

Daniel, J., & Smitherman, G. (1976). How I got over: Communication dynamics in the black community. *Quarterly Journal of Speech, 62,* 26-39.

Deetz, S. A., & Kersten, A. (1983). Critical models of interpretive research. In L. L. Putnam & M. E. Pacanowsky (Eds.), *Communication and organizations: An interpretive approach* (pp. 147-172). Beverly Hills, CA: Sage.

DeJarnett, S., & Raven, B. H. (1981). The balance, bases and modes of interpersonal power in black couples: The role of sex and socioeconomic circumstances. *Journal of Black Psychology, 7,* 51-66.

Delgado, R. (1984). The imperial scholar: Reflections on a review of civil rights literature. *University of Pennsylvania Law Review, 132,* 561-578.

Denzin, N. K. (1978). *The research act: A theoretical introduction to sociological methods.* New York: McGraw-Hill.

De Vos, G. A. (1980). Ethnic adaptation and minority status. *Journal of Cross-Cultural Psychology, 11,* 101-124.

De Vos, G. A. (1982). Ethnic pluralism: Conflict and accommodation. In G. A. De Vos & L. Romanucci-Ross (Eds.), *Ethnic identity: Cultural continuities and change* (pp. 5-41). Chicago: University of Chicago Press.

De Vos, G. A., & Romanucci-Ross, L. (1982a). Ethnicity: Vessel of meaning and emblem of contrast. In G. A. De Vos & L. Romanucci-Ross (Eds.), *Ethnic identity: Cultural continuities and change* (pp. 363-390). Chicago: University of Chicago Press.

De Vos, G. A., & Romanucci-Ross, L. (1982b). Introduction. In G. A. De Vos & L. Romanucci-Ross (Eds.), *Ethnic identity: Cultural continuities and change* (pp. ix-xvii). Chicago: University of Chicago Press.

Dewart, J. (1989). *The state of Black America: 1989.* New York: National Urban League.

Diamond, R., & Hellcamp, D. (1969). Race, sex, ordinal position of birth, and self-disclosure in high school. *Psychological Reports, 35*, 235-238.

Dillard, J. L. (1972). *Black English: Its history and usage in the United States.* New York: Random House.

Diop, C. A. (1991). *Civilization or barbarism.* New York: Lawrence Hill Books.

Donohue, W. (1985). Ethnicity and mediation. In W. B. Gudykunst, L. Stewart, & S. Ting-Toomey (Eds.), *Communication, culture, and organizational processes* (pp. 134-154). Beverly Hills, CA: Sage.

Dorch, E., & Fontaine, G. (1978). Rate of judges' gaze at different types of witnesses. *Perceptual and Motor Skills, 46*, 1103-1106.

Douglas, W. (1983). Scripts and self-monitoring: When does being a high self-monitor really make a difference? *Human Communication Research, 10*, 81-96.

DuBois, W. E. B. (1964). *The world and Africa.* New York: International.

DuBois, W. E. B. (1969). *The souls of Black folks.* New York: New American Library.

Duck, S. W. (1990). Relationships as unfinished business: Out of the frying pan and into the 1990s. *Journal of Social and Personal Relationships, 7*, 5-28.

Duncan, B. L. (1978a). Decision-making and self-disclosure. *Journal of Black Psychology, 5*, 33-41.

Duncan, B. L. (1978b). The development of spatial behavior norms in Black and White primary school children. *Journal of Black Psychology, 5*, 33-41.

Duncan, B. L. (1978c). Nonverbal communication. *Psychological Bulletin, 72*, 118-137.

Duran, R. L. (1983). Communicative adaptability: A measure of social communicative competence. *Communication Quarterly, 31*, 320-326.

Edwards, V., & Seinkewicz, T. J. (1990). *Oral cultures past and present.* Cambridge: Basil Blackwell.

Edwards, W. F. (1992). Sociolinguistic behavior in a Detroit inner-city black neighborhood. *Language in Society, 21*, 93-115.

Emmison, M., & Western, M. (1990). Social class and social identity: A comment on Marshall et al. *Sociology, 24*, 241-253.

Ericksen, J. A., Yancey, W. L., & Ericksen, E. P. (1979). The division of family roles. *Journal of Marriage and the Family, 41*, 301-313.

Erickson, F. (1984). Rhetoric, anecdote and rhapsody: Coherence strategies in a conversation among black American adolescents. In D. Tannen (Ed.), *Coherence in spoken and written discourse* (pp. 81-154). Norwood, NJ: Ablex.

Erikson, E. H. (1959). Late adolescence. In D. H. Funkenstein (Ed.), *The student and mental health* (pp. 66-106). New York: World Federation for Mental Health and International Association of Universities.

Erikson, E. H. (1960). The problem of ego-identity. In M. R. Stein, A. J. Vidich, & D. M. White (Eds.), *Identity and anxiety: Survival for the person in mass society* (pp. 37-82). New York: Free Press.

Erikson, E. H. (1968). *Identity: Youth and crisis.* New York: Norton.

Espinoza, J. A., & Garza, R. T. (1985). Social group salience and interethnic cooperation. *Journal of Experimental Social Psychology, 21*, 380-392.

Eysenck, S. B. G. (1983). One approach to cross-cultural studies of personality. *Australian Journal of Psychology, 35*, 381-391.

Fairchild, H. H. (1985). Black, Negro or Afro-American? The differences are crucial. *Journal of Black Studies, 16,* 47-55.

Fine, G. A., & Kleinman, S. (1983). Network and meaning: An interactionist approach to structure. *Symbolic Interaction, 6,* 97-110.

Fine, M., & Bowers, C. (1984). Racial self-identification: The effects of social history and gender. *Journal of Applied Social Psychology, 14,* 136-146.

Fiske, S. T., & Neuberg, S. L. (1990). A continuum of impression formation, from category-based to individuating processes: Influences of information and motivation on attention and interpretation. In M. P. Zanna (Ed.), *Advances in experimental social psychology* (Vol. 23, pp. 1-74). New York: Academic Press.

Fitzgerald, T. K. (1974). Social and cultural identity. *Southern Anthropological Society Proceeding, 8,* 1-4.

Folkes, V. S. (1985). Mindlessness or mindfulness: A partial replication and extension of Langer, Blank and Chanowitz. *Journal of Personality and Social Psychology, 48,* 600-604.

Foote, N. N. (1951). Identification as the basis for a theory of motivation. *American Sociological Review, 26,* 14-21.

Foster, M. (1989). "It's cookin' now": A performance analysis of the speech events of a black teacher in an urban community college. *Language in Society, 18,* 1-29.

Franklin, J. H. (1988). A historical note on Black families. In H. P. McAdoo (Ed.), *Black families* (2nd ed.) (pp. 23-26). Newbury Park, CA: Sage.

Frazier, E. F. (1962). *Black bourgeoisie.* New York: Crowell, Collier & Macmillan.

Frazier, E. F. (1963). *The negro church in America.* New York: Knopf.

Fugita, S. S., Wexley, K. N., & Hillery, J. M. (1974). Black-white differences in nonverbal behavior in an interview setting. *Journal of Applied Social Psychology, 4,* 343-350.

Gallois, C., Franklyn-Stokes, A., Giles, H., & Coupland, N. (1988). Communication accommodation in intercultural encounters. In Y. Y. Kim & W. B. Gudykunst (Eds.), *Theories in intercultural communication* (pp. 157-185). Newbury Park, CA: Sage.

Ganiere, D. M., & Enright, R. D. (1989). Exploring three approaches to identity development. *Journal of Youth and Adolescence, 18,* 283-295.

Gans, H. J. (1979). Symbolic ethnicity: The future of ethnic groups and cultures in America. *Ethnic and Racial Studies, 2,* 1-20.

Garner, T. E. (1983). Playing the dozens: Folklore as strategies for living. *Quarterly Journal of Speech, 69,* 47-57.

Garner, T. E., & Rubin, D. L. (1986). Middle class blacks' perceptions of dialect and style shifting: The case of Southern attorneys. *Journal of Language and Social Psychology, 5,* 33-48.

Garrett, G., Baxter, J., & Rozelle, R. (1981). Training university police in Black-American nonverbal behavior. *Journal of Social Psychology, 113,* 217-229.

Garza, R. T., & Herringer, L. G. (1987). Social identity: A multidimensional approach. *Journal of Social Psychology, 127,* 299-308.

Geertz, C. (1973). *The interpretation of cultures.* New York: Basic Books.

Geertz, C. (1976). From the native's point of view: On the nature of anthropological understanding. In P. Rabinow & W. M. Sullivan (Eds.), *Interpretive social science* (pp. 225-241). Berkeley: University of California Press.

Geertz, C. (1983). *Local knowledge*. New York: Basic Books.

Gettone, V. (1981). Negative label. *Association of Black Psychologists' Newsletter, 12*(2), 3-11.

Giles, H. (1973). Accent mobility: A model and some data. *Anthropological Linguistics, 15*, 87-105.

Giles, H., Bourhis, R. Y., & Taylor, D. (1977). Towards a theory of language in ethnic group relations. In H. Giles & R. St. Clair (Eds.), *Language, ethnicity and intergroup relations* (pp. 307-348). London: Academic Press.

Giles, H., & Coupland, N. (1991). *Language: Contexts and consequences.* Pacific Grove, CA: Brooks/Cole.

Giles, H., Coupland, N., & Coupland, J. (1991). Accommodation theory: Communication, contexts, and consequences. In H. Giles, N. Coupland, & J. Coupland (Eds.), *Contexts of accommodation: Developments in applied sociolinguistics* (pp. 1-68). Cambridge: Cambridge University Press.

Giles, H., & Evans, A. (1986). The power approach to intergroup hostility. *Journal of Conflict Resolution, 30*, 469-485.

Giles, H., & Hewstone, M. (1982). Cognitive structures, speech, and social situations: Two integrative models. *Language Sciences, 4*, 187-219.

Giles, H., & Johnson, P. (1981). The role of language in ethnic group relations. In J. Turner & H. Giles (Eds.), *Intergroup behavior* (pp. 199-242). Chicago: University of Chicago Press.

Giles, H., & Johnson, P. (1986). Perceived threat, ethnic commitment and interethnic language behavior. In Y. Y. Kim (Ed.), *Interethnic communication: Current research* (pp. 91-116). Beverly Hills, CA: Sage.

Giles, H., & Johnson, P. (1987). Ethnolinguistic identity theory: A social psychological approach to language maintenance. *International Journal of the Sociology of Language, 68*, 69-99.

Giles, H., Mulac, A., Bradac, J. J., & Johnson, P. (1987). Speech accommodation: The first decade and beyond. In M. McLaughlin (Ed.), *Communication yearbook 10* (pp. 13-48). Newbury Park, CA: Sage.

Glaser, D. (1958). Dynamics of ethnic identification. *American Sociological Review, 23*, 31-40.

Goffman, E. (1959). *The presentation of self in everyday life.* Garden City, NY: Doubleday.

Goffman, E. (1967). *Interaction ritual: Essays on face-to-face behavior.* Garden City, NY: Anchor Books.

Goldberg, D. T. (1990). Racism and rationality: The need for a new critique. *Philosophy of the Social Sciences, 20*, 317-350.

Gordon, C. (1968). Self-conceptions: Configurations of content. In C. Gordon & K. J. Gergen (Eds.), *The self in social interaction* (pp. 115-136). New York: John Wiley.

Gordon, L. (1986). College student stereotypes of Blacks and Jews on two campuses: Four studies spanning 50 years. *Sociology and Social Research, 70*, 200-201.

Gordon, M. M. (1978). *Human nature, class, and ethnicity.* New York: Oxford University Press.

Gray, H. (1989). Television, Black Americans, and the American dream. *Critical Studies in Mass Communication, 6*, 376-386.

Gray-Little, B. (1982). Marital quality and power processes among black couples. *Journal of Marriage and the Family, 44*, 633-646.

Greenwald, A. G., Bellezza, F. S., & Banaji, M. R. (1988). Is self-esteem a central ingredient of self-concept? *Personality and Social Psychology Bulletin, 14*, 34-45.

Gudykunst, W. B., & Hammer, M. (1988). The influence of social identity and intimacy of interethnic relationships on uncertainty reduction processes. *Human Communication Research, 14*, 569-601.

Gumperz, J. J., & Cook-Gumperz, J. (1982). Introduction: Language and the communication of identity. In J. J. Gumperz (Ed.), *Language and social identity* (pp. 1-21). Cambridge: Cambridge University Press.

Gurin, P., Miller, A. H., & Gurin, G. (1980). Stratum identification and consciousness. *Social Psychology Quarterly, 43*, 30-47.

Gutman, H. (1976). *The black family in slavery and freedom: 1750-1925*. New York: Random House.

Guttentag, N. (1982). Negro-white differences in children's movement. *Perceptual and Motor Skills, 35*, 435-436.

Haines, V. A. (1988). Social network analysis, structuration theory and the holism-individualism debate. *Social Networks, 10*, 157-182.

Halberstadt, A. G. (1985). Race, socioeconomic status, and nonverbal behavior. In A. W. Siegman & S. Feldstein (Eds.), *Multichannel integrations of nonverbal behavior* (pp. 227-266). Hillsdale, NJ: Lawrence Erlbaum.

Hallowell, A. I. (1955). *Culture and experience*. New York: Schocken Books.

Hammer, M. R. (1989). Intercultural communication competence. In M. K. Asante & W. B. Gudykunst (Eds.), *Handbook of international and intercultural communication* (pp. 247-260). Newbury Park, CA: Sage.

Hammer, M. R., & Gudykunst, W. B. (1987a). The effect of ethnicity, gender, and dyadic composition on uncertainty reduction in initial interaction. *Journal of Black Studies, 18*, 191-214.

Hammer, M. R., & Gudykunst, W. B. (1987b). The influence of ethnicity and sex on social penetration in close friendships. *Journal of Black Studies, 17*, 418-437.

Hammer, M. R., Gudykunst, W. B., & Wiseman, R. L. (1978). Dimensions of intercultural effectiveness: An exploratory study. *International Journal of Intercultural Relations, 2*, 382-393.

Hannerz, U. (1969). *Soulside: Inquiries into ghetto culture and community*. New York: Columbia University Press.

Hansell, M., & Ajirotutu, C. S. (1982). Negotiating interpretations in interethnic settings. In J. J. Gumperz (Ed.), *Language and social identity* (pp. 85-94). New York: Cambridge University Press.

Harding, V. (1975). The black wedge in America: Struggle, crisis and hope, 1955-1975. *Black Scholar, 7*, 28-46.

Harré, R. (1989). Language games and texts of identity. In J. Shotter & K. J. Gergen (Eds.), *Texts of identity* (pp. 20-35). Newbury Park, CA: Sage.

Harrell, J. P. (1979). Analyzing black coping styles: A supplemental diagnostic system. *Journal of Black Psychology, 5*, 99-108.

Harrison, D. S., & Trabasso, T. (Eds.). (1976). *Black English: A seminar*. Hillsdale, NJ: Lawrence Erlbaum.

Hartsock, N. (1983). The feminist standpoint: Developing the ground for a specifically feminist historical materialism. In S. Harding & M. Hintikka (Eds.), *Discovering reality* (pp. 283-310). Boston: D. Reidel.

Haskins, E. W. (1984). Black: Defiance, sensationalism and disaster. *Et. Cetera, 41,* 398-401.

Hatchett, S., & Schuman, H. (1975). White respondents and race-of-interviewer effects. *Public Opinion Quarterly, 39,* 523-528.

Hecht, M. L. (1978). Toward a conceptualization of interpersonal communication satisfaction. *Quarterly Journal of Speech, 64,* 47-62.

Hecht, M. L. (1984). Satisfying communication and relationship labels: Intimacy and length of relationship as perceptual frames of naturalistic conversations. *Western Journal of Speech Communication, 48,* 201-216.

Hecht, M. L., Andersen, P. A., & Ribeau, S. A. (1989). The cultural dimensions of nonverbal communication. In M. K. Asante & W. B. Gudykunst (Eds.), *Handbook of international and intercultural communication* (pp. 163-185). Newbury Park, CA: Sage.

Hecht, M. L., Larkey, L. K., Johnson, J. N., & Reinard, J. C. (1991, May). *A model of interethnic effectiveness.* Paper presented to the International Communication Association Conference, Chicago.

Hecht, M. L., & Ribeau, S. (1984). Ethnic communication: A comparative analysis of satisfying communication. *International Journal of Intercultural Relations, 8,* 135-151.

Hecht, M. L., & Ribeau, S. (1987). Afro-American identity labels and communicative effectiveness. *Journal of Language and Social Psychology, 6,* 319-326.

Hecht, M. L., & Ribeau, S. (1991). Sociocultural roots of ethnic identity: A look at Black America. *Journal of Black Studies, 21,* 501-513.

Hecht, M. L., Ribeau, S., & Alberts, J. K. (1989). An Afro-American perspective on interethnic communication. *Communication Monographs, 56,* 385-410.

Hecht, M. L., Ribeau, S., & Sedano, M. V. (1990). A Mexican American perspective on interethnic communication. *International Journal of Intercultural Relations, 14,* 31-55.

Heise, D. (1977a). Group dynamics and attitude-behavior relations. *Sociological Methods and Research, 5,* 259-288.

Heise, D. (1977b). Social action as the control of affect. *Behavioral Science, 22,* 163-177.

Heise, D. (1979). *Understanding events: Affect and the construction of social action.* Cambridge: Cambridge University Press.

Helms, J. E. (1990). An overview of black racial identity theory. In J. E. Helms (Ed.), *Black and white racial identity: Theory, research, and practice* (pp. 9-32). Westport, CT: Greenwood Press.

Henley, N. M. (1977). *Body politics: Power, sex and nonverbal communication.* Englewood Cliffs, NJ: Prentice-Hall.

Hewes, D. E., & Planalp, S. (1987). The individual's place in communication science. In C. R. Berger & S. H. Chaffee (Eds.), *Handbook of communication science* (pp. 146-183). Newbury Park, CA: Sage.

Hewitt, R. (1986). *White talk black talk: Inter-racial friendship and communication amongst adolescents.* Cambridge: Cambridge University Press.

Hewstone, M., & Brown, R. (1986). Contact is not enough: An intergroup perspective on the "contact hypothesis." In M. Hewstone & R. Brown (Eds.), *Contact and conflict in intergroup encounters* (pp. 1-44). London: Basil Blackwell.

Hill, R. B. (1989). Critical issues for black families by the year 2000. In J. Dewart (Ed.), *The state of black America: 1989* (pp. 41-61). New York: National Urban League.

Hill, S. T. (1984). *The traditionally Black institutions of higher education, 1960 to 1982.* Washington, DC: U.S. Department of Education.

Hoelter, J. W. (1983). The effects of role evaluation and commitment on identity salience. *Social Psychology Quarterly, 46,* 140-147.

Hoelter, J. W. (1985). The structure of self-conception: Conceptualization and measurement. *Journal of Personality and Social Psychology, 49,* 1392-1407.

Hofman, J. E. (1985). Arabs and Jews, Blacks and Whites: Identity and group relations. *Journal of Multilingual and Multicultural Development, 6,* 217-237.

Hofstede, G. (1980). *Culture's consequences.* Beverly Hills, CA: Sage.

Honeycutt, J., Knapp, M. L., & Powers, W. (1983). On knowing others and predicting what they say. *Western Journal of Speech Communication, 47,* 157-174.

Hooks, B. (1984). *Feminist theory: From margin to center.* Boston: South End Press.

Hoover, M. R. (1978). Community attitudes toward black English. *Language in Society, 7,* 65-87.

Hope, D. S. (1975). Redefinition of self: A comparison of the rhetoric of the women's liberation and black liberation movements. *Today's Speech, 23,* 17-25.

Horowitz, D. (1975). Ethnic identity. In N. Glazer & D. Moynihan (Eds.), *Ethnicity: Theory and experience* (pp. 111-140). Cambridge, MA: Harvard University Press.

Horton, J. (1976). Time and cool people. In L. Samovar & R. Porter (Eds.), *Intercultural communication: A reader* (2nd ed.) (pp. 274-288). Belmont, CA: Wadsworth.

Hughes, M., & Demo, D. H. (1989). Self-perception of Black Americans: Self-esteem and personal efficacy. *American Journal of Sociology, 95,* 132-159.

Hyman, H., & Reed, J. (1969). Black matriarchy reconsidered: Evidence from secondary analyses of sample surveys. *Public Opinion Quarterly,* 346-354.

Hymes, D. (1972). Models of the interaction of language and social life. In J. J. Gumperz & D. Hymes (Eds.), *Directions in sociolinguistics: The ethnography of communication* (pp. 35-71). New York: Holt, Rinehart & Winston.

Hymes, D. (1974). *Foundations in sociolinguistics.* Philadelphia: University of Pennsylvania Press.

Ickes, W. (1984). Composition in black and white: Determinants of interaction in interracial dyads. *Journal of Personality and Social Psychology, 47,* 1206-1217.

Imahori, T. T., & Lanigan, M. L. (1989). Relational model of intercultural communication competence. *International Journal of Intercultural Relations, 13,* 269-286.

Isaacs, H. R. (1975). *Idols of the tribe: Group identity and political change.* New York: Harper & Row.

Isajiw, W. W. (1974). Definitions of ethnicity. *Ethnicity, 1,* 111-124.

Jackson, J. S., & Gurin, G. (1987). *National survey of Black Americans, 1978-1980.* Ann Arbor, MI: Inter-University Consortium for Political and Social Research, Institute for Social Research.

Jacob, J. E. (1989). Black America, 1988: An overview. In J. Dewart (Ed.), *The state of black America: 1989* (pp. 1-7). New York: National Urban League.

Jaffe, J., & Feldstein, S. (1970). *Rhythms of dialogue.* New York: Academic Press.

Jaggar, A. (1983). *Feminist politics and human nature.* Totowa, NJ: Rowman & Allanheld.

Jaynes, G. D., & Williams, R. M., Jr. (Eds.). (1989). *A common destiny: Blacks and American society.* Washington, DC: National Academy Press.

Jenkins, A. H. (1982). *The psychology of the Afro-American: A humanistic approach.* Elmsford, NY: Pergamon.

Jenkins, A. H. (1990). Dynamics of the relationship in clinical work with African-American clients. *Group, 14,* 36-43.

Jewell, K. S. (1985). Will the real Black, Afro-American, Mixed, Colored, Negro, please stand up? Impact of the Black Social Movement twenty years later. *Journal of Black Studies, 16,* 57-75.

Johnson, F. L., & Buttny, R. (1982). White listeners' responses to "sounding Black" and "sounding White": The effects of message content on judgements about language. *Communication Monographs, 49,* 33-49.

Johnson, K. (1971). Black kinesics: Some nonverbal communication patterns in Black culture. In L. Samovar & R. Porter (Eds.), *Intercultural communication: A reader* (pp. 181-189). Belmont, CA: Wadsworth.

Jones, R. L. (Ed.). (1980). *Black psychology* (2nd ed.). New York: Harper & Row.

Jones, S. E. (1971). A comparative proxemics analysis of dyadic interaction in selected subcultures of New York City. *Journal of Social Psychology, 84,* 35-44.

Karenga, M. (1982). *Introduction to black studies.* Englewood, CA: Dawaida.

Katriel, T. (1987). Rhetoric in flames: Fire inscriptions in Israeli youth movement ceremonials. *Quarterly Journal of Speech, 73,* 444-459.

Katriel, T., & Philipsen, B. (1981). "What we need is communication": "Communication" as a cultural category in some American speech. *Communication Monographs, 48,* 301-317.

Kealey, D. J. (1989). A study of cross cultural effectiveness: Theoretical issues, practical applications. *International Journal of Intercultural Relations, 13,* 387-428.

Kendon, A. (1967). Some functions of gaze direction in social interaction. *Acta Psychologica, 71,* 359-372.

Kenny, D. A. (1988). Interpersonal perception: A social relations analysis. *Journal of Social and Personal Relationships, 5,* 247-261.

Kerner, O. (Chairman, National Advisory Commission of Civil Disorders). (1969). *1968 Report of the National Advisory Commission on Civil Disorders.* New York: Bantam.

Kim, Y. Y. (1986). Introduction: A communication approach to interethnic relations. In Y. Y. Kim (Ed.), *Interethnic communication: Current research* (pp. 9-18). Newbury Park, CA: Sage.

King, D. (1988). Multiple jeopardy, multiple consciousness. In M. Malson, E. Mudimbe-Boyi, J. O'Barr, & M. Wyer (Eds.), *Black women in America* (pp. 265-296). Chicago: University of Chicago Press.

King, N. G., & James, M. J. (1983, February). *The relevance of black English to intercultural communication.* Paper presented at the annual conference of the Western Speech Communication Association, Albuquerque, NM.

Kitayama, D., & Burnstein, E. (1988). Automaticity in conversations: A reexamination of the mindless hypothesis. *Journal of Personality and Social Psychology, 54,* 219-224.

Klapp, O. (1969). *Collective search for identity.* New York: Holt, Rinehart & Winston.

Knapp, M. L., Ellis, D. G., & Williams, B. A. (1980). Perceptions of communication behavior associated with relationship terms. *Communication Monographs, 47,* 157-174.

Kochman, T. (Ed.). (1972). *Rappin' and stylin' out: Communication in urban black America.* Urbana: University of Illinois Press.

Kochman, T. (1981). *Black and White styles in conflict.* Chicago: University of Chicago Press.

Kozol, J. (1991). *Savage inequalities.* New York: Crown.

Krizek, R. L., & Stempien, D. R. (1990). *Networks and practiced culture: The maintenance of symbolic ethnicity among the Phoenix Irish.* Paper presented at the International Communication Association Convention, Dublin, Ireland.

Kuhn, M. H. (1960). Self-attitudes by age, sex, and professional training. *Sociological Quarterly, 1,* 39-55.

Kuhn, M. H., & McPartland, T. (1954). An empirical investigation of self-attitudes. *American Sociological Research, 19,* 68-76.

Labov, W. P. (1970). *The study of nonstandard English.* New York: Columbia University Press.

Labov, W. P. (1972). Rules for ritual insults. In T. Kochman (Ed.), *Rappin' and stylin' out: Communication in urban black America* (pp. 265-314). Urbana: University of Illinois Press.

Labov, W. P. (1982). Objectivity and commitment in linguistic science: The case of the Black English trial in Ann Arbor. *Language in Society, 11,* 165-201.

LaFrance, M., & Mayo, C. (1976). Racial differences in gaze behavior during conversations: Two systematic observational studies. *Journal of Personality and Social Psychology, 33,* 547-552.

Lampe, P. E. (1982). Ethnic labels: Naming or name calling? *Ethnic and Racial Studies, 5,* 542-548.

Langer, E. J. (1978). Rethinking the role of thought in social interaction. In J. J. Harvey, W. Ickes, & R. F. Kidd (Eds.), *New directions in attribution research* (Vol. 2, pp. 36-58). Hillsdale, NJ: Lawrence Erlbaum.

Larkey, L. K., & Hecht, M. L. (1991, August). *A comparative study of African American and Euroamerican ethnic identity.* Paper presented at the International Conference for Language and Social Psychology, Santa Barbara, CA.

Larkey, L. K., Hecht, M. L., & Martin, J. N. (1991, November). *What's in a name: Expressions of African American ethnic identity.* Paper presented at the Western States Communication Mini-Conference, Annenberg School of Communication, Los Angeles.

Lavender, A. D. (1989). United States ethnic groups in 1790: Given names as suggestions of ethnic identity. *Journal of American Ethnic History, 9,* 36-66.

Lemann, N. (1991). *The promised land: The great black migration and how it changed America.* New York: Knopf.

Lessing, E. E., Clarke, C. C., & Gray-Shellberg, L. G. (1981). Black power ideology: Rhetoric and reality in a student sample. *International Journal of Intercultural Relations, 5,* 71-94.

Leung, K., & Bond, M. H. (1984). The impact of cultural collectivism on reward allocation. *Journal of Personality and Social Psychology, 53,* 793-804.

Leung, K., & Iwawaki, S. (1988). Cultural collectivism and distributive behavior. *Journal of Cross-Cultural Psychology, 19,* 35-49.

Lian, K. F. (1982). Identity in minority group relations. *Ethnic and Racial Studies, 5,* 42-52.

Lincoln, C. E. (1984). *Race, religion and the continuing American dilemma.* New York: Hill & Wang.

Lindesmith, A. R., & Strauss, A. L. (1956). *Social psychology.* New York: Holt, Rinehart & Winston.

Littlefield, R. P. (1974). Self-disclosure among Negro, white, and Mexican-American adolescents. *Journal of Counseling Psychology, 21,* 133-136.

Mack, D. E. (1974). The power relationship in black families and white families. *Journal of Personality and Social Psychology, 30,* 409-413.

MacLaury, S., & Hecht, M. L. (in press). Interethnic relationships across the life span. In R. Kastenbaum (Ed.), *The encyclopedia of adult development.* Phoenix, AZ: Oryx Press.

Maltz, D., & Borker, R. (1982). A cultural approach to male-female miscommunication. In J. J. Gumperz (Ed.), *Language and social identity* (pp. 196-216). Cambridge: Cambridge University Press.

Marcelle, Y. (1976). Eye contact as a function of race, sex, and distance. (Doctoral dissertation, Kansas State University). *Dissertation Abstracts International, 37,* 4238A.

Marcia, J. E. (1966). Development and validation of ego identity statuses. *Journal of Personality and Social Psychology, 3,* 119-133.

Markus, H., & Sentis, K. (1982). The self in information processing. In J. Suls (Ed.), *Psychological perspectives on the self* (Vol. 1, pp. 41-70). Hillsdale, NJ: Lawrence Erlbaum.

Martin, J. N. (1989). Behavioral categories of intercultural communication competence: Everyday communicators' perceptions. *International Journal of Intercultural Relations, 13,* 303-332.

Martin, J. N. (in press). Intercultural communication competence. In R. Wiseman & J. Koester (Eds.), *International and Intercultural Communication Annual.* Newbury Park, CA: Sage.

Martin, J. N., & Hammer, M. R. (1989). Behavioral categories of intercultural communication competence: Everyday communicators' perceptions. *International Journal of Intercultural Relations, 13,* 303-332.

Martin, J. N., Larkey, L. K., & Hecht, M. L. (1991, February). *An African American perspective on conversational improvement strategies for interethnic communication.* Paper presented to the Intercultural and International Communication conference, Miami, FL.

Martineau, W. H. (1976). Social participation and a sense of powerlessness among Blacks: A neighborhood analysis. *The Sociological Quarterly, 17,* 27-41.

Maslow, A. H. (1954). *Motivation and personality*. New York: Harper.

Mayer, A. C. (1966). The significance of quasi-groups in the study of complex societies. *The Social Anthropology of Complex Societies, 4,* 97-122.

McAdoo, H. P. (1988). Transgenerational patterns of upward mobility in African-American families. In H. P. McAdoo (Ed.), *Black families* (2nd ed.) (pp. 148-168). Newbury Park, CA: Sage.

McCall, G. J., & Simmons, J. L. (1978). *Identities and Interaction* (rev. ed.). New York: Free Press.

McCombs, H. G. (1985). Black self-concept: An individual/collective analysis. *International Journal of Intercultural Relations, 9,* 1-18.

McGuire, W. J., McGuire, C. V., Child, P., & Fujioka, T. (1978). Salience of ethnicity in the spontaneous self-concept as a function of one's ethnic distinctiveness in the social environment. *Journal of Personality and Social Psychology, 36,* 511-520.

McLaughlin, M., & Cody, M. J. (1982). Awkward silences: Behavioral antecedents and consequences of the conversational lapse. *Human Communication Research, 8,* 229-316.

McLaughlin, M., Cody, M. J., & O'Hair, H. D. (1983). The management of failure events: Some contextual determinants of accounting behavior. *Human Communication Research, 9,* 208-224.

Mead, G. H. (1934). *Mind, self and society*. Chicago: University of Chicago Press.

Mechling, J. (1980). The magic of the Boy Scout campfire. *Journal of American Folklore, 93,* 35-56.

Michaels, E. (1982, May). *Race and ethnicity: Confused variables in survey research*. Paper presented at the International Communication Association Conference, Boston.

Middleton, D., & Edwards, D. (1990). *Collective remembering*. London: Sage.

Miller, A. G. (1982). Historical and contemporary perspectives on stereotyping. In A. G. Miller (Ed.), *In the eye of the beholder: Contemporary issues in stereotyping* (pp. 1-40). New York: Praeger.

Miller, G. R., & Steinberg, M. (1975). *Between people*. Chicago: SRA.

Mincy, R. B. (1989). Paradoxes in black economic progress: Incomes, families, and the underclass. *Journal of Negro Education, 58,* 255-269.

Minority college attendance rose in the late '80s, report says. (1992, January 20). *The Arizona Republic,* p. A4.

Mitchell-Kernan, C. (1971). *Language behavior in a black urban community* (Working Paper No. 23). Berkeley: University of California Language Behavior Research Laboratory.

Montgomery, B. M. (1984). Individual differences and relational interdependence in social interaction. *Human Communication Research, 11,* 33-60.

Montgomery, B. M. (1992). Communication as the interface between couples and culture. In S. A. Deetz (Ed.), *Communication yearbook 15* (pp. 475-507). Newbury Park, CA: Sage.

Morris, G. H. (1985). The remedial episode as a negotiation of rules. In R. L. Street, Jr., & J. N. Cappella (Eds.), *Sequence and pattern in communicative behaviour* (pp. 70-84). London: Edward Arnold.

Moulton, W. G. (1976). The sound of black English. In D. S. Harrison & T. Trabasso (Eds.), *Black English: A seminar* (pp. 149-170). Hillsdale, NJ: Lawrence Erlbaum.

Musgrove, F. (1977). *Margins of the mind*. London: Methuen.

Mutran, E. (1987). Family, social ties and self-meaning in old age: The development of an affective identity. *Journal of Social and Personal Relationships, 4*, 463-480.

Myrdal, G. (1944). *An American dilemma: The Negro problem and modern democracy* (2 vols.). New York: Harper & Row.

Nakayama, T. K., & Peñaloza, L. N. (in press). Madonna traces: Music videos through the prism of color. In C. Schwichtenberg (Ed.), *The Madonna connection: Representational politics, subculture identities, and cultural theory*. Boulder, CO: Westview.

Natale, M. (1975). Convergence of mean vocal intensity in dyadic communication as a function of social desirability. *Journal of Personality and Social Psychology, 32*, 790-804.

National Opinion Research Center. (1991). *Survey of social attitudes*. Ann Arbor, MI: Inter-University Consortium for Political and Social Research, Institute for Social Research.

Naylor, G. (1988). *The women of Brewster Place*. New York: Viking.

Nobles, W. W. (1979). *Mental health support systems in Black families*. Washington, DC: U.S. Department of Health, Education and Welfare.

Obidinsky, E. (1978). Methodological considerations in the definition of ethnicity. *Ethnicity, 5*, 213-228.

Olebe, M., & Koester, J. (1989). Exploring the cross-cultural equivalence of the behavioral assessment scale for intercultural communication. *International Journal of Intercultural Relations, 13*, 333-348.

Olivas, M. A. (1989). An elite priesthood of white males dominates the central areas of civil-rights scholarship. *Chronicle of Higher Education*, pp. B1-2.

Otto, L. B., & Featherman, D. L. (1975). Social stratification and psychological antecedents of self-estrangement and powerlessness. *American Sociological Review, 40*, 701-719.

Padilla, A. M., Ruiz, R. A., & Alvarez, R. (1983). Community mental health services for the Spanish speaking/surnamed population. In D. R. Atkinson, G. Morton, & D. W. Sue (Eds.), *Counseling American minorities* (2nd ed.) (pp. 181-203). Dubuque, IA: William C. Brown.

Parks, M. R. (1985). Interpersonal communication and the quest for personal competence. In M. L. Knapp & G. R. Miller (Eds.), *Handbook of interpersonal communication* (pp. 171-204). Beverly Hills, CA: Sage.

Patterson, M. L. (1983). *Nonverbal behavior: A functional perspective*. New York: Springer-Verlag.

Patterson, M. L. (1987). Presentational and affect-management functions of nonverbal involvement. *Journal of Nonverbal Behavior, 11*, 110-122.

Pavitt, C., & Haight, L. (1985). The "competent communicator" as a cognitive prototype. *Human Communication Research, 12*, 225-242.

Pearce, W. B. (1989). *Communication and human condition*. Carbondale: Southern Illinois University Press.

Pearce, W. B., & Cronen, B. (1980). *Communication, action and meaning*. New York: Praeger.

Pennington, D. L. (1979). Black-white communication. In M. Asante, E. Newmark, & C. Blake (Eds.), *Handbook of intercultural communication* (pp. 383-402). Beverly Hills: Sage.

Peretti, P. O. (1976). Closest friendships of black college students: Social intimacy. *Adolescence, 11*, 395-403.

Petronio, S. (1990). The use of a communication boundary perspective to contextualize embarrassment research: A commentary. In J. Anderson (Ed.), *Communication yearbook 13* (pp. 365-374). Newbury Park, CA: Sage.

Petronio, S. (1991). Communication boundary perspective: A model of managing the disclosure of private information between marital couples. *Communication Theory, 4*, 311-332.

Pettigrew, T. F. (1979). The ultimate attribution error. *Journal of Personality and Social Psychology, 42*, 1051-1068.

Pettigrew, T. F. (1981). Race and class in the 1980's: An interactive view. *Daedalus, 110*, 233-255.

Pettigrew, T. F. (1985). New black-white patterns: How best to conceptualize them? *American Sociological Review, 11*, 329-346.

Philipsen, G. (1975). Speaking "like a man" in Teamsterville: Culture patterns of role enactment in an urban neighborhood. *Quarterly Journal of Speech, 61*, 13-22.

Philipsen, G. (1987). The prospect for cultural communication. In D. L. Kincaid (Ed.), *Communication theory: Eastern and Western perspectives* (pp. 245-254). New York: Academic Press.

Piestrup, A. M. (1973). *Black dialect interference and accommodation of reading instruction in first grade* [Monograph]. Berkeley: University of California, Language Behavior Research Laboratory.

Rainwater, L. (1967). Crucible of identity: The Negro lower-class family. In T. Parsons & D. Clark (Eds.), *In the negro American* (pp. 160-204). Boston: Houghton Mifflin.

Rampersad, A. (1976). *The art and imagination of W. E. B. DuBois*. New York: Schocken Books.

Ransford, H. E., & Miller, J. (1983). Race, sex and feminist outlooks. *American Sociological Review, 48*, 46-58.

Rawlins, W. E. (1983). Openness as problematic in ongoing friendships: Two conversational dilemmas. *Communication Monographs, 50*, 1-13.

Robinson, C. R. (1983). Black women: A tradition of self-reliant strength. *Women & Therapy, 2*, 135-144.

Robinson, P. W. (1978). *Black quest for identity*. Minneapolis, MN: Burgess Publishing.

Rogers, C. R. (1961). *On becoming a person*. Boston: Houghton Mifflin.

Roosens, E. E. (1989). *Creating ethnicity: The process of ethnogenesis*. Newbury Park, CA: Sage.

Ros, M., Cano, I., & Huici, C. (1987). Language and intergroup perception in Spain. *Language and Social Psychology, 6*, 243-259.

Rosaldo, M. (1974). Women, culture and society: A theoretical overview. In M. Rosaldo & L. Lamphere (Eds.), *Women, culture and society* (pp. 17-42). Stanford, CA: Stanford University Press.

Rosaldo, R. (1989). *Culture and truth: The remaking of social analysis*. Boston: Beacon.

Rose, L. F. R. (1982/1983). Theoretical and methodological issues in the study of Black culture and personality. *Humboldt Journal of Social Relations, 10*, 320-338.

Rosenberg, M. (1979). *Conceiving the self*. New York: Basic Books.

Rosenberg, M. (1986). *Conceiving the self* (Reprint ed.). Malabar, FL: Krieger. (Original work published 1979)

Rosenberg, M. (1989). Self-concept research: A historical overview. *Social Forces, 68,* 34-44.

Rota, J. (1990, June). *Notes on theory, concepts and issues in communication and cultural identity.* Paper presented at the International Communication Association Conference, Dublin, Ireland.

Ruben, B. D. (1977). Guidelines for cross-cultural communication effectiveness. *Group and Organizational Studies, 2,* 470-479.

Ruben, B. D. (1989). The study of cross-cultural competence: Traditions and contemporary issues. *International Journal of Intercultural Relations, 13,* 229-239.

Sachdev, I., & Bourhis, R. Y. (1990). Language and social identification. In D. Abrams & M. A. Hogg (Eds.), *Social identity theory: Constructive and critical advances* (pp. 211-229). New York: Harvester Wheatsheaf.

Sachdev, I., Bourhis, R. Y., Phang, S. W., & D'Eye, J. (1987). Language attitudes and vitality perceptions: Intergenerational effects amongst Chinese Canadian communities. *Journal of Language and Social Psychology, 6,* 287-307.

Saenz, D. S., & Lord, C. G. (1989). Reversing roles: A cognitive strategy for undoing memory deficits associated with token status. *Journal of Personality and Social Psychology, 56,* 698-708.

Sampson, E. E. (1989). The deconstruction of self. In J. Shotter & K. J. Gergen (Eds.), *Texts of identity* (pp. 1-19). Newbury Park, CA: Sage.

Saville-Troike, M. (1982). *The ethnography of communication: An introduction.* Oxford: Basil Blackwell.

Schneider, D. (1976). Notes toward a theory of culture. In K. Basso & H. Selby (Eds.), *Meaning in anthropology* (pp. 197-220). Albuquerque: University of New Mexico Press.

Schonbach, P. (1980). A category system for account phases. *European Journal of Social Psychology, 70,* 195-200.

Scotton, C. M. (1983). The negotiation of identities in conversations: A theory of markedness and code choice. *International Journal of the Sociology of Language, 44,* 115-136.

Seymour, H. N., & Seymour, C. M. (1979). The symbolism of ebonics: I'd rather switch than fight. *Journal of Black Studies, 9,* 397-410.

Sherif, M. (1966). *Group conflict and cooperation.* London: Routledge & Kegan Paul.

Shimanoff, S. B. (1980). *Communication rules: Theory and research.* Beverly Hills, CA: Sage.

Shotter, J., & Gergen, K. J. (Eds.). (1989). *Texts of identity.* London: Sage.

Shuman, A. (1986). *Storytelling rights: The uses of oral and written tests by urban adolescents.* Cambridge: Cambridge University Press.

Shuter, R. (1982). Initial interactions of American blacks and whites in interracial and intraracial dyads. *Journal of Social Psychology, 117,* 45-52.

Sigman, S. (1980). On communication rules from a social perspective. *Human Communication Research, 7,* 37-51.

Slugoski, B. R., & Ginsburg, G. P. (1989). Ego identity and explanatory speech. In J. Shotter & K. J. Gergen (Eds.), *Texts of identity* (pp. 21-36). London: Sage.

Smith, A. (1983). Nonverbal communication among Black female dyads: An assessment of intimacy, gender, and race. *Journal of Social Issues, 39*, 55-67.

Smith, D. E. (1987). *The everyday world as problematic*. Boston: Northeastern University Press.

Smith, D. E., Willis, F. N., & Gier, J. A. (1980). Success and interpersonal touch in a competitive setting. *Journal of Nonverbal Behavior, 5*, 26-34.

Smith, L. E., & Millham, J. (1979). Sex role stereotypes among dyads: An assessment of intimacy, gender, and race. *Journal of Black Psychology, 6*, 1-6.

Smith, R. C. (1982). *Black leadership: A survey of theory and research*. Washington, DC: Howard University, Institute for Urban Affairs and Research.

Smitherman, G. (1977). *Talkin' and testifyin': The language of black America*. Boston: Houghton Mifflin.

Smitherman-Donaldson, G. (1988). Discriminatory discourse on Afro-American speech. In G. Smitherman-Donaldson & T. A. Dijk, (Eds.), *Discourse and discrimination* (pp. 144-175). Detroit: Wayne State University Press.

Spitzberg, B. H. (1989). Issues in the development of a theory of interpersonal competence in the intercultural context. *International Journal of Intercultural Relations, 13*, 241-268.

Spitzberg, B. H., & Cupach, W. R. (1984). *Interpersonal communication competence*. Beverly Hills, CA: Sage.

Spitzberg, B. H., & Hecht, M. L. (1984). A component model of relational competence. *Human Communication Research, 10*, 575-600.

Staiano, K. V. (1980). Ethnicity as process: The creation of an Afro-American identity. *Ethnicity, 7*, 27-33.

Stanbeck, M., & Pearce, W. B. (1981). Talking to "the man": Some communication strategies used by subordinants and their implications for intergroup relations. *Quarterly Journal of Speech, 67*, 21-30.

Staples, R. (1971). Towards a sociology of the Black family: A theoretical and methodological assessment. *Journal of Marriage and the Family, 33*, 119-138.

Stephan, W. G., & Rosenfeld, D. (1982). Racial and ethnic stereotypes. In A. G. Miller (Ed.), *In the eye of the beholder: Contemporary issues in stereotyping* (pp. 92-136). New York: Praeger.

Stephenson, G. M. (1981). Intergroup bargaining and negotiation. In J. Turner & H. Giles (Eds.), *Intergroup behavior* (pp. 168-198). Chicago: University of Chicago Press.

Stern, F. (1991). *Anti-Semitic and philosemitic discourse in postwar Germany*. Paper presented at the Fourth International Conference on Language and Social Psychology, Santa Barbara, CA.

Stewart, W. A. (1970). Toward a history of American Negro dialect. In F. Williams (Ed.), *Language and poverty* (pp. 351-379). Chicago: Markham Publishing.

Stone, G. (1962). Appearance and self. In *Human behavior and social processes*. Boston: Houghton Mifflin.

Strauss, A. (1976). *Images of the American city*. New Brunswick, NJ: Transaction Books.

Stryker, S. (1968). Identity salience and role performance. *Journal of Marriage and the Family, 30*, 558-564.

Stryker, S. (1980). *Symbolic interactionism: A social structural version*. Menlo Park, CA: Benjamin/Cummings.

Stryker, S. (1981). Symbolic interactionism: Themes and variations. In M. Rosenberg & R. H. Turner (Eds.), *Social psychology: Sociological perspectives* (pp. 3-29). New York: Basic Books.

Stryker, S., & Serpe, R. T. (1983). Toward a theory of family influence in the socialization of children. In A. Kerckhoff (Ed.), *Research in sociology of education and socialization* (Vol. 4, pp. 47-71). Greenwich, CT: JAI Press.

Stryker, S., & Statham, A. (1984). Symbolic interaction and role theory. In G. Lindzey & E. Aronson (Eds.), *Handbook of social psychology* (pp. 311-378). Reading, MA: Addison-Wesley.

Sudarkasa, N. (1980). African and Afro-American family structure: A comparison. *Black Scholar, 11*, 37-60.

Sudarkasa, N. (1988). Interpreting the African heritage in Afro-American family organization. In H. P. McAdoo (Ed.), *Black families* (2nd ed.) (pp. 27-43). Newbury Park, CA: Sage.

Swinton, D. (1989). The economic status of black Americans. In J. Dewart (Ed.), *The state of black America: 1989* (pp. 9-39). New York: National Urban League.

Tajfel, H. (1974). Social identity and intergroup behavior. *Social Science Information, 13*, 65-93.

Tajfel, H. (1978). Interindividual and intergroup behaviour. In H. Tajfel (Ed.), *Differentiation between social groups* (pp. 27-60). London: Academic Press.

Tajfel, H. (1981). *Human categories and social groups*. Cambridge: Cambridge University Press.

Tajfel, H. (Ed.). (1982). *Social identity and intergroup relations*. Cambridge: Cambridge University Press.

Tajfel, H., & Turner, J. (1979). An integrative theory of intergroup conflict. In W. Austin & S. Worchel (Eds.), *The social psychology of intergroup relations* (pp. 33-47). Monterey, CA: Brooks/Cole.

Taylor, C. (1977). Interpretation and the sciences of man. In F. Dallmayr & T. McCarthy (Eds.), *Understanding the social inquiry* (pp. 100-131). Notre Dame, IN: University of Notre Dame Press.

Terkel, S. (1992). *Race: How Blacks and Whites think and feel about the American obsession*. New York: New Press.

Thibaut, J. W., & Kelley, H. H. (1959). *The social psychology of groups*. New York: John Wiley.

Tienda, M. (1989). Race, ethnicity and the portrait of inequality: Approaching the 1990s. *Sociological Spectrum, 9*, 23-52.

Ting-Toomey, S. (1988). Intercultural conflict styles: A face-negotiation theory. In Y. Y. Kim & W. B. Gudykunst (Eds.), *Theories in intercultural communication* (pp. 213-235). Newbury Park, CA: Sage.

Traugott, E. C. (1976). Pidgins, Creoles, and the origins of vernacular Black English. In D. S. Harrison & T. Trabasso (Eds.), *Black English: A seminar* (pp. 57-93). Hillsdale, NJ: Lawrence Erlbaum.

Triandis, H. C., Hui, C. H., Albert, R. D., Leung, S.-M., Lisansky, J., Diaz-Loving, R., Plascencia, L., Marin, G., & Betancourt, H. (1984). Individual models of social behavior. *Journal of Personality and Social Psychology, 46*, 1389-1404.

Triandis, H. C., McCusker, C., & Hui, C. H. (1990). Multimethod probes of individualism and collectivism. *Journal of Personality and Social Psychology, 59,* 1006-1020.

Turner, J. C. (1982). Towards a cognitive redefinition of the social group. In H. Tajfel (Ed.), *Social identity and intergroup relations* (pp. 15-40). Cambridge: Cambridge University Press.

Turner, J. C. (1987). *Rediscovering the social group.* London: Basil Blackwell.

Turner, R. (1968). *The self-conception in social interaction.* In C. Gordon & K. J. Gergen (Eds.), *The self in social interaction* (Vol. 1, pp. 93-106). New York: John Wiley.

van Dijk, T. A. (1987). *Communicating racism: Ethnic prejudice in thought and talk.* Newbury Park, CA: Sage.

Vause, C. J., & Wiemann, J. M. (1981). Communication strategies for role invention. *Western Journal of Speech Communication, 45,* 241-251.

Vontress, C. E. (1973). Counseling: Racial and ethnic factors. *Focus on Guidance, 5,* 1-10.

Vora, E., & Asante, M. (1978, May). *The impact of the concept of race versus that of culture on communication.* Paper presented at the Society for Intercultural Education, Training and Research Conference, Phoenix, AZ.

Watzlawick, P., Beavin, J. H., & Jackson, D. D. (1967). *Pragmatics of human communication: A study of interactional patterns, pathologies, and paradoxes.* New York: Norton.

Webb, J. T. (1972). Interview synchrony: An investigation of two speech-rate measures in the automated standardized interview. In A. W. Siegman & B. Pope (Eds.), *Studies in dyadic communication* (pp. 115-133). Oxford: Pergamon.

Weber, R., & Crocker, J. (1983). Cognitive processes in the revision of stereotypic beliefs. *Journal of Personality and Social Psychology, 45,* 961-977.

Weber, S. N. (1991). The need to be: The sociocultural significance of Black language. In L. A. Samovar & R. E. Porter (Eds.), *Intercultural communication: A reader* (6th ed.) (pp. 277-282). Belmont, CA: Wadsworth.

Weedon, C. (1987). *Feminist practice and poststructuralist theory.* New York: Basil Blackwell.

Weinstein, E. A. (1969). The development of interpersonal competence. In D. A. Guslin (Ed.), *Handbook of socialization theory and research* (pp. 753-775). Chicago: Rand McNally.

White, C. L. (1989). Measuring ethnic identity: An application of the Burke-Tully method. *Sociological Focus, 22,* 249-261.

White, C. L., & Burke, P. J. (1987). Ethnic role identity among black and white college students: An interactionist approach. *Sociological Perspectives, 30,* 310-331.

White, J. L., & Parham, T. A. (1990). *The psychology of blacks: An African-American perspective.* Englewood Cliffs, NJ: Prentice-Hall.

Wiemann, J. M. (1977). Explication and test of a model of communicative competence. *Human Communication Research, 3,* 195-213.

Wilder, D. A. (1984). Intergroup contact: The typical member and the exception to the rule. *Journal of Experimental Psychology, 20,* 177-194.

Wilder, D. A. (1986). Social categorization: Implications for creation and reduction of intergroup bias. In L. Berkowitz (Ed.), *Advances in experimental social psychology* (Vol. 19, pp. 213-257). New York: Academic Press.

Wildeson, D. L. (1985, November). *Black identity in transition: 1950-1970*. Paper presented at the Speech Communication Association Conference, Denver, CO.

Williams, A. P. (1972). Dynamics of a black audience. In T. Kochman (Ed.), *Rappin' and stylin' out: Communication in urban black America* (pp. 101-106). Urbana: University of Illinois Press.

Williams, J. A. (1964) Interviewer-respondent interaction: A study of bias in the information interview. *Sociometry, 27*, 338-352.

Willis, F., Reeves, D., & Buchanan, D. (1976). Interpersonal touch in high school relative to sex and race. *Perceptual and Motor Skills, 43*, 843-847.

Wilson, R. (1989). The state of black higher education: Crisis and promise. In J. Dewart (Ed.), *The state of black America: 1989* (pp. 121-135). New York: National Urban League.

Wilson, W. J. (1978). *The declining significance of race: Blacks and changing American institutions*. Chicago: University of Chicago Press.

Wiseman, R. L., Hammer, M. R., & Nishida, T. (1989). Predictors of intercultural communication competence. *International Journal of Intercultural Relations, 13*, 349-370.

Wodak, R. (1991). Turning the tables: Anti-Semitic discourse in post-war Austria. *Discourse & Society, 2*, 65-83.

Wolfram, W. (1971). Black-white speech differences revisited. In W. Wolfram & N. H. Clark (Eds.), *Black-white speech relationships* (pp. 139-161). Washington, DC: Center for Applied Linguistics.

Won-Doornink, M. J. (1985). Self-disclosure and reciprocity in conversation: A cross-national study. *Social Psychology Quarterly, 48*, 97-107.

Wood, J. (1982). Communication and relational culture: Bases for the study of human relationships. *Communication Quarterly, 30*, 75-83.

Woodson, C. G. (1966). *The Negro in our history* (11 ed). Washington, DC: Associated Publishers

Wright, B. H. (1985). The effects of racial self-esteem on the personal self-esteem of Black youth. *International Journal of Intercultural Relations, 9*, 19-30.

Wyne, M. D., White, K. P., & Coop, R. H. (1974). *The Black self*. Englewood Cliffs, NJ: Prentice-Hall.

Yablonsky, L. (1959). The delinquent gang as a near group. *Social Problems, 7*, 108-117.

Zajonc, R. B. (1984). On the primacy of affect. *American Psychologist, 39*, 117-123.

Zatz, M. S. (1987). The changing forms of racial/ethnic biases in sentencing. *Journal of Research in Crime and Delinquency, 24*, 69-92.

Zimmerman, B., & Brody, G. (1975). Race and modeling influences on the interpersonal play pattern of boys. *Journal of Educational Psychology, 67*, 591-598.

Author Index

Subject Index

212

About the Authors

Michael L. Hecht, Ph.D., received his doctoral degree from the University of Illinois. He is a Professor of Communication and the Director of the Communication Research Consortium at Arizona State University. He has edited books on nonverbal communication and interpersonal communication, is currently completing a book on adolescent relationships and drug use, and has authored more than 40 articles and chapters on topics such as communication effectiveness, interethnic communication, communication and emotion, and communication in a social context. Hecht recently completed a NIDA-sponsored study of drug resistance strategies that resulted in an award-winning drug prevention video titled *Killing Time.* He has taught courses on interpersonal relationships, ethnicity, nonverbal communication, communication theory, and research methodology.

Mary Jane Collier, Ph.D., received her B.A. in Communication from the University of Colorado, Boulder. She received her master's and doctoral degrees in communication theory and research from the University of Southern California. She has taught at University of California, Davis, California State University, Los Angeles, and is currently an Associate Professor at Oregon State University. Collier is presently serving as Chair of the International and Intercultural Communication Division of the national Speech Communication Association. Her work appears in the *International and Intercultural Communication Annual, International Journal of Intercultural Relations, American Behavioral Scientist, Communication Quarterly,* and *Howard Journal of Communications.* During the summer of 1992 she was selected as an Overseas Research Fellow at the Human Sciences Research Council, Pretoria, South Africa.

Sidney A. Ribeau, Ph.D., is a Speech Communication Professor and Vice President for Academic Affairs at California State Polythechnic University, Pomona. He is the former Chair of the Pan-African Studies Department at California State University, Los Angeles, and Dean of Undergraduate Studies at California State University, San Bernardino. His scholarly work includes papers in the areas of intercultural communication, Third World rhetoric, and African American expressive forms. Ribeau has taught courses in rhetorical and film criticism, intercultural communication, and African American culture. He is currently studying the impact of Afrocentricity on the identity of African American youth.